EMILY POST'S
BUSINESS ETIQUETTE

EMILY POST'S
BUSINESS
ETIQUETTE

LIZZIE POST AND DANIEL POST SENNING

TEN SPEED PRESS

California | New York

We would like to dedicate this book to business partners everywhere and the meaningful relationships they can have with one another. While writing this book, we found ourselves influenced by and living the advice in it, finding a stronger, better relationship and a more successful business in the process.

Cousin, I will always be grateful for the journey this work took us on and the path that now lies before us.

Cousin, as will I.

CONTENTS

AUTHOR'S NOTE

Dear Reader,

We are so pleased to bring you *Emily Post's Business Etiquette*. This completely rewritten and updated edition is *the* modern professional's guide to the personal skills that bring professional success. For over 100 years, Emily Post has been America's go-to source for advice on etiquette and manners. If you're new to Emily Post, please allow us to introduce you.

In 1922, Emily Post wrote *Etiquette at Home, in Business, in Society, and in Politics*. It was an instant hit, with multiple printings in the first six months of publication alone. It went on to become one of the most influential books of the twentieth century, selling millions of copies and undergoing ten updated editions in Emily's lifetime. The Emily Post Institute was founded by Emily and her son in 1946 so that Emily's work could carry on. After Emily died in 1960, Elizabeth Post, her granddaughter-in-law, took over the brand and continued updating *Emily Post's Etiquette* while producing books on entertaining and other niche topics. In 1995, the torch was passed to the fourth generation of Posts: Peggy Post, Peter Post, and Cindy Post Senning, EdD. This was the first generation to have more than one author carrying the name. The fourth generation added a business etiquette book and built a business etiquette training company from the source material.

Today, we, Lizzie Post and Daniel Post Senning, are the fifth generation of Posts to tackle the topic and carry on the tradition. We continue Emily's legacy of allowing etiquette to change and evolve, as each generation has slightly different social standards and norms that develop for their particular era. We've held on to traditions that serve us well, and changed, adapted, or left behind the ones that don't.

As we set out to explore professional etiquette in a post-pandemic era, our goal was to produce a book you could rely on and turn to throughout your entire career, from application to retirement. Communication methods may change, and work attire has reached unprecedented levels of casual, but throughout it all, business will always be built on relationships, and relationships will always function more smoothly when good etiquette is observed.

If *etiquette* has been a word that sets your spine straight, or maybe it just sounds snooty, we hope to bring it to you in a new light—one that allows it to be a useful tool for making your life and the lives of those around you infinitely easier.

Wherever reading this book finds you on the path of your career, we wish you great success.

Sincerely,
Lizzie Post
Daniel Post Senning

EMILY POST'S
BUSINESS ETIQUETTE

CHAPTER 1

What's the Point?

If you had a commission to give and you entered a man's office and found him lolling back in a tipped swivel chair, his feet above his head, the ubiquitous cigar in his mouth and his drowsy attention fixed on the sporting page of the newspaper, you would be impressed not so much by his lack of good manners as by his bad business policy, because of the incompetence that his attitude suggests. It is scarcely necessary to ask: Would you give an important commission to him who has no apparent intention of doing anything but "take his ease"; or to him who is found occupied at his desk, who gets up with alacrity upon your entrance, and is seemingly "on his toes" mentally as well as actually? Or, would you go in preference to a man whose manners resemble those of the bear at the Zoo, if you could go to another whose business ability is supplemented by personal charm? And this again is merely an illustration of bad manners and good.

—EMILY POST, *ETIQUETTE*, 1922

The point, dear reader, is that manners can make all the difference in business. More than "good manners will earn you business," the lesson here is that it is our choice to use manners and that choice can impact our business. No one forces us. We are in control of this. Understanding and using the manners of the day, which we are all in a state of learning and will continue to learn as they change and evolve over time, is what can set us apart. For five generations, the Emily Post Institute has recommended that business etiquette can make all the difference in business success. We believe it, we see the point, and we hope you will too.

WHAT IS ETIQUETTE?

What does the word *etiquette* mean to you? We can define etiquette as social expectations, but the reality is that the word carries more weight than that definition can hold.

When we start a business etiquette seminar, we often begin by playing a simple word-association game, asking, "What words come to mind when you hear the word *etiquette*?" Without fail, no matter where we are teaching or who is in the audience, we hear "politeness," "manners," "thank-you notes," "respect," "fork," and "mom," or "grandmother" most often. Keep pushing or waiting, and the answers get more interesting: "old-fashioned," "formal," "phony," "stuffy," "elitist," "royal," or worse, "irrelevant."

Some people's responses to the word *etiquette* are very positive and personal, reminding them of someone who really mattered to them: their mother, a grandparent, a favorite aunt, a teacher, or a business mentor. For them, etiquette was a part of a childhood home, a family, a school, or an experience they treasured. Often, this person was someone who initiated or clued them in to a piece of etiquette advice that not only became useful but unlocked experiences and opportunities. For these people, etiquette provides a sense of what is expected of them and what they might expect in a given situation. It is secure, comforting, and thoughtful, and it inspires confidence.

But it's not all roses. Other people remember a time when they felt uncomfortable, unsure, excluded, or judged, and it felt like manners and etiquette were only highlighting how out of place they were, or how unaware they were of how to behave. For these people, etiquette is at best mysterious, and at worst a tool of segregation. Very few feelings are as unsettling as feeling out of place or like you don't belong with others. These two very different associations with the word *etiquette* represent two very different realities about the word and the idea of sharing common social standards.

For those who have experienced the negative impact of the word *etiquette,* we hope to offer a new perspective that helps you move forward with etiquette employed as a trusted skill, a tool to hone that resonates with your life, perspective, and personal integrity. Etiquette can be a powerful part of your life kit to help facilitate cooperation and build relationships. And when behavior is tied to income, as it is in business, it makes etiquette not just a powerful tool but an essential one. Breaking down past negative experiences and feelings of unease around etiquette and manners and allowing light to shine on how etiquette, when properly applied, can be rooted in practicality and thoughtful, self-respecting behavior can be a transformative part of a professional journey.

When etiquette and manners work well, they give us confidence in ourselves and our interactions with others and allow us to feel good. When you have an enjoyable time with someone or a meeting goes well, you leave it feeling great! Quite often, it's because good etiquette skills were being practiced by the people involved. Greetings and pleasantries are exchanged. The conversation is a balanced discourse. People leave the gathering or meeting feeling heard and understood—regardless of whether they agree or solve a problem.

But when etiquette is used poorly to exclude, judge, or, in some cases, reinforce unfair power systems, it breaks people down and divides them. Feelings of insecurity and inequality are the result. We leave that meeting or conversation feeling uncomfortable, disappointed, or deflated. The key to any effort to employ etiquette in the pursuit of good behavior is a willingness to think about how it can work well and to recognize and avoid the aspects that can make people feel excluded and judged.

Good etiquette is about improving oneself or a situation, not judging others or inflating one's own sense of self-righteousness. In the simplest terms, etiquette is a powerful, positive, transformational tool when you use it to assess and improve your *own* behavior. It becomes less useful and even detrimental to relationships when used to judge, critique, or exclude others.

THE GOOD NEWS IS:
IT'S ALL ABOUT RELATIONSHIPS

At the Emily Post Institute, we love the opportunity to share the good news that etiquette is all about relationships. Even with the great divide in how people experience and internalize the idea of etiquette. It's not about rules or knowing the most. It's about how we treat each other and how we experience one another. Here is how Emily Post put it:

> *Whenever two people come together, and their behavior affects one another, you have etiquette . . . it is not some rigid code of manners, but simply how persons' lives touch one another.*

We like to think of this as the heart of etiquette. No matter the circumstances, if another person is involved, the question of how you acknowledge and interact with each other *is* etiquette. It's the care we take with each other. Think about someone who matters to you. Now think about how you behave with that person—not how you feel about them, but how you treat them, respond to them, and communicate with them. The quality of that experience is what we mean by etiquette. Good etiquette is everything you can do to improve the quality of that experience, and bad etiquette is anything you do that makes it worse. The good news is that despite the nuances this book explores, etiquette is not complicated.

The good news doesn't stop there. When we break down the core principles of etiquette, people realize that the foundation of Emily Post etiquette is exactly the kind of foundation they'd like the people they interact with to be working from. You hear it when people express wanting others to have "common decency" and "basic manners" and to "treat each other as human beings." The core principles we use to guide our advice at Emily Post are consideration, respect, and honesty.

CORE PRINCIPLES

At Emily Post, we've identified the core principles of etiquette to be consideration, respect, and honesty. Now, ask yourself: Wouldn't you like to be treated by others with consideration, respect, and honesty? Flip it the other way; can you get behind the idea that it would be good for you to treat others with consideration, respect, and honesty?

We firmly believe that social expectations rooted in consideration, respect, and honesty will serve all kinds of people well in all social circumstances. We see evidence of these core values in all the specific manners that make up the codes of conduct we engage with daily. Our core principles are the values that matter in relationships, and manners are how we demonstrate them to the people in our lives. Let's break down the three core principles before exploring manners and how they function.

CONSIDERATION

Regarding etiquette, consideration is taking the time to think about others, as well as yourself, before you act. It is literally stopping to think first. Consideration helps make us aware of the people, places, and things around us and our impact on them. Through consideration, we cultivate our sympathy and empathy for others by exploring how a particular situation might affect them (as well as ourselves). We aren't necessarily judging a situation; we are just recognizing the people involved and the impact we could have.

RESPECT

A quick Google search for definitions of *respect* brings up phrases such as *admiration for* and *high regard for*, which would lead us to believe that we only respect that which or those whom we look up to, but it is the second definition from Oxford Languages that appears in our search that we appreciate from an etiquette perspective. When we think of respect in connection to etiquette, we think of regard for others. The Oxford definition states "due regard for the feelings, wishes, rights, or traditions of others." "Feelings, wishes, rights, and traditions" covers much of what defines each of us as individuals as well as families and community members. From an etiquette perspective, everyone deserves respect simply by existing. There is no age, financial or educational threshold, or job level that suddenly means you get respect. There is no body type or color of skin that deserves more respect than another. And anyone from *any* station in life can offer respect to themselves and others.

By following the principle of respect, we honor others, not necessarily because of their unique talents, qualities, or ideas, or because we like or understand them, but simply because they *exist*. Respect builds on consideration by encouraging us to be aware of *how* the actions we are weighing as possible solutions or avenues impact others.

By choosing to show respect for ourselves and others (and even places and things), we guide ourselves to make choices that have the best chance of positively impacting others (and ourselves). In doing so, we have the best shot at building relationships—whether with strangers as we hold a door, in a boardroom with colleagues, or at the dinner table.

HONESTY

With etiquette, the truth-telling, sincerity, and authenticity that can all be part of the word *honesty* are at play and are needed in our actions and words to build trust. And great business relationships are built on trust. You have to rise to the occasion with your actions and behavior, not just your words. The boss who says they want everyone to feel like family yet regularly leaves work early without saying goodbye isn't sincere and will not gain the trust of their employees. Honest intentions have to be played out and supported with sincere, genuine, and believable actions. Business is built on trust, and sincere honesty is the path toward it.

PUTTING IT INTO ACTION

Here's how the three core principles of etiquette can be applied in action. If you think about the people involved in a given situation and how they might be impacted (consideration), acknowledge the worth and value of those involved by evaluating the positive and negative effects of your options (respect), and choose a course of action that has the most positive benefit to the most people involved and move forward in a sincere way (honesty), you're likely to respond appropriately and also to honor and improve your relationships with those involved. In our Emily Post business etiquette programs, we use three goals to easily translate the above principles into action:

1. Think before you act. (Consideration)

2. Make choices that build relationships. (Respect)

3. Be sincere in your actions. (Honesty)

When you're unsure of what to do in a given situation, you can lean on these three goals or the three core principles to help you find a way forward. Join us in chapter 2, "The Five-Step Process," for a deeper dive into problem-solving using the three principles.

HOW MANNERS FUNCTION

Answering the question "What is etiquette?" can be more direct when we consider etiquette to consist of a system of manners as well as principles. Manners are specific behaviors. They help us know what is expected of us and what to expect of others. Manners change over time and differ by country, culture, and even social group or family. As a culture changes, new manners emerge, and others become traditions that either continue or become obsolete.

Take the example of a polite greeting; the manner of it will vary depending on the circumstances. You might choose to shake hands, bow, hug, kiss on the cheek, or even just wave or respectfully nod your head. All these gestures are meant to indicate acknowledgment, welcome, respect, or a sense of trust, but they could be considered either polite or awkward depending on who's involved and the nature of the meeting. While the use of these manners varies across the globe, the principle behind them is the same: they demonstrate respect and consideration while acknowledging another.

Since manners change over time and between cultures or even social groups and families, and we interact with people outside our culture, social groups, and families, we are all learning and adapting our manners as we go through life. No one is born with this knowledge, and we are all gaining more of it each day, each week, each year.

While some basics are pretty universal, you'd be surprised how many gaps in knowledge and blind spots there are when it comes to etiquette. These holes are the space that we all have and they give us room to learn and grow and enhance our ability to connect with others and build relationships. If you start to feel nervous or doubt yourself for not having known a particular point of etiquette, remember: it's okay, we are all learning, and anyone who is going to ridicule or judge you over it is a— Oh wait, that's not polite to say.

Mark moments in your life where you learn a new manner as just that, a learning moment. The moment, even if it is a bit embarrassing, gives you knowledge, something to make life a bit smoother next time. No matter your age, make an effort to be observant and use the core principles of etiquette to ground you and guide you as new manners emerge and old ones evolve.

When executed well, manners are the principles (and even the three goals listed on page 8) in action. The handshake is a great example of a manner displaying a principle; it's a very specific social behavior consisting of a defined set of actions that, when done well, not only acknowledges someone, it conveys consideration and respect and is often a symbol of trust, honesty, welcome, agreement, and even friendliness.

Employing manners without principles behind them (a perfunctory handshake, for example, does not feel welcoming) or principles without manners (think of the thoughtful, kind person who is a total slob when they eat or is never on time—like ever) might be something you can get away with occasionally, but they only result in good etiquette when applied together. And in business, using manners and principles together well often results in confidence and trust, two things we all want to instill in our business interactions.

We imagine Emily Post would appreciate this next comparison, as she was a lover of architecture like her father, Bruce Price. If etiquette were a house, our three core principles would be the foundation, a solid, unchanging portion of our house. Manners are like the design details (both interior and exterior); they evolve as the times change and sometimes even as our personal style and preferences or circumstances change. Sure, a few design aspects may be "timeless," just as saying "please" and "thank you" will always be considered good manners, for example. But overall, you could say communication etiquette changes as fast as technology does; maybe it's like the decor, throw pillows, curtains, and bedding you change as your style evolves.

Remember the three core principles of consideration, respect, and honesty can be applied to any situation you find yourself in where you're unsure of the appropriate manners. When we base our actions on them, even when things go badly, others will likely understand and maybe even appreciate our good intent.

TRADITION IN MANNERS

Traditional manners that have weathered societal changes and survived for generations are still in use because they work. There are some things we don't have to reinvent, rediscover, or rebuild. All we have to do to reap their benefits is to learn what they are, why they exist, and adopt them. When we uphold traditions, we participate in a shared practice, and in doing so, we bond with others and, in some cases, can connect to generations past. There may be traditions within your company or team that become treasured moments and memories over time, like doing a "money dance" when a big sale comes in, or choosing a certain way to say goodbye to a team member when they retire.

Looking at the reasons behind our traditions is important to determining which traditions stay and which must be adapted to fit our needs today. When something challenges a tradition, it's important to take a curious attitude, step back, and examine both the tradition and its impact. Doing so can help us protect the aspects of traditions that serve a purpose while leaving room to change or abandon traditions that are outdated.

Given America's history of patriarchal gender dynamics, racial suppression, and inequality, it is imperative to look at the traditions, celebrations, and bonding experiences you are invited and encouraged to participate in and ask yourself if they are inclusive and fair. An invitation to a work golf outing at a famous course might imply you've finally made it to the table, so to speak. However, if other team members are excluded when they also did the work or are even excluded due to gender, race, or religion, you must question if this is a tradition worth participating in. One of the best things you can do to change a tradition is to literally behave differently. In this case, you could decline the invitation and, when you get to be in the position of host, ensure the inviting is done respectfully and inclusively.

WHY BUSINESS ETIQUETTE?

Etiquette is to relationships what grease is to a wheel or oil is to an engine. It smooths the way. Our interactions with others that build and become our relationships are easier and often more productive when we employ good etiquette. Why business etiquette? Because a single interaction can start a new relationship off on the right foot, take a good relationship to great, or even repair a damaged one. Every deal, agreement, trade, exchange, or transaction is based on a relationship. Every organization is built on relationships. Every promotion comes from a relationship (and good work). Etiquette is inherently a part of business, and, thus, business etiquette matters.

Without it, we might as well let the 0s and 1s talk for us and just move our money around—or duke it out until only one person is left standing. Bleak. **Etiquette is how we take care with one another.** And in business, to make it, we *must* take care. Etiquette is essential to your professional identity, the impression you create with those you meet and those you work with and for. It is essential to the relationships you build, the relationships you maintain, and your personal experience of your work. Whether you're just getting started or the longtime owner of a business, etiquette is essential to business success on every level.

ORGANIZATIONAL BENEFITS

The social dynamics at play in any organization can sometimes feel like a mysterious brew, and they will always impact the function of the group. Finding the right balance of actions and expectations, carrots and sticks, leadership styles, and team makeup can be difficult. People have to make an effort, leadership has to guide the way, and money alone can't buy a solution.

When social cohesion starts to break down, the costs are real, but fortunately, the solutions are affordable. Christine Pearson and Christine Porath point out in the seminal book *The Cost of Bad Behavior* that at the time of their research, 95 percent of Americans reported experiencing incivility at work, with a full 10 percent experiencing it daily. The impact of these etiquette offenses resulted in an estimated $300 billion a year in costs to US companies. Civility and etiquette initiatives serve as foundations for addressing hidden costs, from dissatisfied employees to interpersonal conflicts in the workplace to clients who feel treated callously.

When people collectively stop to think about others, make choices that build relationships, and do it sincerely, the values of consideration, respect, and honesty are put into practice and become recognizable attributes of how an organization does business. The results are nothing short of transformational and often lead to better financial outcomes for the organization and happier, more satisfied employees.

THE 24/7 PROFESSIONAL

Before we dive further into the details of professional etiquette, we'd like to introduce the concept of *The 24/7 Professional*. Being a 24/7 professional isn't about wearing a suit to the movie theater or always having a business card handy—although the latter is a *very* good idea. It's about being confident enough in your public behavior that if someone from your professional life ran into you, no matter how you're dressed or what you're up to, you'd feel good about it.

And that can be very freeing. You just never know when the web of human connection that supports and sustains us will connect you professionally in a way that you didn't foresee. When we have confidence in our public behavior and appearance, we can choose to be professional at a moment's notice.

Here are some of our top takeaways for thinking like a 24/7 professional.

1. Acknowledge that how you appear and behave outside of work has the potential to impact you and your business.

2. Ask yourself if you'd be confident running into your boss, an employee, your client, or a new prospect looking and acting like you are.

3. Be able to flip the switch easily from personal you to professional you, without it seeming like a whole new personality has taken over.

CHAPTER 2

The Five-Step Process

Have you ever heard yourself thinking thoughts such as *Should I send this email? Is now a good time to call? Do I need to make an introduction here? Does he know he's coming off a little tipsy? That presentation was a disaster, and I don't think she gets why. Oh no, I won't make it to the meeting!* Rest easy, you are not alone. These problems come up universally in the workplace. No matter who you are or how good you are at your job or in applying good etiquette, we all face difficult situations or choices involving others where we can be unsure of what to do or say, or we second-guess our instincts. We need a process to help us get through these difficult moments and move forward with confidence.

At the Emily Post Institute, we both use and teach a five-step problem-solving process rooted in our key etiquette principles of consideration, respect, and honesty to bring clarity and direction to situational decision-making. When there is no specific manner or black-and-white choice to resolve a situation, core etiquette principles can be used as a foundation to make choices that account for, consider, and honor all parties involved. By systematically applying consideration, respect, and honesty, our decision-making can take into account the human impact of the choices we make.

Additionally, as we practice each step of the process, we carve a deeper neurological groove into our minds, helping us make good behavior a good habit, something we naturally do.

In stressful situations, uncertainty, doubt, conflict, and social and professional pressure can leave us emotionally at a disadvantage and more likely to make bad choices or simply take unconsidered action. Being practiced in the five-step process helps engage the cognitive centers of the brain to make choices that work best for everyone, even under stress.

The process can be used to solve the actual problems professionals face every day and serve as a teaching tool for aligning the intentions, thinking, and actions of whole groups or organizations. With a slight tweak of the language, problems related to time management, giving critical feedback, or addressing a coworker with a hygiene or personal issue affecting work have relevance to all audiences and situations. This process provides a means for addressing these types of problems in situationally specific and universally considerate ways.

THE FIVE-STEP PROCESS

Let's examine each of the five steps in the process and see how they work together to chart a considerate, respectful, and honest path forward. For the last twenty years, we've used the following example to illustrate a high-pressure, in-the-moment decision that can be broken down easily by our five steps: You're at a work function, and your boss has told you she's looking forward to introducing you to a particular client. A very important client. It's your time to shine. As your boss brings this client over to your group to introduce you, the client sneezes into their hand and stretches it right out to you for a handshake. What do you do?

We've watched people's comfort levels and reactions to the question shift and expand over time. Post-pandemic, we're less likely to offer a truly gross, snotty hand to someone. And people have gotten more comfortable declining handshakes, likely not taking offense when others suggest a handshake might not be the best greeting in the moment. The people involved, the pressure of the moment, and the grossness of the situation paint a vivid scene to work with. Let's break apart what in real life would happen in milliseconds, to see how the five-step process unfolds.

STEP 1: WHO'S IMPACTED?

The first step in the process is straightforward: acknowledge the people affected by the situation or decision you need to make. Start with the people most immediately involved and impacted. These will be the key players, decision-makers, and those directly participating in some way.

Now expand to those who might feel the consequences of any choices made. When you expand your list beyond those most immediately impacted, consider people who might experience effects even if they are separated by a degree or two from the situation, like colleagues in other offices or on other teams, managers, or direct reports who could or will be impacted by the outcome. Think about organizations and groups involved as well. Eyewitnesses, while not directly involved, may also be impacted by what they observe. Consider the friends and families of those directly involved, who often serve as sounding boards for their partner, loved one, or friend.

It may seem like a lot at first—the whole thing could snowball, and suddenly the entire world is involved! But in all seriousness, opening the scope of potential people impacted can help you see the ripple effect of any situation, even for those not directly affected. It serves as a reminder of the full impact of our choices on others. Once you've made your list, move on to step 2.

In our example, the people most directly impacted are you, your boss, and the client. We extend the sphere of influence to the company's reputation and other people at your company who work with this client.

STEP 2: WHAT ARE YOUR OPTIONS?

The second step is to develop and consider several options for solving the problem. The natural tendency is to try to come up with a good or correct solution right at the start. Do that. Now, come up with at least two more ways to respond to the situation. They might be good options, or they may be things that you would never act on. Again, the point is to practice thinking.

After many years of teaching this process, we smile at the most common beginning for an answer in step 2, "I know what to do here . . ." It is usually followed by a pretty good option that truncates the whole process and leaves the person who suggests it with only one way to proceed. This isn't the point.

The idea is to stop and think through this step, thereby pausing your automatic response. Defining at least a few options will get us to our goal by forcing you to think creatively and prevent that first impulse from becoming the default solution.

Think you're finished coming up with solutions? Nope. Now, include at least one bad or one extreme option. Allow the inclusion of a few ways to proceed that are clearly not good ideas or might lead to less-than-optimal outcomes. These aren't things you'll do. But it is helpful in expanding the range of choices in front of you, and it can be immensely clarifying to look at the bad options and identify them as such—it can even be cathartic to identify them, much like writing an angry letter and reading it aloud to no one instead of sending it. This helps hone our decision-making skills. And while it's rare, you never know when a bad idea will spark a good one. Don't skip this part of step 2; it's worth it.

In our example, we have these options:

1. Claiming that we are sick and shouldn't shake hands but are so pleased to meet the client (the escape, you think you're so clever!)

2. Shaking the sneezed-upon hand (gross)

3. Refusing to shake hands

    a. without giving a reason why

    b. or explaining your reason directly

STEP 3: EVALUATING THE OPTIONS

In step 3, we examine each solution and ask, "How does this affect each person in step 1?" For those who like analytical thinking, now's your time to shine. Create or imagine a spreadsheet with rows and columns listing solutions and people. Give each cell a plus (positive) or minus (negative) if the person (or group or organization) is positively or negatively affected by the corresponding response in the row.

OPTION	PERSON IMPACTED: BOSS	PERSON IMPACTED: YOU	PERSON IMPACTED: CLIENT
Decline to shake hands by using an excuse	-	+	-
Shake hands	+	-	+
Refuse to shake hands	-	-	-

Again, resist the natural temptation to predetermine which response likely has the most positive marks. Really go through your "solutions" and "people impacted" lists carefully. Sometimes, what initially seems like a good solution doesn't look so good when you see the impact on all parties. Stay with the process: we're trying to build a new mental map here, so it helps to run through the steps in full until they become automatic.

Sometimes a solution that doesn't appear to be the right one at the start of the process emerges as the winner. It might be that it benefits or honors a critically important person, or it allows other departments to move forward with work, even if it's tougher on you. There can be lots of reasons why a solution might surprise you.

More often, though, the answer you initially believe is correct is a pretty good choice. By thoroughly examining several options from the perspective of how all involved are impacted, much can be learned—and your "pretty good choice" might get much better. And it doesn't hurt when terrible choices can be identified and avoided entirely.

A common reality is that competing interests are often involved when a problem arises. Figuring out a way forward can involve identifying those competing interests (you don't want to hold a snotty gross hand; your boss is expecting you to shake hands; the client is expecting you to shake hands) and finding a balance between them or choosing a side with clarity and integrity. Having a complete picture of how different approaches can yield different outcomes for the people involved can help make tough choices easier.

STEP 4: MAKING THE CHOICE

Here, we decide on the best solution we want to employ moving forward. Ideally, this solution will produce the most favorable outcomes for the people involved. From an etiquette perspective, this solution builds or grows the relationships among the people involved.

Step 4 is a chance to be authentic. The word *authentic* gets used a great deal these days, and its importance should not be overlooked in this five-step process. People want to see themselves as authentic, coherent individuals who operate from a clear and strong sense of self. They want their thoughts, words, and actions to align. They want to be genuine in their professional lives and do business with people who are also direct and trustworthy. If you value relationships with others (and if you are reading this, you most likely do), this is where you can choose to take action based on how you *and others* will be impacted.

With the five-step process, the primary consideration is growing relationships. It won't always be the only factor—cost, quality, hierarchy, speed, efficiency, sustainability, familiarity, and other factors may come into play—but by following the steps, we keep consideration for people and how they are affected front of mind. And that is a step in the process that should give your solution an integrity that others will appreciate.

In our example, after having played out in your head how not shaking hands impacts nearly everyone except you negatively and how making up a lie could come to catch you later, you may decide that shaking hands is the best option. You may be taking a hit on the grossness factor, but you're smoothing the way for at least two important people in your life. Or you may decide that you could and would decline the handshake—no excuses or lies—"Pardon my not shaking hands, I'm so pleased to meet you" and bear the social consequences. Call us bonkers but we suggest shaking the hand—don't worry, we have a fifth step to help take care of you as well.

STEP 5: REFINING YOUR SOLUTION

It's important to ensure that your solutions are working as well as they can, and in any good system, there should be a little bit of wiggle room to make refinements when necessary. After working to consider all parties involved, weighing multiple ways to act, evaluating options while thinking of others, and choosing a solution with integrity, step 5 is to fine-tune the details by making practical and thoughtful adjustments to your solution.

When your solution involves having to offer your opinion or feedback, consider how this truth can be delivered in a way that is kind and helpful as opposed to overly frank, inconsiderate, or even cruel. It can be tempting to set yourself apart by identifying how others fall short, but it won't win you fans. Wrapping your solution in care for others and thinking about how to do that well goes a very long way toward positively building the relationship from this moment on.

In step 5, we encourage reflection on how to avoid difficulties that may arise in the future. Take a moment to list some preventative measures you or others can take to ensure your solutions stick or the problem doesn't arise again. Avoiding problems in the future by learning from challenges is the professional way to move forward. Working through a difficult moment helps us hone our decision-making skills and provides us with insight.

Our refined solution is to shake that sneezed-on hand confidently because you have reassured yourself that you can avoid bringing your hand to your face after the handshake and can wash your hands afterward. Your decision honors the client and your boss, and you've represented yourself and the company well in the moment. Now you can go wash your hands.

TEAMWORK

The five-step process is a powerful tool for allowing teams or groups to solve complex, subtle, and personal problems collectively. A benefit of this process is how it empowers teams and groups to approach and solve problems together. Colleagues and executive teams alike can look at a problem with unclear or different ideas about how to proceed and work toward a solution using common language and reference points. Effective solutions and informed choices result when the whole team better understands the solution and how they got there.

By identifying core values and using a step-by-step system for applying those values at work, group members learn to make choices that build relationships for themselves and with each other. Aligning individual and collective goals is how great organizations and businesses are built. Making consistent and coherent choices, individually *and* collectively, is how a trustworthy brand is established and organizational goals find authentic expression. When it is working, it can feel like magic, but it must be taught, nurtured, and practiced.

REFERENCE GUIDES

PRACTICE THE FIVE STEPS

Below are some of the most common situations we use to teach and practice the steps of the five-step process in our business etiquette seminars. Use the following issues to practice going through the five-step process.

- You're running late for a meeting. This has happened before. You would . . . ?

- A coworker has bad body odor, and your boss has asked you, their manager, to fix the problem. You would . . . ?

- You just watched a colleague do poorly during a pitch meeting. He eagerly asks you afterward if you think he did a good job. You would . . . ?

- You're working from home, lost track of time, and you have a video meeting in five minutes. When it comes to turning on your camera, you would . . . ?

Setting up a worksheet like the one on page 22 can be great for organizing your thoughts as you work the five-step process.

WORKSHEET

YOUR QUESTION:

Boss brings over a client to shake hands, client sneezes into hand before extending it to you.

YOU WOULD...

CONSIDERATION (WHO IS AFFECTED AND HOW?):

1. Client 2. Boss 3. ME! 4. Company reputation? 5. My dependents?

SOLUTIONS (WHAT ARE SOME POSSIBLE OPTIONS?):

1. RUN! 2. Refuse the handshake 3. Make an excuse 4. Shake hands

RESPECT (HOW DOES EACH OPTION AFFECT WHOEVER IS INVOLVED?):

1. Bad idea everybody loses 2. Could offend boss and client but good for me
3. Good for me, maybe bad for boss and client? 4. Bad for me, good for everyone else

HONESTY (WHICH OPTION IS BEST FOR EVERYONE INVOLVED?):

Shaking hands is probably best. I can handle the ick factor if it means
I grow the relationship and make my boss proud in the moment.

REFINE (IS THERE ANYTHING THAT IMPROVES ON THE CHOSEN ACTION?):

I won't touch my face after we shake hands and I'll go wash my hands after we're
finished talking.

CHAPTER 3

Professional Appearance

Your professional appearance comprises everything from how you look in person and come across online to the attitude you bring to the table and even the words you choose. You will continue to develop your professional persona throughout your career, but your appearance is the first piece of information that people will have about you. It's how you represent not just yourself, but also your business and the other people that you work with. Since you can hone your appearance, it's an opportunity to tell the story of you as a professional well. Let's look at how to curate a professional appearance to ensure it supports doing work and building the impression we want to make.

INTENTION AND IMPRESSIONS

The way we present ourselves, intentionally and unintentionally, matters and *will* say a great deal about us—even if our professional appearance isn't the whole story. By making intentional choices about appearance, we can help direct what others focus on. It's a powerful tool for taking control of our identity and the impression we make on the world around us—especially when others who don't know you are deciding whether to work with you. The care you take with appearance communicates a certain level of awareness and responsibility.

When we *intentionally* choose to style and present ourselves, we are more likely to create a positive impression on those we meet and even those we already know. Take the time to consider what it is you are dressing for, the environment you'll be in, the people you'll be with, and the work that will be getting done or the goal. By doing these three things, you are intentional about your professional appearance, and that intention will literally show. And you've just made it that much easier for colleagues, the interviewer, or that prospect to focus on you and the good work you bring to the table. You've bolstered the impression that you make and left less room for others to judge you or to walk away with an incorrect or, worse, negative impression.

Without intention or attention in our appearance, we add hurdles and lose control of the impression we want to make. Bad breath, unkempt hair, ill-fitting pants, and a wrinkled or stained shirt create too many barriers for someone to jump through to focus on you and the work you're trying to showcase. You risk making it harder for others to receive you—the one who is excellent at so many things.

Take the same outfit above, but wash and iron the shirt (or add a sweater over it), give our person a shower, a little attention to the hair, and a pair of pants that fit right, and all of a sudden, we have a presentable, even if in a relaxed way, worker. We are focused on what they say and do, not how they look. The hurdles have been removed, and they make a more favorable and positive impression.

Your relationship with professional attire functions in two ways. First, by simply meeting the baseline of the expected standards, you prevent your wardrobe from being a distraction to others. Second, when you demonstrate care and attention to your appearance, the people you work with can literally see the effort you make. The intention that you bring to your professional appearance can help you create the impression you want to leave on others.

YOUR BEST IMAGE

Once upon a time, we used to say, "Dress like this . . ." to advise on dressing appropriately for a particular event, or even just for going out in public. However, today we really can't say that. There isn't one standard that completely reigns as both appropriate and desirable. You might think everyone looks good or "appropriate" in khakis and a sweater. Sure, it's a common outfit that spans the genders, and it's relatively modest depending on the cut of each piece, but not everyone feels like a khakis-and-sweater type of person. Claiming that one style is appropriate would limit us and stifle individual identity. The same is true for hairstyles, makeup choices, body art, and any other aspect of our appearance over which we have control. Instead of adhering to one standard, **the goal for any professional is to present and represent yourself and your business well and to respect the occasion and environment you are dressing for.** The overall impression we create depends upon three things: your appearance, actions, and words. In any situation, think first about the purpose of your interaction; let this be your guide for determining how to groom, dress, speak, and act. Are you presenting to a new client? Attending a colleague's wedding? Going to a religious service with your in-laws? Playing pickup basketball with a direct report? Attending a charity gala dinner where your company has reserved a table? You won't likely wear the same thing or behave the same way at each, but in each case the attention you give your appearance matters both for you and for others.

Here, we'll look at appearance, actions, and words more closely and consider how we can use them effectively to ensure that those we work with encounter our most professional selves. But first, let's learn how to do an image assessment of ourselves.

IMAGE ASSESSMENT EXERCISE

If etiquette is about how we interact with the world, we must understand who we are with others and how others see us. Honest, ongoing self-assessment is a critical skill for making choices about presenting ourselves—daily. Hugely successful people regularly practice all kinds of self-assessments to understand how others experience them, and then they use that to their benefit. Everyone is capable of doing this, and we can do it for many aspects of our professional life, not just our appearance. Our communications (especially email), our work product, our social profiles, and even our Google search results are also candidates for this kind of assessment. In terms of professional appearance, look at yourself as you are right now, with no quick touch-ups or past or future versions in your mind's eye. Now, follow these steps:

1. RESPECT YOURSELF. This is not an opportunity to rip yourself to shreds and validate every critical thought you have about yourself. That won't help. It's also not an exercise in self-congratulation. It *is* about how you can emphasize what's best about your appearance and work on what could be improved. Respect yourself as you challenge yourself.

2. PICK CONCRETE AREAS TO FOCUS ON. Ask yourself the following questions about your choices. These questions are a self-assessment to get you thinking about what others are likely to notice. There are no right or wrong answers. Check in on the following areas:

How do I look? grooming, hygiene, attire, accessories, social profiles, Google search results

What are my actions like? posture, gestures, eye contact/attention, nervous habits

How do I sound? tone, speed, volume, pronunciation, inflection, laughter, word choice, phone greetings

What are extensions of my overall appearance? Email address, phone greeting or answering machine outgoing message, work product, driving/pedestrian habits, text-speak (sometimes these can be more important, for example, someone working remotely)

If you wear a uniform to work, you are more likely to consider aspects other than attire when determining your appearance.

3. UNDERSTAND YOUR COMPLEXITY. We are all complex and multifaceted; sorting out which parts of you will be emphasized in your professional persona is a big aspect of being intentional and taking care with your appearance. Who are you today, for yourself and the different people in your life? How do you shift yourself (your actions, appearance, and words) as you change roles, interacting with different people and environments at different times? You and a colleague might look, act, and even sound different while you work on a project at home versus how you look, act, and sound when presenting the same project in the office or to a client. Same two people, same project, but different venue and a few added people (whether they be colleagues or clients), and you'll be making an adjustment to your overall appearance. Understanding this complexity will let you use it to your advantage. In many ways, you are probably already doing this without even thinking about it. Doing it intentionally to help fine-tune your professional self is another tool for creating successful business impressions and interactions.

Now that you've reflected on who you are right now and in different scenarios, what do you feel good about? Which areas would you like to improve or change? Maybe your grooming and hygiene are great, but you noticed that your wardrobe could use some honing for where you are now going in your career. That's great! It gives you something to work on, something to build toward.

Maintaining a good image is about consistency; improving your image will require a willingness to change. Each change you take on, big or small, can impact your overall sense of professionalism and the impression you create. Take care. Start with small things and take them one at a time. *Think* each potential change through, and make choices that help you present your best self to the world around you. That thinking first is intentionality in practice.

This process will build your confidence and put you more at ease as you interact with others, and it's worth it to return to it periodically. Those hugely successful people we mentioned before regularly incorporate tactics like this into their lives.

APPEARANCE

Our appearance (including hygiene and personal grooming) communicates to others that we are taking care of ourselves, that we are conscious of how we present ourselves to the world around us, and that we understand the difference between an event, our home, and a workday versus an off-work day. We signal with our appearance how ready we are to be in a space, with others, working toward a particular goal. Our professional appearance should facilitate work getting done, not be a distraction from work. We know we've missed the mark if others are so focused on an aspect of our appearance that is under our control that they aren't focused on the pitch we just made, the great idea we shared, or the question we asked.

Things to consider when it comes to your appearance:

- **CLEANLINESS OF YOUR SKIN.** This is especially important for your hands and face.

- **CLEANLINESS OF YOUR HAIR.** The style is less of a concern than that hair (or baldness) should be clean and intentionally managed. Odor-free is important.

- **YOUR PERSONAL SCENT.** Whether your self-assessment results in noticing that you have a strong, neutral, or pleasant aroma, your goal is to have a neutral scent. Pleasantness is a good second goal. But it is very important to know that strong perfumes, colognes, and body sprays can irritate and even sicken those around you. Be very sparing in your use of scent.

- **YOUR CLOTHING SHOULD REFLECT THE OCCASION.** It's important to respect the occasion you are dressing for, whether that's a normal day at work, a work event, or dinner out with the boss and a client. Remember, the fit and condition impact your overall appearance as well.

- **YOUR ACCESSORIES.** Elements such as makeup, jewelry, or wearable tech should be styled and worn to enhance your overall image without distracting or making you stand out too much.

- **BODY ART.** Body art can be deeply meaningful to us and is part of the overall impression that we create with others. Clearly, this is not something you can alter day to day, and is a significant part of your image, so be prepared to incorporate these elements into your professional style.

A note on judging appearance: For all that we talk about how the way you present yourself will create an impression, and how we want to be aware—especially in business—of the impression we make, it's still never in good taste to judge someone else solely on their appearance. And it is unwise. Disabilities as well as cultural and religious guidelines can cause all kinds of attire necessities that you might not be familiar with if you don't experience them yourself. There may be many reasons someone's appearance doesn't match your own idea of attire standards. For example, in speaking with Emily Voorde of Into Strategies, a disability liaison to the Biden administration and Congress, and a wheelchair user, we learned that it's very common and often unavoidable for wheelchair users to have skid marks on their sleeves. By not judging those marks right away, but instead leaving room open for reason, we increase the likelihood of being inclusive and understanding when it comes to professional attire.

Mocking or negatively commenting on anyone's voice, actions, or appearance is a surefire way to make a lasting negative impression. Microaggressions such as eye rolls, silent judgments, condescension, bemused or shocked looks shot behind someone's back, or fake compliments—all of these are rude and far from the behavior of any polite business professional. In business, those actions can be grounds for dismissal. We often think about business as where we must be tough and take what comes our way. However, harassment is not tolerated in the business world and commenting on other's appearance can be harassing behavior. The appearance anyone should pay such attention to is their own.

GROOMING AND HYGIENE

There are always social rewards for meeting the hygiene norms of the day. For example, brushing our teeth regularly can help kill germs and freshen our breath so that in-person conversations can be comfortable. However inconvenient or arbitrary they might seem, expectations around hygiene in any culture are part of what protects us from disease and contagion. Paying attention to these standards is one way of showing care and respect for others and ourselves at work. If you have any questions about company requirements around grooming and hygiene, go to your HR department or manager.

When it comes to hair, "clean cuts" and "neat and tidy" styles were once part of the stereotypical businessperson's appearance. Most workplaces today are more accepting of a variety of hair and hairstyles, recognizing that abolishing certain styles can be exclusionary and even racist. However hair is styled, it's still important to keep it clean and ensure it smells clean. There is a difference between trying a new style (fine) and trying a new style that routinely gets in your way—or in the case of some beehives and buns, gets in others' way.

Keeping our hair groomed and our skin and teeth clean is our best shot at preventing a highly dreaded awkwardness at work: an odor problem. By committing to good grooming and hygiene routines, we greatly reduce the likelihood that others will find our personal aroma unpleasant.

We advise asking a close friend for feedback if you have a grooming or hygiene concern. People don't usually comment on these things (because they are trying to be polite), so inviting someone you trust to do so specifically might help if you want to get advice and make improvements. We all experience physical changes throughout life (a new workout routine, aging, a new diet, hormonal changes; even dental work can change how often food sticks in teeth) that can affect the way we appear. You're not likely to notice the smell of your breath or body odor or to see new (and possibly unwanted) hair growth. We recommend you ask for an outside perspective. Ask specifically and not just as an open-ended permission: "Hey, Liz, do I have coffee breath today?"

BODY

Our posture, facial expressions, and gestures all contribute to people's impression of us. Being aware of our body and how we occupy space, how we position ourselves in relation to others, and how we hold ourselves (we'll get to posture below) all impact our interactions with others. We highly recommend taking the time to pay concerted attention to how your body impacts the space around you as you sit, walk, and move through spaces at work.

POSTURE

When your posture is upright and relaxed, you are approachable and look engaged but not intense. Hunching your shoulders and looking down, purposely avoiding eye contact, or crossing your arms often gives the impression that you are unapproachable, guarded, or unfriendly. Save these for times when they are necessary. If your body naturally assumes this posture, use your tone, words, and gestures to help convey approachability and friendliness.

GESTURES

We all have a unique vocabulary of gestures that contributes to our overall persona. Get to know your own, curate them, and use them well. Large, wild gestures can make someone seem vibrantly alive and wonderfully entertaining, but they can also be perceived as over the top, distracting, or even out of control, depending on the circumstances. While the business world is ever-evolving, it tends to favor moderation. Pay attention to moderating your gestures as you would moderate your voice. Your gestures will be smaller and more intentional in a more serious setting than in a social setting, where you might gesture more impulsively. Touching someone on the arm or shoulder could be a gesture of camaraderie or support in social circumstances, but be aware that in business, the occasion for touching a colleague is usually limited to a handshake.

EYE CONTACT

For most people, eye contact is a sign of trust and confidence. Matching someone's gaze and looking them in the eye shows a willingness to connect. Maintaining eye contact lets the person you're speaking with know that you are focused on them and paying attention. If eye contact is difficult or is too intense, you can also look at their lips or the bridge of their nose. Use your posture to create the same sense of trust, confidence, and focus by keeping your face directed at (and body turned toward) the person speaking as best you can.

FACIAL EXPRESSIONS

Facial expressions have a big impact on our interactions with others. When our expression doesn't match our mood or role at work, we can unintentionally send the wrong signal. When your role is to welcome people, a welcoming expression is essential. This doesn't mean a big cheesy smile (some might even say that could be creepy), but a pleasant and approachable expression—corners of the mouth neutral or slightly upturned (doesn't have to be a full smile), a relaxed brow, and eyes open, not narrowed—will align well with the job at hand. A great tip from the performing arts community is to use a mirror or your phone to practice your facial expressions and see what you look like as you say specific common phrases related to your job. This can be fun! Challenge yourself to keep a straight face but have welcoming eyes or to smile gently while conveying sympathy through your eyes. There are all kinds of combinations to practice and get familiar with. This is an excellent exercise if you get asked if you're okay a lot when you're fine.

DISTRACTING HABITS

Habits such as tapping your fingers, clicking your pen, twirling your hair, pulling your mustache, stroking your beard, biting your nails, or cracking your knuckles can give the impression that you are unaware, nervous, or preoccupied. Finding ways to channel that energy can prevent others from being distracted by it and puts you back in control of your image. For example, if you have trouble maintaining eye contact, try maintaining it for three seconds, then work up to five, seven, or ten seconds. If you bounce your leg in meetings or while on calls, you can substitute pressing your thumb and forefinger together; it makes less noise and doesn't shake the table or ground.

Interrupting a habit is not easy. Changing these behaviors requires action and attention. Frustratingly, we don't always notice these habits in ourselves. Not sure if you have any distracting habits? Ask a friend or partner to help you identify them when they happen; they may appreciate the opportunity to point something out.

APPARENT CONDITIONS

Some of us have or exhibit apparent conditions such as stuttering, tics, trembling, different eating or breathing styles, mobility aids, and more. And many people have difficulty making or maintaining eye contact. Do not ask about or mention someone's condition. If someone has an apparent condition and is comfortable discussing it, they will. If they don't bring it up, you shouldn't either. Staring or being caught off guard is also not polite.

VOICE

You don't need to be seen to make an impression. Your voice is an essential part of your professional image. Tone, speed, inflection, and even our laughter all contribute to how we are perceived by others. Let's look at how to use these elements to enhance our professional image.

VOLUME

Have you ever heard a parent (or maybe yourself) imploring someone to use an "indoor voice"? This essential courtesy is as important in business as anywhere else. It is usually a good idea to speak clearly (for most of us, this means slowly) and at a medium volume level so that we are neither shouting nor whispering. What would it take for you to easily be heard by and hear someone three feet away from you? That's a medium level. Practice lowering your voice if you talk loudly, or speaking up if you talk softly. Unsure? Notice the volume others are using in the conversation. If their voice is lowered, you might want to lower yours, too. You can also watch the other person for cues about your volume. Are they leaning back? Stepping away? Leaning in or turning an ear toward you? Pay attention and you'll find the right balance.

PRO TIP: Imagine you are tossing a ball to the person you are speaking with. This kind of physical mapping can help you direct your volume in the situation.

TONE AND INFLECTION

Practice different tones and pitches with your voice: serious, friendly, concerned. How do you sound? By being aware of your different tones and honing them so that they register with others when you use them, you'll be able to access them more easily at intense moments when you may be tempted to use a less-than-business-polite tone. Save your angry and even humorous inflections for when they are truly needed—they will be more effective if they match the moment rather than become a default.

SPEED

Enunciating words properly can help slow down speech and make it easier for others to understand. However, over-enunciate and you may appear stiff or patronizing. It's a delicate balance. Reflecting on your own speed is tough. Your brain thinks the words before they are spoken, so it's primed to understand them. If you find others asking you to repeat yourself regularly, you may speak too fast for them to catch what you are saying and separate the words. If you find that others tend to jump in regularly and intrude on your thoughts as you try to express them, it could be a sign that you speak slowly and your audience is wondering if you've finished. Asking a colleague about your speed of speech can help you gauge where you're at.

VOCAL FILLER

Like, ummmmmmmmmmmmm, be careful that unintended . . . uh . . . , verbal . . . , like . . . , filler words don't . . . um creep into your . . . , like . . . , um . . . , speech patterns unnecessarily . . . like okay? We're not talking about stuttering here, or altered speech. We're talking about letting yourself get lazy with your language. We all do it, whether it manifests as a bunch of "umms" or "errs" or "likes," you want to kick this habit if you hear it starting up in yourself.

These habits can be deeply ingrained and may require persistent attention to correct—you may need to ask someone to be on you about it when they catch you doing it. It's worth the effort. In business, the more that your speech can be clear and concise, the more easily you and your great ideas will be understood.

PRONUNCIATION

Once upon a time, how someone pronounced words indicated the social spheres they belonged to. Today, we are much more interested in clarity of communication than in one's particular vocabulary. Use words that *you* understand well, both the meaning and the pronunciation. You don't want to give the impression that you are talking about something you don't understand. That said, *never* snicker or laugh at someone who mispronounces a brand name or location. It's a direct route to othering, and it's rude. See page 139, To Correct or Not to Correct?

ACCENT

An accent can be a charming, even disarming, part of your image. You do, however, want to minimize the chance of being misunderstood. If you have a regional accent that you are aware of or are doing business in a second language, stay open to signs that someone is having trouble understanding you. Show self-awareness by being ready to slow down, repeat something, or even use a different word to help someone else understand.

> **PRO TIP**: Get to know yourself better by recording your voice and listening to yourself. You can try it in different situations. Record and then listen to yourself reading materials from work such as an email, taking part in half of a business call, or practicing a presentation. You can even read from a favorite piece of literature. Hearing yourself will help you assess yourself. Additionally, AI can help you if you choose a program that can analyze emotional tone, speed, and clarity.

ATTIRE

There is one outfit in particular that has always been a staple of the business world: a buttoned shirt, tucked in, with a pair of nice slacks and closed-toed shoes. This wardrobe basic can work for almost any setting and almost every person, regardless of gender or body composition, especially with the many variations for dressing it up or down and making it more personal to you, your style, and your needs. There are thousands of outfits we could discuss as being professional—entire books have been written—but for now, we're going to focus on this classic, and we encourage you to imagine how you can make it your own. For example, if you don't wear pants, a mid-length to tea-length skirt will substitute nicely.

KNOW YOUR WARDROBE

Understanding the formality and style of the attire that corresponds to your industry isn't always easy. Overall, you'll fare well in business by trading on your good ideas, not your good looks, so we recommend starting out with conservative attire in a new job or when meeting a new client. Not every industry will require this. If you're a Colorado River Guide, shorts and tank tops will likely be expected in your profession, but for those working in office environments (even home office environments), skewing conservative—especially while you are still getting to know your company and position there (or a client)—is a safe bet. Trends will come and go, but having foundational pieces to work with will help you be prepared for any professional situation. Let's look at a few basics of classic professional attire.

THE CLASSIC DRESS SHIRT

The dress shirt is an iconic staple, whether blue or white (or almost any other color). It symbolizes professionalism and work, and it can be worn by anyone. You'd think a shirt with a collar and buttons is obvious enough that you don't need instruction on how to wear one, but some specifics are worth knowing and will help you style yourself well professionally. The overall goal? Don't allow your clothes to speak louder than you.

1. Collar buttons determine the name and style of the shirt. If there are no collar buttons, it's simply a *dress shirt* or sometimes a *collared* or *buttoned shirt*. This is the most formal and easy to wear a tie with. A *button-down shirt* has buttons that help hold the collar tabs down (a more casual style).

2. The hem style, whether for a button-down or dress shirt, is either a wave or undulation meant to be worn tucked in or straight across, allowing the shirt to be untucked if the wearer wants.

3. Collars come in different shapes. The most common is the *American-style collar*, with longer collar points and a narrow gap between them. A *European-style collar* has less of a peaked point and a wider spread. Both are common and appropriate. With no tie, the top button is usually left unbuttoned, regardless of whether the collar is buttoned.

4. Cuffs come in different shapes as well. A *French cuff* is long and folds back over itself. It's held in place with *cuff links,* which are formal and most common with a tuxedo. A *standard cuff* with the button secured is a great professional look. A standard cuff with the button undone and the cuff and sleeve rolled up is more casual. This is literally where we get the phrase "roll up your sleeves," meaning "get to work."

5. On color. The most formal color for a dress shirt is white, followed by ecru. Dress down the shirt by taking it to a shade of light blue, and then you can go further if you want to have fun by entertaining other colors, textures, and patterns.

PRO TIP: If you are not wearing a tie with your button-down or collared shirt, ensure your undershirt's neckline does not show (it might be time to pick up a pack of V-necked tees).

PANTS

Suit pants are often fine wool or refined fabric with the option of pleats or a crease on the front of the leg, with an optional cuff. This is the most formal option and worn only with a suit jacket. *Slacks,* also made of fine fabrics and styled like a suit pant, are the next most dressy option and do not have to be part of a suit. *Khakis* are constructed of heavier cotton fabric. They are more durable than the dressier options and can be easier to clean. They are a step down in formality from slacks and a step up from chinos. *Chinos* are also cotton but usually a lighter version, and they typically forgo pleats, creases, and cuffs, bringing these pants one step up from jeans. *Jeans* were originally rugged work pants. We see them worn with jackets and sports coats today to dress them up, but they are still considered casual pants. Leggings made an impressive attempt at working their way into the workplace in the aughts; even up-styled, they are casual wear. Sweatpants and athleisurewear are gym, recreational, and at-home appropriate. Shorts of any kind are not pants. Unless your boss is wearing fashion shorts or you work in an industry where shorts are standard attire, consider them inappropriate for work.

THE WORK DRESS AND WORK SKIRT

There is so much variability in the work dress and work skirt. Typically, this dress or skirt falls at or close to knee-length. While longer and shorter styles are certainly seen in the work environment, this is a "safe bet" measurement to go by until you know what's appropriate for your particular company and the everyday situations you encounter there. A work dress may or may not have a collar, but generally we suggest you avoid a deep plunging neckline unless you're wearing something underneath the dress. It's not that cleavage must be hidden, but the question to ask yourself is how much of it feels appropriate to you, for your industry, your company, or this particular event. Whether you wear tights or pantyhose with a work skirt or dress is up to you unless it's part of a uniform. Colors, patterns, and materials can all vary for dresses and skirts, the ever-present goal being not to allow your clothing to speak louder than you.

SHOES

Black patent leather is the most formal shoe and has the highest shine, with matte- or satin-black leather and both patent and matte or satin-brown leather being the next most formal. Closed-toed loafers, lace-ups, flats, pumps, heels (under three inches), and the like are commonly considered office-appropriate. Fashion sneakers can be an option if you know what you are doing (we see you, Jordan 3s). Go for it. However, gym shoes or dirty, well-worn sneakers are not work wear. Open-toed shoes are breezy and comfortable but not traditional office attire, except for some peep-toe styles. Sandals (Tevas, Birkenstocks, Kinos, or similar) are usually a no-go at work. Flip-flops are not work appropriate, and the noise drives many people up the wall. Fashion boots and booties occupy a strange space in work attire. Even though they bring a lot of style and look fantastic, even elegant, they are often considered more casual and semi-formal wear. Boots that function to protect us from the elements are definitely considered casual wear, and many people have "office shoes" to change into once they're at work. Know your company's dress code so that you can know what footwear is appropriate.

YOUR TECH

Your phone, tablet, smartwatch, and computer, the condition they are kept in, and the protective cases and covers you use are an extension of your professional persona. These devices are accessories to your overall wardrobe and appearance. Don't make our mistake and walk into a presentation for one company flashing a laptop made by a competitor. Oh, yes, we did. Obviously, we weren't going to buy a new computer for one presentation, but using an on-site one with our presentation on a thumb drive or cloud account would have made a better impression. Make sure the appearance of your devices matches the impression you'd like to be making.

JEWELRY AND WATCHES

Wearing jewelry or watches is a personal choice. Beyond any restrictions for safety or sanitary reasons, it's really up to you how much and which types you wear. One thing to be aware of when wearing multiple items is the amount of noise they can make when bumping together. Watches that chime or offer alerts can also be distractions. Like many aspects of our attire, accessories can be distinctive, and intriguing or distracting. Avoid letting them steal the spotlight when it comes to business.

THE SUIT

A matching jacket and pants or skirt is a symbol of professionalism, and for much of the twentieth century it reigned supreme in office settings. For some it's an everyday uniform. For others it's the outfit we turn to for interviews, presentations, evening work events, and more. If you need a suit either in pursuit of your career, for everyday use, or for special work occasions, you'll want to wear it well. When we think of a business suit, we think of confidence, success, power, capability, and more. The suit symbolizes a transition into adulthood for many, a shift from casual to professional. The suit sends a signal that says, "I am prepared and capable, and I look it." What matters the most about a suit isn't the name on the label but instead how well it is fitted, the purposes you have for it, and the care you take to keep it in good shape.

Shirts, belts, ties, shoes, and sometimes a vest or pocket square will enhance your suit and allow you to dress it up or down. If you can have only one suit in your wardrobe, we highly recommend a dark blue color and a medium-weight fabric that's easy to care for. Let's look at the components of the classic suit.

> **PRO TIP**: If suits are going to be part of your regular professional wardrobe, we highly suggest you find a tailor that you like. They can help you with simple alterations, making sure your suit always fits right. And it's a lot cheaper to make a small adjustment than to purchase a whole new suit.

JACKET

A well-fitted jacket is a thing of beauty no matter who is wearing it. Everyone looks fantastic in a suit jacket that has been fitted to their body. Each body is different, and we cannot recommend enough finding a local tailor to adjust your jacket for you and to you. Here are some things to consider as you pick out a suit jacket.

- Whether your suit has *two or three buttons* on the jacket front, always leave the bottom button undone and the other(s) buttoned while standing. Unbutton a jacket to sit or while standing to adopt a more casual look.

- The shape and width of *lapels* and the size of *shoulder padding* change with trends. A *single-notch*, neither narrow nor wide, lapel is a safe bet for most business purposes. Shoulder pads that naturally enhance and avoid exaggerating your shape are another safe bet. When purchasing, make choices that don't push the envelope on style trends if you want your suit to wear well for as long as it was designed to and be universal for you. Save the peak lapels for more formal occasions, and wear them with distinction.

- *Vents* allow your suit to fall well as you stand, sit, and move. *Single-vent* jackets are often described as American, but no American should feel out of place in a double-vented jacket if it is preferred. *Double-vented* (also referred to as having *side vents*) jackets suit more body types, as the side fabric can fall evenly and oftentimes look better when sitting down.

- A proper *vest* instantly creates a *three-piece suit* of distinction. Snug through the middle, this extra layer also adds formality. Have fun with it or use it to dress up a favorite suit, but be aware of its old-timey appeal and relatively minimal use as a common everyday item. It makes a statement.

- *Double-breasted suits* have two rows of buttons on the front, creating a formal, old-fashioned feel. They are traditional, but not to the degree that they are silly or costume-like. One might call them stately.

- It's up to you whether to add a *pocket square, lapel pin, brooch, tie bar* or *watch chain,* but be aware that the general rule is to add only one of these things at a time. Be sure that a pocket square is folded thoughtfully. You can do a quick online search to see which styling of pocket square best suits you and your situation.

SUIT PANTS/SKIRT

Whether your suit jacket is paired with pants or a skirt (or a dress that goes under the jacket) is totally up to you; however, with both types of bottoms, we highly advise not going too short. Even with high hem styles coming and going in fashion trends, with pants a nice clean hemline (with or without a cuff) that comes down to the shoes (whether you go for the "break," a single fold appearing on the top of the foot, or not) has always been a good, clean, professional look. Pleats or a flat front is a style choice based on body shape. Both can look good, and will not be seen unless the jacket is unbuttoned. The creased leg front adds a cared-for formality that will fade with wearing. So, if you go this route, keep it sharp and get these pants pressed regularly. Whether your skirt is pleated is entirely a style choice; however, some pleated styles, especially if they are pushing the limits of being short rather than knee length, will evoke a younger or more playful feel. A pencil skirt in comparison is more elegant and serious in tone.

TIES

The tie may be a very masculine symbol of the business world, but people of all genders have incorporated it into their outfits for years. No matter what you pair your tie with, know that how you style it will add to the overall impression of your appearance. A loose tie over a scoop-neck T-shirt has a very different impact than a half-Windsor knot with a crisply starched white collared shirt. Know the difference between wearing your tie creatively or classically, and you'll give yourself options for this great accessory.

The most important advice to give anyone who does not already wear ties is to practice tying them. Practice so you don't have to stress when the moment arrives and you're trying to get out the door or prepare for the meeting.

Learning how to tie a tie (or a few different tie knots) is a life skill that can help you feel confident dressing for many different events, from formal functions to business scenarios, and any time you want to sharpen—or even get playful with—your look. The four great knots to know are the four-in-hand, the partial or half-Windsor, the Windsor, and the bow tie. Become familiar with these, and you'll have nothing but options!

CHOOSING LENGTH When tied well, the front and broad side of the tie should fall to about, but not below, the belt line.

MANAGING WIDTH The knot you choose will be based on the width of your shirt's collar spread. Wide collar spreads can accommodate bigger or wider knots, while narrower collar spreads require narrower and longer knots.

THE DIMPLE The tie dimple, a small crease or fold in the center of the knot, has been a consistent desired fashion choice for years. When set right, it's like the perfect punctuation to the sentence that is your outfit. Practice tying your ties so that you get a dimple you like.

REPP TIES Diagonal stripes going up and to the right indicate an American tie, and British repp stripes go up to the left (cutting the heart).

BOLOS AND SKINNY TIES Bolos and skinny ties have their place in formal attire particularly on festive formal occasions.

CLIPS AND BARS Whether you choose to wear a tie clip or tie bar is up to you (though you wouldn't wear both at the same time).

SCARVES There are hundreds of different ways to wear scarves, from small ascots that fit tightly around the neck to beautiful silk scarves draped around the shoulders and tied with stunning or chic knots. Pinterest is one of our favorite places to search for scarf-tying videos and tutorials.

OUR KNOT OF CHOICE

We at the Emily Post Institute have been waiting for years to share this with everyone: Not the four-in-hand, the half-Windsor, or the Windsor. Not the standard, Kelvin, Prince Albert, or Pratt. We think of it as the family knot and refer to it affectionately as the Post. Tied well, this knot is medium sized, well-shaped, symmetrical, and durable. For visual guidance, see How to Tie the Post Knot on page 52.

1. Drape the tie over the back of your neck so that the wide length hangs down over your right shoulder and chest and the skinny length drapes over your left. The seam of each should be against your chest. Adjust the lengths so that the wide one is longer than the thin one by about five inches.

2. Now, create the base of the knot by bringing the wide length to the left and crossing it over the thin length as you do. Next, bring the wide length back to the right side by going behind the thin length. You've now wrapped the wide length one full time around the thin length and have created the base of the knot.

3. Wrap the wide length up in front of the base of the knot and then down through the neck opening, coming out underneath the neck loop and to the right (where you started). You are essentially going all the way around the right side of the neck loop one time. The seam of the wide length will now face outward.

4. Bring the wide length to the left by going over the front of the knot so that its edge is horizontal; this new layer covers the base of the knot you created in step one. With the wide length on the left side now, take it behind the knot and up through the neck hole. Pull it down into the knot by going behind the top layer of the knot but on top of the base of the knot.

5. Pull the wide length down and pinch and work the knot, tightening it as needed until it's snugly under the spread of your collar. To create a dimple, pull down on the tie while holding the knot. The thin end should be short enough that it doesn't stick out below the wide length, and it should be long enough to tuck into the little bit of ribbon on the back of the wide end of the tie that is meant to hold it in place.

IMAGE EXERCISE

We find the following exercise really impactful. Find an exemplary person who you think presents well professionally. You can observe from a distance, but be specific about what you look for in them. What choices are they making with their clothes? What stays the same? What do they change day to day or based on the occasion? If they are someone you are close with or know reasonably well, you can even ask them for advice. "I admire how you dress. Do you mind if I ask what stores you shop at or how you think about your wardrobe?" If done well, it can be a flattering conversation. The image you aim for might be a composite of a few people, and you could ask each of them this same question. You might look for a peer to emulate, but challenge yourself to aim for the example of someone in a job or position you want. Making an effort to

EMILY POST'S BUSINESS ETIQUETTE

dress like them can help you prepare for when the time comes. And could help someone see the potential in you.

ATTIRE DESIGNATIONS

Attire designations can be super clear ("black tie") or they can be vague ("dressy casual"). Let's explore some of the expectations with the most common attire designations we see in business.

FORMAL ATTIRE

Formal attire is an opportunity to break out your very best, to live outside the everyday for a moment. Most often we put on formal attire for weddings, galas, graduations, formal charity events, or performances where it is traditional, such as the opera, ballet, or opening night at a theater or Broadway performance. When these functions double as work events for us, it's even more important to get our attire right and rise to the occasion, playing our role of the good guest well.

For formal wear, well-fitted is usually the goal. It will look out of place if the garment is too small, short, or tight or too large, long, or loose. Aim for the midrange of your size unless your persona supports an appropriately creative or festive look. While ornaments such as sequins, sparkles, fringe, and tassels are fabulous, traditional formal wear finds ways to use these elements sparingly and opt instead for more elegant details. Here are some common attire designations and the proper wardrobe elements for each. Any of the following items may be worn by people of any gender.

WHITE TIE

The most formal traditional attire, white tie is reserved and required for occasions such as the Nobel Prize banquet or a state dinner. Expect black jackets with tails and black trousers, wing-collared white shirts (fly or stud-front shirts are also options), white pique vests with matching bow ties, cuff links or stud sets, and black Oxford lace-ups at these events. Top hats, scarves, gloves, and pocket squares may also be worn as accessories. Chesterfield coats, which are formal, dark-colored, knee-length coats with velvet collars, may also be worn as outerwear if the weather is cold. If the event takes place during the day, you would wear a morning coat (a longer coat that drops below the waist in the back, landing around mid-thigh) instead of white tie. (It's the same level of formality, but white tie is reserved for the evening and a morning coat for the daytime.) For those not wearing tails, the expected white tie options are ball gowns and long formal dresses with formal shoes. On a rare occasion, you might see their counterparts: formal pants and dress tops or formal skirts and dress tops—but they must be very formal versions. Dresses, gloves (of varying lengths), and tiaras are other possible accessories.

BLACK TIE

Black tie as we know it today was born in the social club of Tuxedo Park, New York (which Emily's father, Bruce Price, designed, and where Emily grew up and lived for many years), and came of age in the social revolution of the late 1960s. Black tie is the next most formal dress option for occasions after 6:00 P.M. (except when you are asked to wear it to an afternoon wedding with an evening reception following it). Often worn only a few times in a person's lifetime (if ever), black tie can be found at a prom, wedding, or gala. Expect guests to wear tuxedos (see the Attire Guide, page 50, for details), evening and formal dresses or outfits, formal shoes, and jewelry. You could wear a very dark suit and a black necktie (particularly if black tie is listed as optional). White jacket tuxedos are an option for summer; they're thought of as more of a cocktail jacket for warm-weather outdoor events. You could wear a velvet smoking jacket if you want something different for a winter option.

BLACK TIE CREATIVE

Black tie creative (or sometimes festive) was born of the need to break the rules, and tuxedo wearers should feel okay going outside the traditional black-and-white color scheme. Elements of flair or fun can also be added. Play it up! This goes for gowns and formal two-piece sets, too. The attire should still be formal black tie, but a bit splashier and more playful—perhaps a colorful bow tie and matching cummerbund.

SEMIFORMAL ATTIRE

Semiformal attire is a step up from dressy casual but two or three steps below formal. Expect suits, jackets and ties with slacks, blazers, sports coats, dress tops and dress pants, long dresses (typically a maxi dress instead of a gown), tea-length (knee to above-ankle-length) or cocktail (knee-length) dresses, or two-piece outfits. Here's where you can mix and match to set the right tone for the event. You might wear a long maxi dress in a casual jersey knit to your friend's beach wedding or a jacket with corduroy pants and suede dress shoes to a new gallery opening. We see semiformal attire frequently requested on invitations; it's also when we see most of the "creative" attire labels on invitations, like "diamonds and denim" or "dressy Western," which are generally best used for specific events or when guests will truly understand them. Semiformal events can be everything from school dances, office holiday parties, charity events, art openings, and weddings to retirement parties, milestone birthdays, and anniversaries. Remember, you can easily remove a tie or tone down the jewelry if you feel overdressed. It's usually better to aim for more formal and take it down a notch than show up on the casual side and be underdressed.

BUSINESS ATTIRE

Your business dress code will vary depending on the industry you work in and the company you work for. Many industries, such as law or finance, are traditionally conservative in their work attire, but for others, such as the fashion industry where the players create the styles of the day, it would be a mistake not to be of-the-moment. If you work at a tattoo studio, proudly displaying and talking about your own body art might be encouraged. Ask your company what their dress code is and what any confusing terms mean to feel confident you're meeting expectations. When in doubt, fall back on clean and classic items: a buttoned shirt of quality fabric, fitted well and in good condition, and a pair of slacks or a skirt with simple, closed-toe shoes will work almost anywhere for anyone. Keep a simple, well-fitted jacket on hand to easily polish almost any look. For business attire, open-toed shoes, shorts, short skirts or dresses, low-cut shirts or dresses, cut-out styles, and anything exposing a shoulder are typically avoided. Patterns and colors aren't necessarily muted, but are not usually bright and bold either (unless you've cultivated a personal look based on loud patterns and colors).

DRESSY CASUAL

Dressy casual means the best of our casual wardrobes. Not all T-shirts, jeans, or sweaters are created equal in regard to formality. For dressy casual events, choose nicer fabrics, newer items—rather than your old favorites that are looking worn—and more flattering cuts. You may be in jeans and a sweater, but a bit more dressed up than you might look when running errands or visiting friends. Stylish shoes, jewelry, or other accessories dress up an everyday outfit. How you style your hair and, if you wear it, how you apply your makeup can also dress up a simple outfit. This is not the time for rips and tears, though it might be the time to wear super-styled sneakers.

BUSINESS CASUAL

Business casual is a slightly dressed-down version of traditional business attire. For some companies, this will be the everyday dress code and you'll want to check with your employer regarding expectations. In other workplaces, it's allowed periodically as a relaxation of the usual company dress code, for example, when a company has *casual Fridays*. You might not go so far as to wear shorts and sandals to the office, but a non-buttoned shirt, polo shirt, or casual sweater might replace a buttoned shirt and jacket, and loafers might replace lace-up shoes. Patterns and colors can be more expressive. Anything too revealing is still a no-go for work. You can always ask to be sure you're relaxing the dress code to the right level.

CASUAL

Casual attire today covers everything from jeans and T-shirts to athleisurewear, shorts, skirts, tank or tube tops, flip-flops, and sneakers. It's important to continue to be clean with your casual look and avoid appearing unkempt. A casual tank top and pair of shorts is acceptable in these instances, but a stained tank top, dirty hair, or body odor from lack of hygiene will take you out of casual and signal that you don't care about the situation or yourself. Dressing casually does not mean that you can dismiss the importance of appearance. When it comes to good etiquette and making choices that build relationships, people will respond to what they see. Being clean and presentable as a baseline for our appearance when interacting with others is worth aiming for.

A NOTE ABOUT "FESTIVE" ATTIRE

The designation "festive attire" conjures images of ugly Christmas sweaters, red, white, and blue on the Fourth of July, or glitz and sparkle on New Year's Eve. But festive can quickly cross into cultural appropriation if you aren't careful and aware of your selections. Cultural appropriation refers to using objects or elements from a particular culture in ways that reinforce stereotypes, don't respect their original purpose or meaning, and/or don't credit their source. It's generally inappropriate to wear clothing or iconography from cultures that aren't yours when attempting to "festivize" your look. Turning someone else's culture or identity into a costume is hurtful and in poor taste. When considering "festive" attire, always remember that you can be festive without being disrespectful or inappropriate (see the Attire Guide on page 50).

DIGITAL IMAGE

The best advice we have for your professional image when it comes to your digital life is to be smart and be in control. If you're going to participate in social media and online spaces, it's imperative as you enter the workforce, and periodically throughout your lifetime, that you cultivate and maintain an image that you not only feel good about but would feel okay exposing your professional life to. Employers and clients will notice your image in these spaces, whether they look for you in them or happen across you in them.

LINKEDIN LinkedIn is specifically a social site for business interaction. Think of your LinkedIn profile as an online business card and the site itself as a giant work mixer. The focus is on everything from building connections to getting jobs. Many professionals use LinkedIn as a networking and marketing tool, as a business-focused social network, and as a public place to get more information about potential contacts. Maintaining a complete, current, and accurate LinkedIn profile is a best professional practice. Use a headshot that represents you well. Google plays well with LinkedIn and will yield first-page search results related to your name. This is often the first impression someone can get of you online, and you have control over it. Be honest about your experience, skills, and achievements; there is no need to inflate or exaggerate your qualifications, and doing so can cause more trouble than it is worth. *The big picture is that your profile should accurately reflect you as a professional.*

SOCIAL PROFILES Your personal social media profiles are one of the easiest online spaces for you to control. Be smart about whether you let friends of friends contact you, and check notifications for tagged photos so that you are aware of the photos and videos of you that are posted on profiles beyond your own. It's okay to untag yourself or ask someone to untag you from a photo, or even black you out from a photo that does not align with your self-image or preferred online persona. "Hey, Jerry, even with weed being legal in California, I'd prefer not to have pics online of me hanging around with joints and bongs. Do you mind untagging me from that one or, even better, taking it down?" This is a perfectly reasonable request.

EMAIL Your email address (the actual letters and numbers that make it up) and the subject line, greeting, body text, closing, and signature that you include represent you. Think of making these choices like you would picking out professional stationery. Make sure that when you email professionally you consider each aspect before you hit send to help you maintain your professional image when communicating via email.

VOICEMAIL GREETING The outgoing message that you have recorded for when someone leaves a voicemail for you can be an opportunity to get playful and cute, but once you're in the professional world, if your personal phone doubles as a work phone, it's important to make sure you sound professional in your outgoing message. Keep it simple with a message like "You've reached the voicemail for Alexander Post at 555-893-9938. I'm sorry, I can't pick up. Please leave a message, and I'll get back to you as soon as I can." If it's possible to have work calls go to a separate voicemail, it's a great option to look into.

GOOGLE SEARCH It sounds self-serving to google yourself; however, this is one of the only ways to know what shows up when a quick search of your name is done by someone else. Think of it like looking in the mirror to check how you'll look to others. No matter what browser you use, go through a few pages to ensure that you aren't also popping up further down in the search results. Search for image and news results related to your name. There are lots of services available to help you clean up any search results that pertain to you, the real you, not the Wendy Melin who lives in Tulsa and raises alpacas or the Wendy Melin who just graduated from the University of Miami and is offering shots shots shots at Calli-o's on Saturday for happy hour.

TEXTING If texting is part of your work communications, paying attention to your text speak, as well as general spelling and grammar, will be key to your success in professional communication. For some industries and contacts, you'll be fine using emojis or all caps, sending gifs, you name it. But when in doubt, start formal with your texting and then move into the fun stuff as you build text rapport with an associate. This doesn't mean formatting your text like a letter, but take the time and effort to avoid abbreviated language, use proper spelling and punctuation, and address each thing that was stated or asked of you. (See Texting in Business on page 99.)

CALENDAR Be aware of the personal items you might be putting on your shared work calendar. "Vasectomy at 4 P.M." on a personal or family calendar is important, for sure, but is too much information for the office shared calendar. (See the Calendar section on page 101.)

FOR—EV—ER

The horizon of your life is not just as far as you can see; it is also determined by how long it takes to get there. Online behaviors are not just potentially public; they are potentially permanent. The digital world is saved, stored, copied, and recorded more times and in more ways than most of us will ever understand. Everything we do online is potentially permanent. Every search, every keystroke, every query, every email, every IM, every picture shared. Take just a minute to let that sink in.

The choices you make online accrue into a semipublic record. The line between public and private information and spaces is blurry at best. Take the lead in managing your online behavior with enough integrity to navigate the ambiguity around privacy with confidence.

CLASSIC ATTIRE QUESTIONS

Some attire traditions are worth knowing—or debunking, as the case may be. Here are some classic attire questions we get at the Emily Post Institute.

Must you remove your hat indoors?

Today, hat etiquette is still about allowing eye contact, letting your face be seen, and showing respect. Anyone going indoors should remove their hat once they have reached their destination. If you're in a large building, the lobby and elevators often count as outdoor spaces where hats are acceptable to leave on, but hallways, dining areas, rooms, and offices are considered indoors, so hats are to be taken off.

Always remove brimmed hats, such as cowboy hats and ball caps, for dining. Eating with others with your face shielded is not polite. Cowboy hats are sometimes worn in professional dining situations—especially outdoor events, but again, try to make sure your face is visible. At formal meals, you can give your hat to the coat check, or as a last resort hang it on the back of your chair. At an ill-planned event where you have no options but your lap or the floor, choose your lap—this isn't your fault.

Brims or no brims, hats are removed for the national anthem if they are not pinned to your head. Chemo caps, hats, or scarves worn for temporary hair loss due to a treatment or condition never have to be removed, nor do head coverings worn for religious purposes.

What is the etiquette for sunglasses?

Sunglasses can be a fashion statement, a favorite accessory, a health precaution, and a security blanket. Unfortunately, when interacting with others, they also cover our eyes. During conversation, and especially when being introduced, take your sunglasses off if you are able. Once you're inside, or when they are no longer needed to shield your eyes from the sun, remove them so they don't shield you from others. Whenever we can, we want people to be able to see our whole face, and make eye contact if possible.

Are blue jeans office attire?

Jeans were long forbidden in formal situations and were not considered possible office attire until the early aughts. Today, they are still discouraged or considered casual wear in many business settings—even though fashion jeans have been a staple of wardrobes since the 1960s and 1970s. Your best bet is not to wear jeans to an interview and to wait until you've been at a job for a while and are familiar enough with the dress code to know if jeans are appropriate, and which styles would qualify.

If no one's around, does dressing for work matter?

We think so. While it's true that many of us work jobs where we go days without interacting directly with others, we think that it can make a difference to dress up for work. Not because more rigid clothing makes us pay attention or focus more, but because of the readiness it affords you. By cultivating and executing a professional appearance you are proud of, you prepare yourself for any situation your workday could throw at you. At Emily Post, our bacon has been saved more than once by simply being showered and in clean office attire for the day—even though we both work from home most days and are usually in control of whether we are on camera for calls. An ounce of prevention is worth a pound of cure.

REFERENCE GUIDES

ATTIRE GUIDE

Use this guide to help you determine what to wear to events with different formality levels. Remember, it's always easier to dress up and take it down a notch than to dress up a more casual outfit.

WHITE TIE	BLACK TIE	BLACK TIE CREATIVE/ FESTIVE	SEMIFORMAL
White bow tie, black jacket with tails, matching trousers with a satin or braid stripe, plain front wing-collar French cuff shirt, stiff white vest, cuff links or studs, black or white braces, black socks, black formal (patent leather) pumps or black lace-up Oxfords

Or, a floor-length gown, possibly a *very* formal two-piece outfit, optional long gloves, formal shoes

Rarely if ever would a dress pant and dress-top combo be worn for white tie | Black or midnight navy tuxedo jacket and trousers, wing- or regular-collar white formal shirt (fly or stud-front or pleated or bibbed front), black bow tie, braces or suspenders, vest (if you wear a vest, do not also wear a cummerbund), cuff links or studs, cummerbund (should match bow tie and lapel fabric), black socks, black formal (patent leather) pumps or black lace-up Oxfords

A white dinner jacket may be worn in the summer or in warm climates. Or floor-length gown (material and structure can be more casual than white tie but still usually very formal), a very formal cocktail dress—at or below the knee (no shorter), formal shoes | Same as black tie but with colors or elements added to spice it up a bit

For dresses and two-piece outfits it's the same as black tie but with more room to experiment with color, texture, and accessories | Suit and tie or jacket and slacks, buttoned shirt, belt, and dress shoes

Or more casual long dress (nicer than a casual maxi dress but more casual than a gown), formal cocktail dress at or below the knee; a dressy skirt and top or dressy top and pant outfit; and dress shoes |

BUSINESS	BUSINESS CASUAL	DRESSY CASUAL	CASUAL
Suit and tie, buttoned dress shirt, belt, dress shoes

Dress slacks/trousers with dress top. Or more conservative dress or two-piece outfit (nothing too low cut, short, or luxurious in material or color); close-toed shoes if not in a fashion-forward industry | Suit (no tie) or seasonal coat with trousers, dress jeans (if allowed), button-down, polo, sweater, or open collar shirt, belt, socks, loafers or dress shoes

Dress slacks/trousers with more casual top

Dressy jeans and top or dress or skirt-and-top combo can run the gamut (nothing too short or low cut, even when casual); ask first if open-toed shoes are okay | Jeans and sweater or casual buttoned shirt

Dress pants and casual top

Casual pants and dress top

Dress or skirt-and-top combo that is comfortable; any shoes | Jeans, shorts, T-shirts, pullovers, hoodies, tank tops (as long as you're covered and clean, you're likely in good shape)

Dress or skirt with any top (as long as you're not topless, you're good); any shoes |

GROOMING AND HYGIENE CHECKLIST

If you check each item on this list, your grooming and hygiene will likely be on point for whatever event you are attending, even if it's an average workday.

☐ Hair clean and free of odor

☐ Face and body washed and smelling pleasant or free of odor

☐ Teeth brushed and flossed

☐ Hands washed, nails clean

☐ Facial hair intentionally groomed (don't forget ears, nose, brows, and neck), or removed if unwanted

☐ Minimal scents for perfumes, colognes, and body sprays (double-check with HR on any fragrance policies they may have)

Ask someone you trust to give feedback on body and breath odor and errant or unwanted hair. We recommend asking them directly—"Liz, do I have coffee breath today?"—rather than saying, "Let me know if you ever smell bad coffee breath on me." This way, you're more likely to nip the problem in the bud.

HOW TO TIE THE POST KNOT

This is how to tie the Post family's favorite tie knot. For additional detailed instructions see page 41.

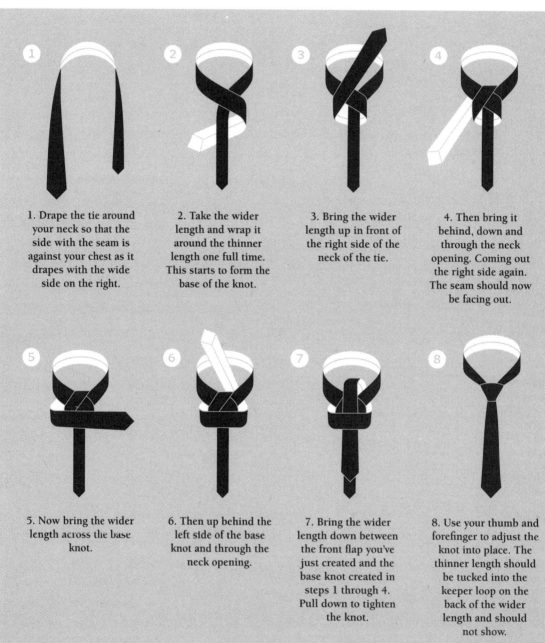

1. Drape the tie around your neck so that the side with the seam is against your chest as it drapes with the wide side on the right.

2. Take the wider length and wrap it around the thinner length one full time. This starts to form the base of the knot.

3. Bring the wider length up in front of the right side of the neck of the tie.

4. Then bring it behind, down and through the neck opening. Coming out the right side again. The seam should now be facing out.

5. Now bring the wider length across the base knot.

6. Then up behind the left side of the base knot and through the neck opening.

7. Bring the wider length down between the front flap you've just created and the base knot created in steps 1 through 4. Pull down to tighten the knot.

8. Use your thumb and forefinger to adjust the knot into place. The thinner length should be tucked into the keeper loop on the back of the wider length and should not show.

CHAPTER 4

Getting the Job

Whether fresh out of school, changing up a lifelong career, or returning to the game after some time out of the workforce, starting your job search can be exciting and intimidating. You can find openings through career fairs, college career services, guidance counselors, career counselors, LinkedIn, online job sites such as ZipRecruiter, Indeed, and CareerBuilder, internships, company postings, and word of mouth. Once you have identified a position or company that interests you most, a long-understood hiring process can be engaged. How you navigate this process is the beginning of a professional opportunity and will set the stage for future opportunities.

STARTING THE SEARCH

Job fairs, online searches, word of mouth, LinkedIn—whether the job is coming to you or you're actively searching for it, a great place to begin is with a digital check-in. Even just googling your name can show you what's out there about you and what someone else might see. Use the advice in chapter 3, "Professional Appearance," to help you review your digital image, as you prepare to apply and respond to potential jobs.

PRO TIP: Treat job fairs and meetings with career counselors and headhunters with the same seriousness as a job interview. These people may assess, recommend, and share opportunities with you, and your chance to build a strong and professional image begins here.

SOMETIMES THE SEARCH FINDS YOU

We should all be so fortunate as to be recruited for a position or a professional opportunity. Even if you aren't actively looking for a job or changing jobs, you might be approached by a career consultant or professional headhunter, or just flat out offered a job by someone hiring or in charge of those decisions. You are not obligated to reply in a particular way, but take this as the compliment that it is. Even if you don't plan on taking the job, acknowledging the offer and thanking them for it is smart and has potential to build your relationship, even when you say no, thank you. If you are open to the opportunity or even just curious, it is okay to find out more.

Again, the key, no matter what the outcome, is to acknowledge the opportunity and say thank you. Enjoy the moment; it's really great to hear someone has confidence in you.

APPLICATION

There are two main ways that you can apply to a company. The first and most common way is to answer a request for applications, via the company website, a career counselor, a professional recruiter, or a hiring website such as Indeed.

Show that you can understand and follow directions as a first step toward illustrating your ability to do the job and fill the position. Read the job description and any directions about how to apply carefully. Complete all forms, submit your resume or application, and provide the requested materials and credentials per the directions given by the company. Pay particular attention to details about deadlines, timing, and the preferred format for receiving anything you submit.

The second way that can also work is to reach out and express your interest in a job or company by sending in your resume and cover letter to the most available contact information you can find. You can inquire about any potential positions, while also asking if it's possible for your resume to remain on file for the future. Whether via the mail or email, be prepared for the company to say they aren't hiring. A digital version is usually easier for companies to deal with, but there is something memorable and durable about a physical copy.

RESUME AND COVER LETTER

Your resume and cover letter are a snapshot of you. No pressure, but how you choose to represent yourself on file matters. Let's look at some standards and best practices for cover letters and resumes. Once you've got the etiquette down, you can experiment with different styles. A quick internet search will give you many examples, but be warned, not all sites are reputable. Be sure the example you emulate is from a trusted site that gives quality business advice for the specific industry you are working in. Making your resume bright blue might make it stand out, but it can also make it hard to read, and therefore easy to cull. Choose substance over style. It's worth it here.

GENERAL STANDARDS

Your cover letter and resume each should be formatted as follows: left aligned with a 1-inch margin, one page, single-spaced, 10- to 12-point font size, and in a professional font such as Times New Roman or Arial. If you submit the cover letter in physical form, use resume-weight paper between 24 and 32 lb. One hundred percent cotton paper will give the document a unique and softer feel; it is another recommended way to up your resume game and distinguish yourself. Save your resume and cover letters as PDF files for online applications so they are unalterable and easily shared. Name the file with your name and either *resume* or *cover letter*. Let's look at each document separately so you can confidently build yours.

> **PRO TIP**: Do not use letterhead from your current job or position. Avoid social stationery as well.

COVER LETTER

A cover letter is your opportunity to share some of your personal voice with those making hiring decisions. Rather than a chore, it's a chance to highlight or address specific details about your qualifications, fit for a position, and even objectives you would accomplish if offered the role. It is a professional opportunity to get a little more personal about why you want a job, what you bring to the work, and what you can offer an employer. It also presents your written voice to whomever reads it.

Spend some time thinking about your qualifications, the person you are writing to, and the organization they represent. A cover letter allows you to show your interest and address specific attributes of the organization that you find admirable, attractive, or a good fit. If you learned of the job through a specific person or channel, you can mention that person here in the cover letter. "After running into Vishal Gupta at the Crypto 2025 conference last month and hearing the goals of NewWay Financial, I knew I wanted to apply for the position of Chief Technical Officer." Rather than "I've known Vishal Gupta since high school, we were close then because his father and my father golfed together. Upon his encouragement and recommendations I am applying for the position of Chief Technical Officer."

COVER LETTER STRUCTURE

The basic body layout is that of a business letter. If you don't have your own stationery, you'll put your contact information across the top in a stylized format. Your name, centered, with some combination of email, phone, and either city and state or full address centered and in a smaller size font below it is a clean and modern way to go. Choose a style that feels right to you.

For the body, in the top left corner, include the date, then two lines down from it goes the name of the recipient, then the next line down contains the address of the company, the next line down you put their phone number, followed one line down by their email address. You then skip two lines and begin your salutation.

WRITING YOUR LETTER

The body of the letter begins with a salutation on its own line. We are fans of "Dear Ms./Mrs./ Mr./Mx. Important Person," and try to avoid "To Whom It May Concern" unless no other option is available. Even beginning with "Dear Hiring Manager" or another position title can give what follows a more direct feel.

Write clearly and succinctly; the first paragraph is your first impression. Demonstrate your understanding of the position you are applying for, share how you learned about it, and briefly touch on why you and your experience make you a suitable candidate. There is no need to do all your "standing out from the crowd" in your first few sentences; keep it clear, direct, and specific to the job.

The second paragraph is your chance to shine. Expand on your qualities and how you can fulfill the expectations outlined in the job description. Focus on specific experiences or skills and how they show your capacity and fit the employer's requirements. Now, highlight your key achievements related to what you hope to do at this job. This is not the time for false modesty.

The third paragraph is your closing statement and written sign-off. Now is a good time to share a vision. Without restating your skills and how they could benefit the company, share how you could bring the work you'd be doing forward. What do you envision being able to do with this position and for the company if given the chance? Keep the focus on what you can do together. Close with a thank-you for the effort, consideration, and time that goes into reviewing applicants and your enthusiasm for a reply or any next steps. Before you get to your closing, write, "Thank you for taking the time to review my resume." Keeping this as its own sentence, separate from a closing, is a nice touch.

"Sincerely" should close your cover letter, with a comma after the word. If you are not physically signing, your name goes on the next line, or leave a few lines to make room for your written signature above your printed name.

PRO TIP: To give the signature on your cover letter a more personal touch, get a digital version of your actual signature for digital applications.

PROOFREAD

Now, set your cover letter aside for at least half an hour, if not overnight, and then *proofread*. Put it down for a while again and then proofread it again. Even better, ask someone else to proofread it for you as well. Some find it helpful to do multiple reads from different angles:

1. Review the content.

2. Assess the tone by reading it out loud.

3. Copyedit for grammar and spelling.

4. Read for accuracy of names, numbers, statistics, and more.

> **PRO TIP**: Keep a current draft of a cover letter that focuses on you and your qualifications. Then, modify it with details about each specific position or company as you submit your resume to different places. See the Reference Guide on page 76 for a sample cover letter.

RESUME

The objective of a resume is to communicate important information about you and your professional experience to decision-makers in the most direct and comprehensible manner possible. A traditional resume structure is both functional in organizing this information and familiar to those who are hiring. Be ready to pare down to present a concise, professional picture to someone who might not have a lot of time or attention to spare.

RESUME STRUCTURE

Less is more; omit logos, graphics, special fonts, or colored text, and do not include photos or emojis. Use a 1-inch margin. Unlike cover letters, resumes have headings differentiating sections and will likely include bulleted lists within sections. Use consistent font sizes for your name (16 to 18 point), section headings (12 to 16 point), and body text (10 to 12 point).

Use bold, underlining, and/or capitalization on section headings so the eye can easily jump to the most relevant information. Then, stay consistent throughout the document. Use left-aligned text to define subsections and bullet points to list information within a section.

We'll look first at the sections you can include and then at different ways to organize them.

NAME AND CONTACT INFORMATION

In many ways, this is the most important information on your resume. Place your full name at the top in a 16- to 18-point font with contact info directly below in your chosen body font and size. Include the town and state/country you live in—for privacy reasons, do not include your street address—followed by your phone number and email address. You may also include links to professional social accounts, portfolios, or websites directly related to your work. This information can be centered or left-aligned.

SUMMARY

Not every resume will have a summary section, but it is a great way to begin since it serves as a mini cover letter. If you are including one, place it just below your name and contact information and use a clear heading so it is easy to locate. In no more than a couple of sentences, highlight your most important skills and experience, then share how they make you a strong candidate for the position.

PRO TIP: Use language from the job description when defining your skills and responsibilities.

EXPERIENCE

In this section, list the verifiable work experience that qualifies you or prepares you for the position you seek. The job position, company, and duration of employment should all be present, typically followed by a brief bulleted list of responsibilities and accomplishments. Balancing thoroughness with brevity is the goal of this section. Never add to or embellish your experience. You may have to make a tough choice about which jobs and positions to include. Keep the focus on experience that is relevant to the job you're applying to, and that presents a coherent picture.

PRO TIP: Don't be shy; be specific when sharing achievements: "Number 1 regional and national sales associate, 2024 and 2025."

EDUCATION AND CERTIFICATIONS

List educational degrees by the highest and/or most recent that you've received. Consider whether the credentials are necessary for or relevant to the position. There is no need to list primary or secondary schools, or even undergraduate degrees if your professional credentials, experience, or postgraduate degree already qualify you. However, if you've got the space, and want to, you certainly can include them. You never know when the hiring manager might be an alum of your institution!

> **PRO TIP**: Academic titles and post-nominals can be communicated with your name and contact information to save space on the page.

SKILLS

If you have particular skills that apply to the job you are seeking, this is a place to list them. In a functional resume, each skill becomes an independent section, with an explanation of the skill and how it was acquired or demonstrated listed in the body of the skill's section (for an example of a *functional resume*, see the Reference Guide on page 79).

> **PRO TIP**: Share both *hard skills,* like experience with software or equipment, and *soft skills,* like creative problem-solving or team leadership.

WAYS TO ORGANIZE YOUR RESUME

Generally, there are two ways to organize your resume. The first is *reverse chronological,* where experience is listed with the most recent position at the top to the least recent at the bottom. For someone who has been working for a number of years, it presents a clear picture of progress over time or, at a minimum, highlights the most recent and relevant experience. Sections listing education, credentials, or important skills can be added after experience.

> **PRO TIP**: Don't include experience that is more than fifteen years old.

The *functional resume* prioritizes skills, with experience listed below. This is a great option for skills not acquired through work experience. Someone who is transitioning from one industry or field to another may have developed skills not directly related to the job that would still be very useful.

A combination approach that works well for many creative professionals highlights skills near the top of the page but still includes a chronological experience section afterward.

STEPPING IT UP

Customize your cover letter and resume for each job you apply to. Look for the hiring contact at the company for the job listing, use language from the job description and mission statement, and tweak the description of your experience to highlight the aspects most relevant to the job you're applying for.

An achievements or interests section could be added as an optional section to expand a resume that shows less experience or has too much empty space at the bottom of the page. When you are confident with the content, proofread one final time to be sure that no typos or grammatical errors speak louder than all the work you put into presenting yourself in your cover letter and resume.

INTERVIEW PREPARATION

Congratulations! You got an interview! Regardless of how many interviews you have lined up and whether they are spread apart or back to back, you want to stay prepared. To get ready, try envisioning your interview so that you can feel confident and familiar when the actual interview day arrives. We'll look at what you'll wear and bring, how you'll get there or connect, and, yes, what you might say.

Before we jump into prepping for an interview, we want to highlight that every company is obligated to make the interview process as accessible as possible. All companies should be asking about accessibility and accommodation needs that you the applicant may have when they reach out to schedule the interview. If no one has asked you about accommodations or accessibility needs, it is perfectly polite and encouraged that you ask about them. "You hadn't mentioned anything about accessibility, so I'd like to share that I use a wheelchair. Does your facility accommodate wheelchair access, and if not, how would you like to proceed?"

YOU

We already know it's important to be clean, presentable, and free from odor during our workdays; it's not rocket science to conclude that it's also essential during interviews. Even if you are going to be attending your interview via video, it's still best to shower, put on deodorant, and wear work-appropriate shoes (and pants; pants are important!). The goal is to present an attentive, competent, and amiable version of yourself.

The internet is filled with sample interview questions that you can use to practice, but overall, be prepared to talk about yourself, your work style or work ethic, and even how you might envision yourself in the position. Being able to articulate these things out loud and practicing them a few times will help you feel ready for the standard interview questions. There are certain basic qualities, such as punctuality and meeting deadlines, that are always desirable, but others, like "I try to be appreciative and complimentary of my colleague's work because I know it contributes to a more positive team environment," communicate more about you and how you like to contribute to your work environment. Identify a few specific things about yourself and examples that would apply to the types of jobs that you're interested in and will be applying for. Interview prep is all about thinking things through beforehand so you have answers ready during the interview.

WHAT TO WEAR

Other people are reading you for cues all the time, and nearly 70 percent of hiring managers surveyed by CareerBuilder noted that dressing *inappropriately* was the biggest reason for rejection when considering applicants.

When interviewing, do your best to dress in accordance with the industry or the position—even if the job is remote or uniformed. Consider the culture of the place you're applying to (conservative law firm? creative at a tech start-up? teacher at an elementary school?) and the position you're applying for (entry level, managerial level, c-suite?) *and then dress one notch up from what you would expect your everyday wear to be if you were hired.*

You can always call or email to ask about the company dress code; for example: "Before I come in, I wanted to know the company's dress policy." Or, "I know the job is remote, but I was wondering if there is a suggested dress code." If you have already met your interviewer, or you know the team you'd be applying to work on, aim to wear something that matches what the interviewer will likely be wearing.

Whether your interview is virtual or in person, you'll want to dress for it from head to toe. It's very tempting to tell you that a classic suit or a buttoned shirt with dress slacks will always be the right call (and for the record, it's usually a safe bet), but with the variety of dress codes we see in the workplace today, it's more important that you focus on making sure that you are clean and your clothing is clean, unwrinkled, and well fitted to you and the type of interview you are having (boardroom = fitted suit; community farm center = clean garden wear). Looking dressed and ready for the interview will certainly impress a potential boss, even via video.

There are times when disability or cultural or religious requirements come into play for our attire. If, for example, you have a disability that requires you to wear stable shoes, such as sneakers, and the work environment is formal, it's appropriate for you to mention it. While the hope is that more and more people will assume the best, thinking *they must need sneakers for a reason,* it's not uncommon for people to assume the worst (*they are trying to get attention* or *they don't know what's appropriate*). If you feel comfortable mentioning it, do. All the work shouldn't be on the part of the person with the disability, but speaking up is always an option from an etiquette standpoint. How you do it, of course, matters, but when others haven't figured it out or been gracious, it's perfectly polite to clue folks in by saying, "I wear them for stability."

WHAT TO BRING

Bring three copies of your resume or portfolio to the interview: one for the person you will meet with and a couple to have in case the opportunity arises to share it with someone else. Also, be ready with a link or file-sharing system that allows you to distribute the same information easily to anyone in electronic form.

Bring a pen, notepad, or notebook to jot down anything. This isn't as necessary, but having them on hand signals your investment in the interview: it's not beneath you to come prepared and ready to take notes. Think of it as the opposite of a power move; maybe call it a humble move.

Most importantly, bring a friendly, interested, curious, intelligent, confident, and upbeat attitude. There is nothing disingenuous about putting your best foot forward for an important first meeting or big opportunity. It shows both respect and self-awareness to put effort into engaging positively.

> **PRO TIP**: What you *don't* bring could also make a big difference. Leave behind the bad attitude, cynicism, sarcasm, and off-color humor. Put it with your unwanted phone, tablet, and smartwatch alerts, dings, rings, and reminders.

GETTING THERE ON TIME

For a job interview, being on time means being early. Your goal is to arrive at the interview site five to fifteen minutes before your interview, with enough time to collect yourself before going in. Some people choose to set their arrival time an hour before the interview and wait in the car, go for a walk, or grab a cup of coffee nearby to kill the extra time (maybe decaf today to keep the caffeine jitters at bay). The relief achieved by not putting it to chance is worth the wandering-around time. You can't be late if you're early!

You may think you know your city or town, but throw an important event into the mix, like an interview, and Murphy's Law might strike. Time out your route to get to the interview and test it at the same time of day as the interview is scheduled so that you know how much traffic to expect or what delays could get in your way. If you cannot do your own test run, use Google Maps to get recent traffic information. We have so many tools to alert us to issues on our route that there is no excuse besides an unforeseen accident blocking your way. Use this information to help you set your "leave the house by" time. Now add ten to twenty minutes (or more if you want) to that time, and you'll create a reasonable buffer to ensure you get there on time or early, which is the best-case scenario.

Interview start time	11:00 A.M.
- Travel time to interview (20 minutes)	10:40 A.M.
- Buffer time (20 minutes)	10:20 A.M.
- Early arrival time (5 to 10 minutes)	10:10 A.M.
Time you need to leave by	10:10 A.M.

THE INTERVIEW

It's time. Whether you're meeting in person, over the phone, or via video, the time to shine has come. This is the moment when your skills and experience come off the page, and you get to introduce yourself in person to your potential new employer. Here are some tips to ensure your interview etiquette skills are as polished as possible.

IN-PERSON INTERVIEW ARRIVAL

From the moment you cross the threshold, you are on display. Knowing this shouldn't send you into a panic; instead, use this knowledge to be confident and aware that your every move, from how you speak with the receptionist to how you act in the parking lot or sidewalk on your way out, is visible and could add to the impression you create with your interviewer. If you're short with the receptionist or take a phone call loudly (or worse, on speakerphone/video chat) in the lobby or waiting area, there is a good chance it could get back to the interviewer and might negatively affect their impression of you. (*Boy, he's great in person, but what a jerk in the waiting room!*) Conversely, if you wait patiently while the receptionist finishes his phone call to announce yourself ("Good morning, I'm here for an interview with Ellie Brandson") and say thank you to anyone who escorts you around the building, you'll likely have them saying *yeah, he was nice* at the minimum.

IN-PERSON INTERVIEW INTRODUCTIONS

A confident introduction will go a long way in making you a viable candidate in the eyes of the company you're applying to. Your top goals are to greet your interviewer(s), engage in a handshake if you are able, and introduce yourself, saying something such as "Alison Crowning, thank you for taking the time to interview me. It's a pleasure to meet you" in response to their likely having said, "Hi, I'm Justin Ferguson, thanks so much for coming in today."

Wait to be invited to sit or shown where to sit. Don't take a seat until you are invited to do so by your interviewer, or unless they have already taken a seat and are waiting for you to join them without having said anything. And certainly don't point out that the invitation was not forthcoming if this should be what happens. See pages 158 to 160 for proper introductions and handshakes.

VIDEO INTERVIEW CONSIDERATIONS

Unless otherwise specified, your camera is expected to be on during the video interview. Before the call, settle on a neutral and non-distracting background. It's commonplace today to use digital or blurred backgrounds if your current location warrants it. This can also work in your favor by keeping the focus on you.

If possible, test your microphone and camera before you enter the shared space so you can troubleshoot any issues on your own and spare the interviewer any awkward feedback or glitchy connections. Once you're on the call, be sure to say, "Hello, and thank you for taking the time to meet with me today." Your interviewer will likely act as host and introduce you to anyone participating in the call. Follow their lead for introductions and the agenda of the interview.

Frame your head and shoulders in the picture and direct your attention to your camera lens so it appears you are looking directly at your interviewer. Avoid fidgeting or turning away from the camera frequently, and do not set yourself up so that the screen you are looking at is different from where the camera is positioned. This is also true for interviewers; make sure your body and face are directed straight at your camera so that you demonstrate that your interviewee has your full attention. If you have notes pulled up on your screen, avoid making it obvious that you're reading off them. These notes should be visual reminders of things you'd like to say or ask rather than scripts. It can disrupt your connection with the interviewer if they feel like you're reading lines.

PRO TIP: Place the camera up high and point the camera down at your face rather than up to achieve the most flattering angles.

QUESTIONS TO EXPECT

Some questions are pretty standard interview questions, and others will vary for each industry and each job, but typically you'll be asked about your qualifications—so your education, training, and skill sets. You'll be asked how well you think you can satisfy the job's requirements (the interviewer will either list the requirements or they will have been in the job description, and you can use that to guide you). You might also be asked about leaving previous jobs or any past disciplinary action.

The interviewer is trying to gauge your qualifications and reliability for this position, as well as how well you'll fit in with the team or the rest of the company.

RESPONDING TO INAPPROPRIATE
INTERVIEW QUESTIONS

There are questions the interviewer should not ask, and you do not have to answer them. According to the US Equal Employment Opportunity Commission, the following are questions that an employer should not ask during an interview. Don't worry; we'll offer a general response to questions that shouldn't be asked.

- Questions about race, religion, or ethnicity, such as: "Are you biracial?" and "Which church do you attend?"

- Questions about age, excepting age verification for age restrictions.

- Questions about pregnancy or plans to start a family, as well as questions about health or disability, including: "What medications do you take?" and "Have you ever filed for workers' compensation?"

- Questions about relationship status.

- Questions about military discharge.

- Questions about your current salary information. (This is true for roughly twenty states. Learn the standing for the state you're interviewing in/for and whether this question is appropriate in advance.)

- Questions about if you've been arrested. However, you can be asked if you've been convicted of a crime. (An arrest is not the same as a conviction.)

If you are asked a question that falls under these categories, we recommend that you gently and politely decline to answer: "I'd rather not say." Or, more firmly, "I respectfully decline to answer." If pressed, you can say, "This is one of the questions an interviewee is not required to answer during an interview." This version removes the accusation that you are *not allowed to ask me that*.

QUESTIONS *YOU* CAN ASK DURING THE INTERVIEW

While a job application process can feel like you are being scrutinized and all the pressure is on you to perform, you are also interviewing the company to see if you'd want to work there. Don't let this puff out your chest too much, but remember that you are evaluating them in this process, too. Knowing that can give us a bit of a confidence boost to help calm any natural anxiety about the process. The more you can focus your questions on your specific experience versus asking generic questions, the better off you'll be. In some cases, it may even help paint the picture for the interviewer of you in the position.

You can ask about the specifics of the job, the team, or the department you'd be working with. *What would a typical day for me look like in this role?* This is a great one because it gets the interviewer visualizing you in the position doing the work. Asking questions about how the role functions, is supported, and is evaluated shows interest and investment in the job.

1. How do you measure success in this position?

2. How do you help employees grow professionally?

3. What is the salary and performance review process for this position?

As you close the interview, here are four questions that are worth asking and give you something solid to end on. Whatever you do, do not end your interview without having asked a question. You want the information, and it shows the company that you are invested in your own career path. If you've already asked or covered the questions listed above, you could close with any or all of these four.

1. What am I not asking you that I should?

2. Is there anything else I can provide you that would be helpful?

3. Is there anything I can clarify for you about my qualifications?

4. What are the next steps in the hiring process?

QUESTIONS TO *AVOID* ASKING IN A JOB INTERVIEW

WHAT IS THE STARTING SALARY? For most interviews, it's too early in the hiring process to go there. Discuss salary once they have shown that they are very interested in you. Avoiding this number early on can literally pay later. This is true too for questions about benefits such as health insurance and paid leave. These are matters to address once the job offer is made.

SO, DO I HAVE THE JOB? Danger, Buck Rogers, this question is a major red flag you want to avoid. It's tempting, especially after a great interview, but it can sound cocky, presumptuous, and disrespectful of the interview process. It is so rare that a company would offer you a position on the spot. Even if they did, you can always say you need time to think about it and that you're looking forward to getting back to them with an answer. You don't want to be rushed, and the excitement you experience could prevent you from having a clear head about it. "Thank you for the offer; I'd like to take some time to think about it. I can get you an answer by Friday if that works for you."

FOLLOW-UP

At the end of the interview, thank your interviewer. Thank them once, twice, and maybe even three times. First, thank them verbally as you leave. "Thank you for taking the time to interview me today. I appreciate you and the work being done at XYZ Company." Whether you get this job or not, or think the interview went well or didn't, it is imperative from an etiquette standpoint to thank your interviewer(s) for their time.

Second, follow up with a written thank-you note. Over the years, we have heard from employers that a handwritten thank-you note not only showed effort on the part of the applicant, but also demonstrated both consideration and a knowledge of tradition. Even if that tradition isn't always expected, it's almost always appreciated and creates a good impression. Now, the reality is that we live in a world where that note might not be possible. Or where the note—being an older form of communication—could look out of touch. You know the industry and job you're applying to, and once you've met with an interviewer, you probably have a sense of what the company values. Use this information and the timing of the hiring process to know if you should send a handwritten note versus an email. If you know they are on a tight turnaround to hire, it's probably best to email first. You can always follow that up with a handwritten note (and yes, that would be the third time you thank them).

PRO TIP: If you have more than one interviewer in the room, write a separate thank-you note to each.

SUPER PRO TIP: Write thank-you notes for interviews that don't go well. Even if you feel like you won't get or take the job, still write that note. It is a thank-you for the interview. See Thank-You Notes, page 112, for more on how to write one.

SAMPLE THANK-YOU NOTE

Here's a sample of both a handwritten and an email thank-you so that you can see the formatting differences.

EMAIL VERSION

Dear Anisha,

It was a true pleasure to meet with you today. Thank you for taking the time to interview me for the position of Director of Learning and Development at Rickley Industries. It was wonderful to get to see the office and meet a few of the team members. I also enjoyed hearing about your expansion plans—very exciting, and something I'd be proud to be part of if I am chosen for the position. I'm looking forward to hearing from you.

Thank you again for your time today.

Sincerely,
Katie Kaplan

Katie Kaplan (she/her/they/them)
KKaplan89@gmail.com
830-994-9865

HANDWRITTEN NOTE VERSION

June 15, 2026

Dear Anisha,

It was a true pleasure to meet with you today. Thank you for taking the time to interview me for the position of Director of Learning and Development at Rickley Industries. It was wonderful to get to see the office and meet a few of the team members. I also enjoyed hearing about your expansion plans—very exciting, and something I'd be proud to be part of if I am chosen for the position. I'm looking forward to hearing from you, and again, I thank you for your time today.

Sincerely,
Katie Kaplan

JOB SEARCH OUTCOMES

There are only a few ways that the job search ends. Let's examine each scenario, the etiquette for it, and how you can clean up your search once you've finished looking.

YAY! YOU GOT IT

Oh, happy day! Did you do a happy dance? Do a dance! Securing a job is a moment worth celebrating! Whether you gather friends for a celebratory drink, cook a special dinner with your family, or call Mom, we hope you celebrate big time. A new job, and especially a first job, is a *BIG DEAL*. And *you* did it! You got the offer. Now you have to decide if you will accept.

No matter how much you wanted to be offered this job, you might be in a position where you cannot say yes right away. You could be holding out for another job you applied for, or you could just be considering your options before jumping ship on your current job. We apply for all kinds of reasons and accept for all kinds of reasons. Once you know that the offer of the job is on the table, ask how much time you have to make the decision and gather some basic facts: start date, wages, benefits, vacation days, personal days, and anything else that might influence your decision. You may already know some of these things, and if so, that's great. At the very least, find out when your potential employer would like a reply. Then, make sure you get your answer in before that deadline.

CLOSING YOUR SEARCH

When the search is over and you're no longer looking, it's time to clean up after yourself. Here are some tips for moving out of search mode:

- Do what you can to withdraw resumes and applications from online services and let those you've had interviews with who have not yet made their decision know that you are no longer available.

- Contact leads, recruiters, and recommendation writers, share the good news, and thank them for the support or help.

- Send thank-you notes to anyone who interviewed you whom you have not thanked yet (in the heat of battle), whether it was for a position you took or one you did not.

- Change your status on any websites that show you looking for work, to reflect your new employment, or take down the posting.

- Notify the correct people if you will be leaving your current place of employment.

- Update contact and employment information on any profiles, member groups, and with those whom you wish to remain in professional contact after you transition to the new job.

GIVING NOTICE

If you decide to take the job and have started telling family and friends, you need to consider how to let your current employer know as well. It is much better to give notice yourself than to let your employer find out on their own. And it is certainly preferable to just not showing up one day, or worse, just quiet quitting until that day arrives. Don't destroy your reputation by failing to leave a job with integrity, whether through the complete lack of effort you are putting in, a resume you left in the copy machine by mistake, or chatter overheard at the water cooler. You want to be in control of how important information about you is shared. To avoid being the object of rumor, speculation, or negative gossip, it is best to give your notice both in writing and verbally to your boss or supervisor as soon as you can.

Show respect for your close colleagues by letting them know as soon as possible so they can prepare for any changes in work routines and responsibilities. Just as you will greet new colleagues at your new job, having the presence of mind to say goodbye well shows your care and consideration for those you have worked with and serves as an opportunity to leave those relationships on solid footing with a positive, lasting impression.

What does that look like?

1. Give notice in a timely manner. Two weeks is standard but it may vary by industry, field, or even position. Tell people once you have made your decision and you are free to share the information.

2. Say goodbye as warmly and as personally as possible. When possible, meet in person. Send a note, message, or memo to those you are not able to speak to.

3. Thank friends and colleagues for the time you spent well together or acknowledge things you accomplished.

WAITING . . .

It can be difficult—especially when you are ready to work or switch jobs—to wait while the company you're applying to interviews other candidates or circulates information about your interview to decision-makers. Waiting is rarely fun.

If you've been given a date that you'll hear by, wait for that date to arrive and pass before you reach out to your interviewer (or anyone else you may have been in touch with). Once it has passed, you can email your contact and ask.

> *Hi Jeff,*
>
> *I hope this email finds you well. I am writing regarding the position I applied for. During my interview, it was mentioned that a decision would be made and communicated by August 12. I am checking in to see if a decision was made and, if not, if there's anything else I can provide. Thank you for your time and for any insight you can offer.*
>
> *Sincerely,*
> *Jamie*

Note to those hiring: It's considerate, respectful, and honest toward your candidates to let them know whether they got the job or not.

SORRY

It can be crushing not to be chosen for a position. If you felt the job wasn't really for you after the interview and you were just curious if you might get picked anyway, hearing a rejection might bring relief. However, most people are disappointed when they hear the position went to someone else. Just as you were taught as a kid when playing with others to be a good loser, being gracious about losing out on this job opportunity is important.

Getting angry toward the interviewer or whoever has shared this news with you will not benefit you. It will do the opposite and guarantee you won't be considered for other positions. In the moment, take a deep breath. Whether you're replying via email or over the phone, and especially if you find out in person, your best move is to thank the interviewer or person who has told you news about the job and to let them know that you would love to be considered again for any other open positions in the future. Many people have been passed over for one job, only to be offered something else at a company—maybe even a position that is a better fit. It's wise and worthwhile not to burn the bridge behind you. "Thank you so much for letting me know. I appreciate the time you all took to interview me and consider me for the position. If something else opens up, I'd love to be considered." Saying something to this effect—we call it taking the "etiquette high road"—will ensure that even though you weren't chosen for the job, your integrity and reputation remain intact.

REFERENCE GUIDES

COVER LETTER FOR CHRONOLOGICAL RESUME

Chris Austin
[Address—Optional]
[City, State, Zip Code]
[Phone Number]
[Email Address]

[Date]

Established Bigwig
Hiring Manager
Earthjustice
[Address]
[City, State, Zip Code]

Dear Mr. Established Bigwig,

I am writing to express my strong interest in the Earth Justice Community Partnerships Program's Managing Attorney position. As a recent graduate from Vermont Law School with a Juris Doctor degree and a passion for environmental law, I am excited about the opportunity to contribute to your important organization.

During my time at law school, I excelled in courses related to environmental law and actively participated in legal clinics with the Environmental Law Center, which equipped me with a solid foundation in legal research, writing, and analysis. My internships at the Environmental Law Center provided me with practical experience in case research, where I honed my ability to craft legal arguments.

I am drawn to Earthjustice due to its outstanding reputation for excellent environmental advocacy. I am eager to contribute my dedication, work ethic, and passion for the law to your team and mission while also embracing the opportunity to learn from the experienced attorneys in your organization.

Furthermore, I am confident that my strong research and analytical skills and ability to communicate complex legal concepts effectively would make me a valuable asset to your firm. I am also committed to upholding the highest ethical standards and professionalism in all aspects of my work. I am looking forward to the possibility of discussing how my background, skills, and enthusiasm for the practice of law align with Earthjustice's needs

Thank you for considering my application. I am eager to bring my energy and commitment to Earthjustice and contribute to its success. I am available at your earliest convenience for an interview and can be reached at [phone number] or via email at [email address]. Thank you for your time and consideration.

Sincerely,

Chris Austin

CHRONOLOGICAL RESUME

CHRIS AUSTIN
[City, State, Zip Code]
[Phone Number]
[Email Address]

SUMMARY
Dedicated and detail-oriented recent law school graduate with a Juris Doctor degree seeking to leverage legal knowledge and skills in a challenging role at a reputable legal organization.

EDUCATION
Juris Doctor (J.D.), Vermont Law School, Royalton, VT, 2023, Bachelor of Arts (B.A.) in Land Use and Public Policy, Hampshire College, Northampton, MA, 2016

ACTIVITIES
President of the Pioneer Valley Trails Assoc. 2016–2021

HONORS/AWARDS
Summa Cum Laude

LEGAL EXPERIENCE
Legal Intern, [Law Firm/Organization Name], [Location], [Dates]
- Conducted legal research and analysis on [specific legal issues]
- Drafted legal memoranda, motions, and other legal documents
- Assisted in case preparation and trial support

Legal Intern, [Legal Organization/Company Name], [Location], [Dates]
- Supported attorneys in preparing for depositions, hearings, and trials
- Conducted client interviews and drafted client correspondence
- Researched and analyzed statutes, regulations, and case law

ADDITIONAL EXPERIENCE
Legal Research Assistant, Vermont Law School, Royalton, VT, 2021–2023
- Supported law professors with legal research for academic publications
- Assisted in compiling research materials and drafting scholarly articles

SKILLS
- Legal research and writing
- Case analysis and preparation
- Client communication and interviews
- Strong understanding of environmental law
- Proficient in legal research tools and databases [You might also include the standard workplace applications that you're proficient in—for example, Microsoft Excel.]

BAR ADMISSIONS
Admitted to the State Bar of New York, 2024

MEMBERSHIPS/AFFILIATIONS
Member of [Law Student Association or any related organizations]—Affiliation with [any relevant legal associations or groups]

COVER LETTER FOR FUNCTIONAL RESUME

Daniel Schibuk
[Address—Optional]
[City, State, Zip Code]
[Phone Number]
[Email Address]

[Date]

Sally Forth
Hiring Manager
Earthjustice
[Address]
[City, State, Zip Code]

Dear Ms. Sally Forth,

My name is Daniel Schibuk, and I am writing to express my interest in the developer position at Brain Games Designs. I have three years of experience working in game development and a passion for making fun and educational games. My skills, experience, and dedication perfectly fit a company like yours that is looking to build highly engaging software for learners.

I worked for over three years as a game developer for Learning Studio, where I successfully planned, built, and launched three games that went on to achieve distribution in more than 600 schools, reaching more than 10,000 early readers between the ages of 7 and 10. Each game has sold better yearly than in previous years, and this performance trend with my product library is expected to continue.

Before this, I worked in child development as a writing tutor at The Reading Room, as well as 4 years directing programming at The Reading Room. As director, I guided program development to meet the needs and challenges of struggling readers. I have dedicated myself to building curriculums and games for my students that help them achieve their goals.

I've attached my resume for further review. I would like to bring my unique combination of experience, skills, and passion to the developer role at Brain Games Designs. Please do not hesitate to contact me if you would like to speak about my qualifications and interest in more detail.

Thank you for your time and consideration.

Sincerely,

Daniel Schibuk

FUNCTIONAL RESUME

DANIEL SCHIBUK
[City, State, Zip] | [Phone Number]
[Email Address]

CAREER OBJECTIVE
Dynamic and dedicated professional with a strong background in game design and children's learning center management. Seeking a challenging role at an educational software company to utilize my expertise and passion for creating innovative educational products.

SUMMARY OF SKILLS
- Proven game design and development expertise, with a keen focus on learning objectives and interactive design principles.
- Leadership experience in managing and directing the operations of a children's learning center, including curriculum development and staff management.
- Outstanding communication and interpersonal skills, dedicated to fostering a positive and inclusive learning environment for children.

EDUCATION
Bachelor of Science in Education | University of Vermont, Burlington, VT | 2011

WORK EXPERIENCE
Director of Programming at The Reading Room, Learning Center | Claremont, CA | 2012–2017
- Directed daily operations of a children's learning center, overseeing a dedicated team to ensure the delivery of high-quality educational experiences.
- Created and implemented age-appropriate curriculums to support children's cognitive, social, and emotional development.
- Maintained communication with parents, addressing concerns openly and providing regular updates on children's progress.
- Managed budgeting and finances of the center, ensuring cost-effective operations while upholding high quality standards.

Game Designer | The Learning Studio, Pasadena, CA | 2017–2019
- Contributed to designing and developing interactive educational games, aligning gameplay and design with educational objectives.
- Collaborated with cross-functional teams, including developers, artists, and educators, to improve learning experiences for targeted age groups.
- Conducted user testing and feedback analysis to enhance game designs and ensure educational value and a positive user experience.

VOLUNTEER EXPERIENCE
- Volunteer Coordinator, Local PTA | 2019–2023
- Organized and facilitated extracurricular literacy activities for children in the community, with more than 400 children and more than 200 families participating.

KEY SKILLS
- Proficiency in game design software
- Strong project management and organizational abilities
- Exceptional communication and collaboration skills
- Deep knowledge of educational principles and child development
- Proficiency in Microsoft Office Suite

LINKEDIN PROFILE ELEMENTS CHECKLIST

☐ Professional headshot

☐ Current job

☐ Previous experience (honest version)

☐ Education (bachelor's degree and higher)

☐ Trade organizations, professional memberships, other qualifications

☐ Current contact information

PRE–JOB HUNT CHECKLIST

☐ Digital image check—LinkedIn, social profiles, Google search

☐ Current resume, transcripts, credentials, IDs

☐ Contact info—phone number, email, mailing address

☐ Interview or first-day wardrobe

☐ Software, technology, transportation, tools required to do the job

☐ Hygiene and grooming check—hair, skin, teeth, breath, body odor

CHAPTER 5

Methods of Communication

Taking care with your communication is one of the marks of a great professional. The way we reach out to and talk with one another (verbally and digitally), even how we set up meetings and appointments, are all part of fostering great relationships with our colleagues, collaborators, clients, prospects, suppliers, and others we work with. Spending time honing, clarifying, and improving the following areas of communication will go a long way toward maintaining your working relationships. Good communication skills will quickly and effectively identify you as a great person to work with.

TIME AND ATTENTION

In business, attention is time, and time is money. So, asking for someone's attention is no small thing. We control our attention and how we ask for attention from others. Every act of communication requires something of us; even in the simple act of declining a meeting invitation or request, you must take the time to consider it first. To be polite, taking care with how we ask for attention means we think first before reaching out to someone. Do we really need to make this ask or have this conversation about this issue? Right now? In business, if you come across as too forward, intrusive, oblivious, or disrespectful of someone's time and attention, they will write you off without a thought or be frustrated when interacting with you. There are a million fish in this sea. And as Emily Post has pointed out, why work with someone disrespectful and unaware when you can work with someone thoughtful and attentive?

Consider this, more than 361 billion emails are sent daily (as of 2024), a number that is expected to increase. The average person sends 40 and receives as many as 120 emails a day. Anything we can do to support each other in minimizing the number of emails we send and receive will help make a difference to us all. Use lists and reply-all features carefully and sparingly to avoid wasting or intruding on other people's time and attention.

THE NEW SPAM COURTESY Today, the courtesy of not cluttering the information spaces we work in and asking for attention only with things people want or need to see applies across email, text, DM/PM, channel messages, social media, watch alerts, and whatever comes next. You want to channel, tag, write a subject line, and reply in a way that makes the information contained in the message easy to identify, sort, and find again later. Another consideration when thinking about not spamming others is the timing of your communication. Do you *have* to hit send right now? Just because we can doesn't mean we should.

CHOOSING HOW TO
COMMUNICATE

With a colleague, direct report, manager, supervisor, vendor, supplier, or client, before you reach out—even if it's in response to them—ask yourself:

Is this the right time to broach this?

Is it the most respectful way to deliver this message or ask this question?

Is this the best method for delivering this message or asking this question?

We have so many ways to communicate, which means we have to carefully choose *how* to communicate the message. These decisions demonstrate your awareness of how important communication and relationships are to business. Some types of communication lend themselves to certain methods better than others.

WHEN IT'S PERSONAL When discussing opinions, catching up, getting to know someone, or discussing the "why?" of something, choose verbal communication. Pick up the phone, initiate a video chat, or meet in person. Your tone, volume, and cadence support your ideas and feelings in ways written words on a page or screen cannot do justice to.

COMMUNICATING FACTS Scheduling and sharing the details of a situation (the who, what, where, or when) is best supported by a written medium so you can keep track of everything and integrate it into your calendar more easily. Writing it down serves both to stay organized and to have a record of your communication. You might call your client to discuss an upcoming project but send an email afterward with the scope of work, actionable items, and deadlines from the meeting. Having details organized in one place or message thread is the best way to ensure you communicate well regarding schedules, details, assignments, and deadlines.

SHARING YOUR CONTACTS

Back in the day, when you left a job, it was a big deal whether you got to take your Rolodex with you. This was the physical (and mechanically operated) address book on many desks. Based on your job, the contacts you build through your work may or may not be something you can take to your next position. If you find yourself in a stage of transition, you can ask the HR department at your company about their policy.

When it comes to managing contacts, most businesses have specific systems that should be used, unless you've been permitted to do otherwise. Regardless of whether your contact list is yours or not and whether we're talking about someone's phone number, address, or a link to their personal Zoom room, you mustn't share this information without first determining that it is okay to share it. You can usually ask if it's okay to share someone's contact information; the question shows care and forethought.

Take care with how you organize and utilize your business contacts. Acknowledge who will be with you for a season, a reason, or a lifetime. You think that saying works well for describing different personal relationships? It's equally excellent for business relationships.

A SEASON usually means we're in touch for a definitive period of time, and for anything outside of that, you'll want to be delicate in your outreach because it will be in relation to a new project or situation. Essentially, with this contact, you want to acknowledge that while you've been in touch before, you don't assume you can or will be in touch again.

A REASON often means that we are in touch with this person periodically because they offer a service or provide information that we need, not regularly but enough throughout our work, so getting back in touch would be welcome for both parties.

A LIFETIME means this is one of your "business nearest and dearest." These are the people you stay in touch with no matter your current job and can call on for favors or insight, and who you'd happily do the same for if the offer or request came your way.

Just like with friendships and romantic relationships, these categories can be fluid, but thinking about where you stand with someone and where they stand with you before reaching out can help you set the right tone for your communication.

Most businesses will have preferred means of communication. There are times when it may seem like having a direct contact (someone's email or phone number) is the golden goose of communication. But with all the incredible systems at our disposal today for things such as media forms, general inquiries, booking services, and customer service systems, to name a few, this isn't always the case. Make sure you're using the system the business you're trying to contact prefers or has set up.

PRO TIP: To avoid disrespecting someone who has said they don't need your services, only reach out if you have something new to offer or discuss.

EMAIL: THE BUSINESS STANDARD

Although many offices have exchanged their internal email threads for Slack and Teams channels, and now text and DM seem to dominate some job communications, email is still essential to our professional and personal lives. A more formal, structured approach is the default standard in professional emails.

An email was originally fashioned to mimic a letter, and many people still use it this way, following the classic format below:

Greeting (Person's Name),

Followed by the body of the email in standard paragraph format, with no indentations.

Closing,
Your Name

Contact information if necessary

SETTING UP YOUR BUSINESS EMAIL

Because our business email is an extension of our image and it makes an impression every time we use it, there are some basic points to consider when writing business emails.

TO AND SUBJECT FIELDS

Be extra careful with selecting or typing in the correct email address. One wrong click and your line of communication is effectively dead. Deals and jobs have been lost over such errors. With so much at stake, make sure to triple-check that your email is headed to the right recipient(s).

The "Subject" field is your attention-getter. If your name alone doesn't get someone to open your email, the subject line is your next opportunity to grab their attention, so make it count. Be aware of words that flag spam filters. Choose your words wisely, being as brief but clear as possible about the contents of your email or the nature of the outreach. "Pics" is rather useless because it is so generic and could be problematic when the recipient has to search for this email later. "Edited Proofs—Swift Launch Shoot" is concise and clear.

Tagging and labeling our emails correctly and effectively is a courtesy to everyone we contact. Stay on topic in back-and-forth email threads to avoid confusion.

CC, BCC, AND REPLY-ALL FEATURES

Carbon copy (CC) and blind carbon copy (BCC) are two features that hail from letter writing. In email, we use these to include others in our communications. When we include them openly, we use the CC feature. When we want to disguise recipients from each other, we use the BCC feature. CCing is a great way to keep folks in the loop and a part of conversations, even if they only need to be a fly on the wall. BCC is great when you want to send to a large group of recipients, but you don't want them all to receive each other's contact information or be part of the reply chain.

When you're on an email with yourself or others CC'd, you want to use Reply All when replying so that everyone stays included. If someone no longer needs to be on the thread, removing them is always an option. The courtesy is to move someone to BCC and announce you're doing so. "Jane, thanks for your help on this. I'm moving you to BCC to spare your inbox." They won't see any replies to the CC group from then on.

YOUR SIGNATURE

Your signature is some valuable real estate in business emails. It communicates your identity: your position in your company, your contact information, and a plethora of other details, if you'd like to include them *and* it makes sense for the work you do. If your organization has a standard format, use it. We like to include our business titles, common links, and our mailing address in our signature since these seem to be things we get asked for a lot. Your signature will vary from job to job, but being comfortable crafting an effective signature will help you better establish yourself and your business persona. Choose from the most common elements below, and build a signature that is right for you and your position.

ELEMENTS OF SIGNATURE	EXAMPLE
Title Full Name (pronouns):	Ms. Emilia Cloyes (she/her)
Position or Job Title:	Co-Founder
Organization:	Cloyes & Rizzi Real Estate
Street Adress:	1253 Canyon Road
City, State, Zip	Park City, UT 09876
Country (optional)	USA
Phone office:	604-998-0987
Phone cell/direct:	872-960-1814
Website (hyperlink):	CloyesandRizzi.com

Here are some options that illustrate both a choice of information and some different options:

ESSENTIAL	USEFUL	ALL INFO
Emilia Cloyes (she/her) 604-998-0987	Emilia Cloyes (she/her) Co-Founder Cloyes & Rizzi Real Estate CloyesandRizzi.com 604-998-0987	Emilia Cloyes (she/her) Co-Founder Cloyes & Rizzi Real Estate 1253 Canyon Road Park City, UT 09876 604-998-0987 CloyesandRizzi.com

You can add logos and links to social media accounts or other aspects of your business. Whether to include things such as addresses and phone numbers is up to you. Some people choose not to due to privacy reasons; others find it's crucial to keeping business moving.

PRO TIP: Avoid using graphics in your signature that mail servers read as attachments. You don't want every email you send to look like extra information is attached.

EMAIL GREETINGS

In most professional emails, a formal greeting is a smart and respectful choice when initially emailing someone. Once you start a back-and-forth thread, the formality usually drops to first names with no greeting or no names and no greeting in subsequent emails, as the thread itself mimics the flow of a conversation.

From formal to casual, the greetings we choose set the tone of the email. Often, the best thing is to choose something with a tone that matches the circumstances of your writing to them.

FORMAL	INFORMAL	CASUAL
Dear (recipient's name), To Whom It May Concern, Good Morning, Good Afternoon, Good Evening,	Hello, Good Morning, Good Afternoon, Good Evening, Greetings,	Hi, Hey All, Everyone, The recipient's name or initial ("Yasunori," or "Y,")

BODY OF THE EMAIL

The body of the email should be written in complete sentences and paragraphs utilizing correct grammar, spelling, and punctuation. We cannot recommend strongly enough that you utilize some type of grammar and spell checker software. Google has a good system, and many are familiar with Microsoft Word. However, we noticed a significant decrease in the need to edit our work when we started using Grammarly. None of these tools are perfect. You won't say yes to every suggestion they make and you'll still want to read your emails aloud before hitting send, but, wow, they've made a difference for us. Try installing free versions of Grammarly or a similar editing software on your computer or browser—you will not regret it, and neither will your email recipients.

When it comes to the actual content of an email, the body of the email is where you get your work done. It's where you'll build and enhance relationships, ask questions, make requests, and give feedback or support; it's the heart and soul of your email.

Different stages of an email thread will result in different styles of emails. But when you start out, especially if you're emailing someone for the first time, it's best to be concise and complete. A balancing act for sure, but it will help you communicate a considerate, respectful, and competent image of yourself to the recipient.

WHEN REACHING OUT, we find that this is one of the most effective ways to structure your email:

1. Inquire about the other party or state that you hope they are well.

2. Get to the purpose of your correspondence. And get to it quickly and directly.

3. Ask questions clearly.

4. Paint a path forward.

WHEN REPLYING to an email, hitting these marks can set you up well:

1. Offer well-wishes to the person reaching out to you.

2. Address the subject they bring up and contribute any of your own thoughts.

3. Reply to all questions asked, or state that you cannot answer a particular question now.

4. Agree to or adjust the suggested path forward.

Keep consistent with replies, and try to use communication channels set up for certain tasks rather than introducing a new system. You want to avoid being the person who begins an email with "Hey, I saw your Slack message and wanted to reply." 🙄 (Reply over on Slack.)

EMOJIS

In a survey conducted by Slack, 53 percent of workers said they use emojis in workplace communications with colleagues, and 67 percent said they feel more bonded with a colleague who understands their emoji use. Gone are the days when emojis were inappropriate altogether. For casual work communications, they are appropriate and helpful in many cases.

That said, 48 percent of Americans have seen a misinterpreted emoji create an uncomfortable situation, found a Preply report, and it further indicated that this increasingly happens at work. As of 2024, the most easily misinterpreted emojis are 👋 , 🤙 , and 🙃 . Be sure you are using emojis that are mutually understood by all parties.

It's important to recognize, not only for those working globally but for those whose organizations employ people of multiple nationalities, that hand-gesture emojis should be used with care. They can mean very different things to different cultures. The "okay hand" emoji is obscene in Brazil and parts of southern Europe. And in some Middle Eastern cultures and for the aboriginal people of Australia, it's a symbol of evil. In America and other Western cultures, it represents *understood* or *perfect*.

> **PRO TIP**: Consider custom emojis or even just company-specific emoji use as a way to bond and build company culture. Companies that use them find their employees enjoy and look forward to using company-specific emojis and that it helps foster a sense of unity.

EMAIL CLOSINGS

For formal or first-interaction emails, definitely use a proper closing followed by your name. You might forgo closings for casual emails or work emails with those you communicate with daily but still use your first name or initials to "sign off."

One thing to watch out for is saying "thank you" or "thanks" preemptively and/or as a closeout. If your email asks for a favor or task to be done, it's best not to close with "thank you," as it assumes the answer is yes. Instead, close with something such as, "Many thanks for any help or direction you can offer. Best, [Your Name]." By specifying that your thanks is for the "help or direction" someone "can offer," you recognize that they might not be the one who ends up helping you. You also remove the thank-you from the closing position, allowing it to stand independently and not requiring it to do double duty of being both the thank-you and the close. Instead, it's a direct acknowledgment at the end of the email, independent of the close. Or you could say, "Thank you again," if you've thanked them properly in the note already. "Best" works for just about everyone, but it can sound stiff when writing to someone you are close with, similar to signing an email to a close friend or family member with your full name.

Remember that in business, we generally don't show affection; it's best to leave out hugs and kisses (X's and O's), *love,* and other affectionate closings. Here are classic options for closing a business email:

FORMAL	INFORMAL	CASUAL
Sincerely,	Best,	A dash followed by your name or initial
Best regards,	All the/my best,	("- Brian" or "-B")
Kind regards,	Regards,	Best,
Gratefully yours,	Warm regards,	Take care,
With high regard,		Bye for now,
		Cheers,

> **PRO TIP**: Avoid using a closing in your preset signature. It will discourage you from customizing the sign-off—which is a mistake. You want even your closing to create the feeling that you're being attentive and appropriate to the recipient and the communication.

ATTACHMENTS

Remember to attach them.

When possible, make attachments visible as icons, rather than the full image of the file. File size can also affect someone's ability to receive, download, and read attachments. For many email services, 25 MB is the upper limit for all attachments. Try to keep file sizes comfortably below this, or upload the file to a shared folder that you can link to.

INTRODUCTIONS VIA EMAIL

Depending on the circumstances of the introduction, you might direct an email to one particular person and introduce another person to them, or you might address both (or all) of the people needing introductions. Be sure to include full names, pronouns, and job titles when applicable, as well as the reason the introduction is being made. If one person is higher ranking than the other, you would address this person first and introduce the other person to them. In the following examples, the first would be the best if Frederika was superior to Alex in the organization, or if she was a client.

Dear Frederika,

I'm looking forward to working together. I'd like to introduce Jesse Ritvo (cc'd). He is our point person and will be working with you on next year's rollout.

Or:

Hi Frederika and Jesse,

I wanted to take a moment to connect the two of you. Frederika, this is Jesse Ritvo, our point person for next year's rollout. Jesse, this is Frederika Roland of Acme Jet Packs.

I'll leave you to it!

Best,
Kyle

It is not uncommon for people introduced via email to move the introducer to BCC once the introduction has been made. "Thanks for the introduction, Kyle. Frederika and I will take it from here and move you to BCC."

COURTESIES FOR CALLS

We still make and take *calls* today, but the format they take is now a question we ask daily, often multiple times. We use video and phone calls so interchangeably at work that both are regular features of the average office and work-from-home jobs. Let's look at the etiquette of both.

PLACING AND ANSWERING WORK CALLS

Many new hires and younger generations report anxiety around phone calls in general. How we conduct ourselves on the phone will impact our success when we do business with others. Building strong phone etiquette skills can take a lot of that anxiety and turn it into confidence, and it might even help you stand out from the crowd at work. Whether you're dialing someone for the first time or answering the phone after it rings unexpectedly, confidence and engagement come through to the person on the other end. It's one more step in building a great relationship with them.

PLACING WORK CALLS

Before you dial, think about the purpose of the call and what you need to say when the call is answered. Prepare responses and have a path forward for yourself depending on what the person on the other end says.

OTHER PERSON: "Yes, now's a good time to talk."
RESPONSE: "Great, I was hoping to talk with you about . . ."

OTHER PERSON: "No, I'm not interested."
RESPONSE: "Thanks for letting me know. Should I try again in X amount of time, or should I leave my contact information with you in case you find yourself needing XYZ service?"

OTHER PERSON: "Could we talk another time?"
RESPONSE: "I'd be happy to; what works best with your schedule?"

Now that you've thought through how to handle any answer you get, let's break down your opening lines step by step:

1. Greet the person on the other end and identify yourself. "Hi/Hello/Good morning/Good afternoon, this is Lorna Peters."

2. State who you are trying to reach and why: "I'm calling for Coco Turner. I have a meeting scheduled with her at ten o'clock."

3. Listen to what the person on the other end says.

4. If this is an assistant or receptionist who connects your call, thank them. "Thank you, Tony."

Coco may or may not know that it's you who is being transferred to her direct line. When she greets you, you'll either be addressed by your name when she picks up the line—"Lorna! I've been looking forward to our call"—or she'll answer with a generic greeting, and you'll return her greeting and announce yourself again. "Hi, Coco, this is Lorna Peters. Is now still a good time?" Checking that now is still a good time is always a thoughtful courtesy. Then you can carry on with your conversation.

ANSWERING WORK CALLS

Isn't it such a relief when you call somewhere and the person answering is pleasant, and it's easy to tell you've reached the right place? That's what to aim for with incoming business calls. What you say will depend on your company, your role, and whether or not you can tell who is calling. For a call where you cannot identify the person calling in, it is appropriate to be a bit more formal and present the company and yourself with your greeting: "Hello, KushKards, this is Lauren. How may I help you?" It might sound like a mouthful, but it only takes two seconds to say and offers so much to the person calling. A shorter version: "KushKards, how may I direct your call?" would let the caller know immediately that this person was the operator or receptionist and could get them to where they needed to go.

If you're not receiving incoming calls directly from outside lines but instead receiving calls forwarded by reception or an assistant, answering with your name is also acceptable: "Hello, this is Arriana," or "Hello, this is Arriana Arroyos." This is particularly common for in-company calls and those using a dedicated extension. If you have caller ID and the contact calling in is a close one, it's quite typical today to answer that call by greeting the person directly: "Ann! I'm so happy to hear from you!" However, if you can tell an outside number is calling in and you're going to answer it, it's still best to issue a greeting, and then state your company, and your name: "Hello, Common Sense PR, Arriana speaking."

If calls are only ever announced by an assistant, who is likely letting you know, "Sebastian Rainer is on line one for you," you could certainly answer, "Sebastian, how wonderful to hear from you," or "Hello, Sebastian, I've been looking forward to our call today." In this case, your assistant acts as the initial greeter, and you can focus on the person and the purpose of the call rather than announcing yourself.

YOUR BEST PHONE VOICE

One of the very best tips for a pleasant call is to smile. The other person cannot see you, but they will hear your smile on the other end, which makes all the difference to the tone of the call. You'll also want to be aware of your volume and tone to have a successful call.

LEAVING A MESSAGE

Having an idea of what you need to say in a message, if you need to leave one, is another way to prep well before placing a call. Jot down notes if you need prompts. If you are sent to voicemail or need to leave a message with an assistant, include your name and callback number (better than spelling out your email address) twice and the reason for your call. If you'd like to offer a good time to reach you and it makes sense to, then do so.

While it's technically preferable to be formal with anyone in business, more and more people are defaulting to first names, even in messages to someone they've never spoken to before. Judge whether to be formal or familiar based on your industry, company, and whom you are calling. You might even consider using titles as a sign of respect if you are a new hire or this is your first job.

FOR A FORMAL MESSAGE

"Hello, Mr. Erickson; my name is Robin Miles from We Train 'Em Right. We met at the SHRM convention last week, and I'm calling to set a time to discuss your training needs.

Please call me back at 555-212-5656 when you can, or I can try again on Friday. Again, this is Robin Miles, and my number is 555-212-5656. Thanks for your time, and I wish you my best. Goodbye."

FOR A CASUAL MESSAGE

"Hi, Milton. It's Robin from We Train 'Em Right at SHRM last week. It was great speaking with you. I was hoping to set up a time to talk about training. Feel free to reach me at 555-212-5656, again, that's 555-212-5656, or I'll try you again on Friday. Take care, bye."

THE ETIQUETTE OF PHONE FEATURES

This section might feel like we're telling you how to boil water, but a few of the most common phone features can be better utilized if we apply a bit of etiquette to how we use them.

SPEAKER

Anytime you use a speakerphone, you are responsible to two groups: anyone on the call who is being broadcast, and anyone around you who might hear the call. Announcing those present to those on the call is a common courtesy: "Hi, Jim, I've got you on speaker; Jenn is here with me in the truck." On the flip side, rarely do the people around you want to hear a conversation if they aren't involved. Try to minimize your impact on those you are with.

Whether your speakerphone is being used on a landline in an office, at your home office, or coming out of your cell, it's loud and obnoxious unless everyone present is on the call. Walking down the street? Have it up to your ear, or use headphones. Hallway at work? Have it up to your ear, or use headphones. In the taxi with your boss? *Why are you on the phone now? That's so rude!* (Unless it was for work, but still, not on speakerphone.)

MUTE

With mute, we can stay on a call and have a coughing fit, eat a sandwich, take a whiz (yup, we said it), call the dog in from the yard, or even block out ongoing background noise such as construction or kids. Be careful with the mute button. Forget it's on, and you can have entire conversations without being heard. Forget to turn it on, and the multitude of mea culpas you may need to issue goes up exponentially. "Gerry, you forgot to mute" isn't a phrase you want to hear (especially in the case of that whiz!).

HOLD

The biggest courtesy with a hold feature is to let someone know you are going to put them on hold: "Dr. Mehta's office, hold one moment please," or "Oh, Arya, I just got an incoming call from Puj, can I put you on hold for a sec while I check in with her?" Second biggest courtesy: don't forget you placed someone on hold!

MERGE

The etiquette around the merge feature mostly involves announcing that you'll merge a call. All parties should be able to see the numbers or contacts that have been merged, but it's worth making the announcement and double-checking that the merge was successful before launching into the substance of the call.

VOICEMAIL

While it's true that with caller ID and texting, voicemail is less prevalent than it used to be in our personal lives, voicemail has remained relevant in our professional lives. Leaving messages is a professional skill. Keep it short and direct: speak clearly, state your name, where you're calling from, the reason for the call, and times you're available to be reached back at. Repeat contact or important information. See Leaving a Message, page 95, for sample scripts.

VIDEO CALLS

We'll take a look at tips for video meetings in chapter 8, "Meetings." Here, we'll focus on using video calls for everyday communications.

While some might work on teams that prefer using video calls and are comfortable with casual video call experiences, most of us need to bring our "professional appearances" to the table when we hop on a video call. For this reason, most people do not just initiate a video call out of the blue. Instead, they are planned events; sometimes they truly are a meeting, not a call. Let's look at how to be polite with video call features.

CHAT

The chat feature of a video call, done via a platform like Zoom, is a tough space. On the one hand, it's so useful to send messages to other participants or the whole group without interrupting the ongoing conversation, and with the wide range of uses for these calls, it can be an integral way of sharing information. However, it can also be distracting and hard to tell if you are sending a message to an individual or a group, even though having the option to do both is great. Be careful and go slowly with your communication in the chat. It can be tempting to make a comment on the side to just one person, and it only takes one little, easy-to-make slip-up for that comment to go to the host or the group.

MUTE

Join a video meeting with the mute on as a best practice. Be familiar with your mute button. Know what it looks like, where to find it, and which symbols indicate that you can be heard or are muted. You also want to be familiar with your device's mic (input) and speaker (output) settings so that you can quickly and easily adjust them if you need to without causing a fuss or taking up too much time on the call.

RAISING A HAND

This was a really smart feature to build into video call platforms. We give it a tip of the hat for sure! By selecting the "hand raise" feature, you allow the host and others to know you have something you'd like to ask or contribute without interrupting. For groups smaller than three or four participants, this feature is often unnecessary and could come across as overdoing it. When you have one quarter of the right to the conversational pie, it's easier to manage a fair share of speaking time or in-the-moment questions or thoughts. But once you start to get above five people, it's an incredibly helpful tool to manage the group.

AI NOTES AND SUMMARIES

We may not be fans of our work being used to teach AI without proper compensation and respect for copyrights, not to mention the fact that there is no guarantee AI is learning from the latest editions of our books, but we are fans of AI for transcriptions, summaries, closed captioning, and meeting notes; there are even features that can let you get caught up if you're joining a meeting late. It's incredible! But it comes with its own etiquette. First acknowledge or ask if anyone minds your AI taking notes. Second, ask if anyone on the call would like a transcript or meeting summaries or follow-ups afterward. You can also offer to turn on the closed captioning during the call. If someone doesn't want to be recorded or would prefer some of the AI tools not be in use, it's best to respect their wishes. If you are unable to, be prepared for them to not participate in the call.

TEXTING IN BUSINESS

Texting is an ongoing conversation space, one you can pop in and out of. It's one of our least formal and somewhat intimate form of communication. Much like a nickname, you can use it when you know you're on the in; it's great, convenient, and even natural. But when you're not in someone's inner work circle, it's a bit forward and assumptive to just text them out of the blue and expect a response, kind of like skipping the spaces they expect to be reached for business (email, work phone) and instead just going straight to their pocket. It can be a bit too soon.

Always check with your company and work contacts as to whether text is an acceptable form of communication. There can be teams, companies, and industries where the name of the game is speed: everyone texts each other and shares numbers without permission, and it's okay. You'll know if you're in a field like this or if a work relationships requires it, much like that nickname territory. It will be explained and expected as part of the job. Outside of this, use caution. Keep your work communications in work channels and on work devices.

GET THE RECIPIENTS RIGHT. This one is pretty obvious. The wrong recipient could be a big deal in business. It could stop a deal dead in its tracks or, in the worst cases, provide someone access to privileged, private, or even confidential information. Some people add nicknames to their contacts to help them avoid mistakes with autofill and voice commands, especially when you have thirteen Justins in your phone. Double-checking the "To" field of your text before you hit "Send" should be a constant practice. Another common mistake is using group texts to exchange information that is best done directly. Remember that the courtesy of not spamming or distracting colleagues with unnecessary information applies in the world of texting too. Keep your group texts focused.

SAY WHAT YOU MEAN. Using only emojis in your texts, saying "LOL" just because you don't know what to say, or continually replying with "K" or a thumbs-up emoji is unprofessional. All of these responses are fine, but they're obnoxious when done constantly or to reject text messaging as a form of communication. It's one thing if now isn't a good time to text and you want to give some sort of response, or the simple answer of a thumbs up really is the answer, but whenever possible, say what you mean and say it clearly. Business communications aren't the place to make others decipher hidden meanings.

BE CLEAR IF NOW ISN'T THE TIME. There are many reasons you might not want to get into a text conversation or respond right away: you're in the car, with other colleagues, or unable to focus on the content of the conversation. In these moments, send a simple "Busy now, will respond later," or use an auto-reply like "I'll get back to you as soon as I can" if you need to. Specifics are helpful when possible, and any response is preferable to no response. That being said, it should also be understood that if someone isn't replying (or isn't replying in kind), they are likely busy and will respond when they can. Badgering someone for a reply isn't likely to help matters.

RESPOND PROMPTLY. Even though "promptly" might mean "thirty seconds" to some and "within the week" to others, it's important to note and honor expectations that develop in your working relationships. Pay attention to the content and context of a message. Don't let important things sit. The stress you can create by not responding promptly when you should be available isn't worth the sense of freedom or autonomy you seemingly gain from not responding immediately. If you have a reason, sure, but you can tell the other person, "I can't answer right now, but I should know by Monday," rather than just not responding until Monday.

PAY ATTENTION TO YOUR TYPING. When texting with friends and family, we're used to rapid-fire texts that often don't present as a coherent conversation because the replies don't align in a perfect script. Certain features, like being able to couple the message you're replying to with your reply, even if other texts have come in while you're typing, can help. When texting for business, slowing down and allowing someone to finish typing when we can see their "typing text" bubble is akin to not interrupting them midsentence or midthought in live conversation (and just like interrupting, there are times when you might just need to do it). We can also use good texting etiquette by ensuring we send one longer message instead of six short ones in reply. The reduced notifications are the consideration here—and they are so worth it.

SKIP THE SALUTATION AND CLOSING. When texting with someone you have an established or ongoing text chain with, there is no need to use salutations or closings. When reaching out to someone via text for the first time or from a new or different number, making an effort to use a greeting and identify yourself will help the recipient, given the circumstances.

MAKING INTRODUCTIONS VIA TEXT. When introducing someone via text message, first ensure that both parties are okay with sharing their information. Then proceed to send a group text: "Drew, I'd like to introduce Marc Winters. Marc, this is Drew Rawlings. Hopefully, you two can connect for the meeting; I'll leave you to it!" Drew and Marc may say thank you for the introduction and let you know they'll start their own thread.

OUTREACH. Outreach texts to business contacts are often to ask for favors or information, share news, generate interest, or stay connected. It's important to remember and respect the nature of your "pop-in" with these texts. Acknowledging that it's been a while, or that you recognize you're reaching out with a request, and closing your text by saying something like "Thank you for considering this" can help to soften the outreach and keep it in the friendly business category. "Hey! We need your help! Can you send us a testimonial by EOD tomorrow?" after not reaching out in a year is gauche. Keep your tone gentle and clear and show self-awareness to maintain trust in this relationship. "Hi Allisha, I know it's been a while. I hope you and the team at JJM are doing great. I'm reaching out with a request [insert request]. Thank you for considering it. I completely understand if now isn't a great time, but we'd love to have you on board if you can. Take care!"

CALENDAR

Your calendar is a communication tool. Yes, it is used to organize your time, but depending on how you share it, it also tells others when you are available and what you are doing.

Most people are used to putting appointments and meetings on their shared work calendars. If this is standard practice for your company, be conscious of what you are communicating to your colleagues through your availability. Effectively setting up appointments is key to using your calendar politely. Be sure that reminder and alerts are set up conveniently, but not obnoxiously—you don't likely need more than one reminder email or alert to go out.

Sharing pertinent information in the actual calendar appointment is incredibly helpful when it comes time for participants to join the call or attend the meeting. When creating a calendar invitation, make sure to include meeting locations, contact information for you or the person managing the meeting should attendees need to reach out, log-in or dial-in information, links, or any attendance information the participant might need. The notes section of the appointment is a great space for this. Materials or pre-work that would be helpful, such as an agenda for the meeting, could also be included or attached in email reminders about the appointment. Take note that some calendar systems send notifications anytime the entry is changed. This can result in a lot of unnecessary notifications to the participants.

SCHEDULING

Taking care and being respectful when we ask for someone's time is essential. Whether it is a job interview, a catch-up lunch with a former coworker, an annual executive meeting, or anything else, the care you take as you plan and organize it is the first step in ensuring the meeting goes well.

OFFERING VERSUS ASKING VERSUS TELLING

There is a big difference between *offering* to meet, *asking* to meet, and *telling* someone you're going to meet. In the offer, you express interest and make yourself available. In the ask, you are directing the conversation. In both situations, there's a focus on the agreement or consensus that people will get together, and it is important to establish and respect that. The tell is our least favorite, but it has its necessary place. There is an authoritative tell and an informative tell, and the difference is in how you deliver it. Let's look at all three approaches.

THE OFFER Keep your offer an offer by giving a range of dates and times if you're "starting the bidding" to schedule a time. Ask others involved what works best for them. Keep your language open by giving the recipient options or choices, since you're initiating the scheduling and you don't yet know their reaction to the offer. "I'm available mornings, your time, next week if there is a day that works for you, or I'd be happy to share a scheduling link to my calendar if that is easier."

THE ASK When you ask someone who reports to you to meet, or are tasked with organizing a meeting that is already agreed to, your language and approach should reflect that. You can be more direct about finding a time while staying gracious about the unknowns that might be in play. "It looks like we all have Tuesday morning open. I suggest 10:30 A.M. as a good time for the Blue Sky meeting about the new flavors they'll launch this spring. Please let me know if this works for everyone."

THE TELL Be very judicious in how you use the *tell*. While it may be *your* prerogative, your team deserves respect when told to do something. "Mandatory Employee Meeting Monday at 3 P.M. Be There or Be Fired" sends a message, but it's a bad one. The tell can be respectful and without threats. "All-Staff Meeting Monday at 3 P.M. Attendance is required" communicates the exact same message but is more inclusive, presenting the company as one with "all-staff," instead of "employees," which can create an "us versus them" mentality. Even with the latter's message of required attendance, it is a more inviting, informative tone. Since people interpret commands in different ways, consider the impact on your relationships and to company culture when you make demands about time.

No matter if you are *suggesting a meeting* ("I know everyone is busy, but I think it might be helpful if we all jumped on a call and talked through the issue that came up on this channel today"), *tasked with planning it* ("I'm reaching out on behalf of Jaya to plan the directors' meeting for next month. I'm hoping to get best and worst dates from everybody to generate some options"), *requiring it* ("I know this is short notice, but I need all engineers on the follow-up call this afternoon"), or *trying to change it* ("Hi, Lee Ann, I ended up with a sick kid today and have to ask to reschedule our sit-down for tomorrow or Wednesday at the same time. Would either work for you?"), showing awareness and respect for all the demands that people have on their time is a communication courtesy that others will appreciate.

COMMON SCHEDULING COURTESIES

- Offer a client or superior the option of booking directly with you or through a scheduling link if you have one. Providing both options lets the other person decide, and that's what makes it a courtesy.

- If the other party hasn't chosen to use your booking link, offer to send a calendar invitation once a time is selected. Remember to include everyone who will be on the call.

- When setting up the calendar appointment, include the necessary details, such as phone numbers or links, in the notes section. As the recipient, pay attention to the notes section of a calendar appointment. It may contain call-in info or links to connect for a call, meeting, or interview.

- If someone responds to a request for a meeting time with "Well, what works for you?," feel confident stating what does work best for you.

- Accept or decline calendar appointments as soon as possible so that either they appear on your calendar for recordkeeping, or the host knows you cannot attend.

- Choose intentionally and wisely whom you give access to book directly on your calendar and pay attention to whether your booking link allows recipients to use the link again.

SAMPLE SCHEDULING EXCHANGE

FORMAL CALL SCHEDULING EXCHANGE: "A call sounds great. I'm available Thursday and Friday this week from 2 P.M. Eastern on, and if you'd like to look into next week, I've got openings on Tuesday and Wednesday."

"That sounds great! I can meet at 11 A.M. ET on Tuesday and anytime between 2 and 5 P.M. Eastern next Wednesday."

"Awesome, let's do 3 P.M. Wednesday, ET. Shall I send a calendar invite? If you want to connect via phone, please send a number and I'll give you a buzz, or you can reach me at 802-867-2334. I'm also happy to connect via video if you want to send a link."

CASUAL CALL SCHEDULING EXCHANGE: "A call sounds great, late this week or the middle of next week are looking good on my end. Here's my scheduling link if you'd like to pick a time that works for you, or I'm happy to schedule directly if you prefer."

[Books on scheduling link] "Great, thank you. I just booked us for 3pm on Wednesday."

> **PRO TIP**: If you have an assistant, let them do their job. Jumping in will only complicate the process, even if your intent is to make it more personal.

OFF HOURS

Personal and private time is important. We have all heard of job creep and maybe of the opposite, life creep. In an increasingly connected world, we need to pay attention to the blurring line between personal and professional time and set boundaries and expectations for ourselves and those with whom we work. Using that phone in your pocket to get an answer from your team anytime you need it might sound appealing until you answer that work call at your daughter's wedding reception. Think about how you will manage your availability and accessibility during your time away from work and decide what types of communication are acceptable for you.

If you are in a position to set your own availability, be clear with clients and collaborators about your hours and whether you can respond outside of working hours. We know many wedding and event planners who have had to clearly explain to clients that emails and texts sent after 5:00 P.M. will be responded to the following business day. With clients calling at all hours and expecting replies to 3:00 A.M. emails immediately, these boundaries are necessary. Managing expectations politely and confidently is essential to having boundaries around your off hours.

> **PRO TIP**: Use texting sparingly for communication outside of work hours. Texts can be harder to get away from than email or other office messaging systems when people don't want to be reached.

DISPLAYING WORK TIME

Calendars don't have to be only for booking shared work time with others. Networked calendars can function as a work planning and communication tool as well. In addition to planning and accepting meeting invitations and adding them to your calendar, block off time for independent work so that your manager, colleagues, and direct reports can see an accurate representation of your availability and understand the full scope of your workday. The boss used to see you sitting at the desk out front, showing up on time, working through your tasks, and meeting with colleagues. Now, they can look at your calendar and get a sense of your work schedule and routine, whether you're at the office or working remotely.

THE ADVANTAGES are that it is transparent, it lets others know when you aren't available, and it can help you manage and plan your work.

THE DISADVANTAGES are the risk of overbooking yourself and not leaving enough time for others to contact you. Yes, it might be true that you will be working on the new proposal all week, but that probably doesn't mean you can't plan a thirty-minute check-in meeting with the department chair. Even though your calendar is packed. Use permissions and features that label your work blocks, such as Outlook's *Busy, Tentative,* and *OOO (Out of Office),* to help folks know when they can schedule over blocked time and when they can't.

DISPLAYING PERSONAL TIME

Think about how you display non-work-related appointments on your calendar as well. You should include personal appointments that take your attention away from your workday for transparency and scheduling's sake. On teams where folks can book time and invite each other to meetings, it's easier to have that time blocked off as Time Out of Office (it doesn't have to say why) so that your colleagues know you aren't available.

THE ADVANTAGES are that it is transparent, lets others know when you aren't available, and can help you manage the times when your personal life crosses over to work time.

THE DISADVANTAGES are the risk of oversharing personal information (doctor appointments, kids' activities, dates, health and fitness plans or goals, personal to-dos). If you become too comfortable with the practice, you might accidentally include the reason for that doctor's visit or details of your personal life that you'd rather not share.

By avoiding too much detail on personal calendar appointments and by being a team player with the way your company wants to manage shared calendars, you're going to set yourself up well to communicate effectively and efficiently with those at work.

MESSAGING AND WORK MANAGEMENT APPS

Slack, Microsoft Teams, G Suite, Basecamp, SalesForce, Zoom, and even Monday.com and Canva are all cloud-based communication and work management platforms that can be godsends for businesses. The Emily Post Institute was transformed when we started working with Monday.com. We understand from a very personal point of view that these systems are vital to a company's productivity and efficiency. From an etiquette standpoint, there are several ways to use these platforms well with others and demonstrate professionalism at work.

ORGANIZATIONS

Because these tools are so powerful and customizable, whether for work management, scheduling, communication, or data organization, each company must define their usage and take responsibility for educating the teams or clients who will use them. Plan the time and attention it may take to bring new users up to speed and get them using these systems well. There are several things to consider when planning your training or deployment.

- What are the most essential features and capabilities of the work you do?

- What are the customizable settings and profile setup options for each user, and what is their direction for how each user will configure them?

- What are the specific use patterns that work for your group?

Be sure to have a plan to address these areas and be ready to review it as necessary.

INDIVIDUALS

You are responsible for what you say and do on these platforms. Ignorance about how they are supposed to be used is not an excuse. Pay attention to how your company uses these systems and learn them properly. As you get your feet wet, there can be little hiccups everywhere. Does the message send or feed you a new line if you hit return? When you reply to this message, does the whole team see it? Do clients ever see this message board? Are you sure? *Really sure?* Well, keep it safe for now.

Keep your good etiquette foot forward as you message in these spaces. Remember, familiarity with the tool does not make your use correct. You still need to be considerate and pay attention to the *quality* of what you do in these spaces. Remember that people are still at the other end of every message, alert, and status update notification. Don't send a chat until you're ready to engage in the conversation. Sending a request via the company messaging app and then ignoring the chat or taking more than a minute or two to reply leaves the person you're making a request of wait on you. This is not polite.

Beginners, go slow at first. Don't just dive right in; take your time as you learn to swim in these waters. Maybe you grew up with a tablet in hand and social accounts at your fingertips, but messaging at work, in your first job, is a whole new body of water. Cannonbaaaaaaaaaaall! No.

CHANNELS

Etiquette for channels on messaging apps, like Teams and Slack, has become a big component of professional communication in the last decade and a half. So much work is run through these systems that courtesies have emerged and deserve some attention. Let's look at the top manners for messaging channels.

STICK TO THE TOPIC. Think of a channel as an in-person meeting for work on a certain project or task. Keep your communications on the channel focused on the topic. Drawing attention away from that purpose is disrespectful to others and the work.

KEEP MESSAGES SHORT AND SWEET. Literally, be nice and concise. For longer exchanges and more detailed messages consider meetings, calls, and emails instead. No one wants to read a 7-inch-long unformatted message when an organized attachment would have worked better. (That said, be careful about responding in other spaces to a channel topic, as DM might be drawing the conversation away from the space it's supposed to happen in. If it does happen, be sure to return to the channel with a response so the conversation there isn't left unfinished. Paper trails are mighty useful.)

USE @TAGGING TO DIRECT ATTENTION. In the steady stream of information flowing back and forth, an @name tag can help recipients filter out and see the most important information for them. In most cases, tagging an individual also sends them a direct notification to call the message to their attention.

ACKNOWLEDGE. You are accountable to channels like you are to your work email and phone calls. Don't leave messages unacknowledged, and don't leave direct questions unanswered. Reply in a timely manner. Thumbs-up, likes, and similar acknowledgments can be helpful, but words work best. Follow up directly with someone if you message them on a channel and don't see a response or the work product itself. Saying, "Well, I put it on Slack" isn't always enough, and while each employee is responsible for this space, you must bottom-line your work with more direct follow-ups when necessary.

> **PRO TIP**: You can always reply saying you don't know or don't have time to address it or will reply with an answer later, even if you don't have the answer now.

KEEP IT PUBLIC. Even if it is just two people on a channel, the channel might include others at some point in the future or be referenced as the work continues elsewhere. Channels can be like conversations in public places, private one moment and public the next. Communicate confidential information, negative feedback, and personal information in more private forums. And definitely don't gossip on a channel.

WORK-SOCIAL CHANNELS ARE EFFECTIVE. Many organizations find substantial value in providing a channel for messages that would function the way kitchen or water cooler talk does in shared workspaces. Allowing off-work conversations builds social cohesion and provides more relationship opportunities. Everything from "Go Tigers!" so everyone can talk about the local team to "Easy + Yum Recipes" or "Pets of Vermont Public" can have an important place at work—just not on the client channels.

KEEP YOUR STATUS CURRENT. Understand how your status appears to others and manage it accurately. Conversely, observe and respect the status of others so as not to bother them and to get a sense of how reasonable it is to expect a reply. Some systems allow you to set your status; others default to certain positions depending on your activity.

EMOJIS, GIFS, TEXT ABBREVIATIONS, EXCLAMATION POINTS, AND ALL CAPS. These can give written communication more emotional context and dynamic range. They can also be confusing, distracting, or come across as unprofessional. Keep their use to a minimum on external channels and in larger groups. They are best reserved for side channels and long-established relationships. Correct spelling, grammar, and punctuation are still the baseline standards for *every* written business communication on *any* platform. Maintaining this standard is the best way to ensure that you are understood, and it also shows that you care enough not to make others edit or interpret your communications for you.

MANAGE THE VOLUME OF COMMUNICATION. As the number of channels you follow increases and connections become more complex, it can be like trying to follow several conversations at once, and things can slip through the cracks. Use features such as *save for later,* just as you would flag an email to build reminder lists of things that you could not respond to or need extra attention at some point.

BE THOUGHTFUL WITH CHANNEL CREATION, BOTH IN TOPIC AND WHO YOU INVITE. Don't involve people who don't need to be involved. Label channels thoughtfully and clearly so that anyone can tell what the subject and purpose of the channel are. This will also help the organization track the work being done on the platform.

KEEP IT CIVIL. Creating a good environment on your channels greatly affects the overall work environment. These tools can keep distributed and remote workforces connected in amazing ways. Bringing common civility and care for others into these spaces is a great way to support civil workplaces for years to come.

THE NEXT THING. Remember that when you ask anyone in business to join your channel, you ask them to adjust to you. Consider the relationship and how worth it the convenience is for you. How much are you asking the other person to adjust? Clients who don't use these systems at their own companies may not use them well enough for you to get the streamlined communication you're hoping for.

> **PRO TIP**: Make a separate channel for feedback on how the platform is managed or functions. Solicit feedback from those using these tools to allow for constant adaptation and evolution. This can also be a great place to share organizational ground rules, best practices, tips, new features, common practices, and gold-standard user acknowledgment.

PRIVATE CHANNEL	PUBLIC CHANNEL
Greg: Hey, I need that copy by 3pm. Susan: On it now!	Greg: Hi Susan, I'm checking in to see if you will have that copy by 3 p.m. today? Susan: Hey Greg, Yes, I'm working on it now.

SOCIAL MEDIA

We are not here to tell a social media manager how to do their job. Every business will have its own social media strategy and policies, and you should know yours and follow them. But we will say that you should be cautious and deliberate when making choices around your *own* social media presence once you're in the working world. (See Digital Image, page 46, for more on how to make sure your digital appearance matches your professional appearance.)

Maintain a sense of public accountability on social media and keep private things off it. Before you post, comment, share, or even like, ask yourself if you would post it on the bulletin board by the front desk of your office or in the chat space of your next meeting. Social media content, even when shared with private connections, has a habit of getting shared widely in unexpected ways. Think of everything you share and do on social media platforms as potentially public.

It might be helpful to use the three tiers for managing conversation (See The Three Tiers of Conversation, page 134) to make choices about what to share on social media.

While we used to advise that you should never send a direct or private message to a company or service via social media and expect a response, increasingly people do rely on these message centers to communicate with their clients and audience, vendors, and other business affiliates. That said, we still believe that when you are looking to do business, it is smart to do a little detective work and visit a company's website (if it does not exist solely in the social media sphere) and see what their CONTACT US page looks like. If they have a preferred method for inquiries, follow it. If your detective work has provided you with nothing, then by all means, hit up that DM for this business request or proposition and see how it goes. If no one replies to your outreach within a week or two, it's okay to reach out again.

> **PRO TIP**: While it can be tempting to mix it up and clap back at people who are wrong or, worse, rude to you or your organization on social media, let the jerks and trolls be jerks and trolls. Keep your public voice professional in all your exchanges. Don't get dragged into arguments that diminish you. Remember, the etiquette high road is worth it. The trolls are often looking to get you to respond.

STATIONERY

A well-appointed "stationery wardrobe"—consisting of basic pieces such as cards, note sheets, letter sheets, blanks, and envelopes—should have you well set up for handwritten correspondence. What matters is to include the pieces that meet your needs. Personal professional stationery will have your company name, your name, title, initials, or logo engraved or printed on it. Generic company stationery, also known as letterhead, can be used by anyone from the company. Usually, the company's name, address, phone number, and website are all positioned nicely on the 8.5 by 11–inch sheet, with the elements not interfering with the page's main content area. You could handwrite something on a sheet of letterhead or insert it into your printer and print out a letter, proposal, or scope of work.

Type, color, and graphics options are infinite. But in business, we suggest blue or black ink for the body of the letter, using standard professional fonts such as Times New Roman or Caslon. Informal social stationery can use playful colors, fonts, patterns, and images. For formal business styles, choose simple, clean lines and dark or deeply saturated classic colors—a traditionalist will advise you to avoid black. Cards and sheets are paired with matching envelopes. A local stationer can be a great asset when making decisions.

Correspondence cards are the most typical cards you'll use for both written business correspondence and messages such as thank-you notes, sympathy notes, and congratulatory notes. If your company has supplied you with something like a fold-over card instead of a correspondence card, it's fine to use that, even though the latter is more commonly associated with business correspondence.

YOUR BUSINESS CARD

Your business card is probably the most used piece of business stationery, and the most common. This is you on a card, and it will be how you are remembered for future reference. Take care of the details and respect the business cards you receive. You have a lot of room to be creative with the design if you freelance or own your own business. For many others, the company you work for will issue your business cards, which will be on a set template. Regardless, the card should include your name, the company name, your title/position, and the contact information you wish to share. Beyond that, websites and QR codes are examples of additional options.

Heavier-weight paper is of higher quality, more durable, and more expensive. Use a font no smaller than 8 points to ensure it's legible. See "Business Social," chapter 9, for more information about properly giving and receiving business cards.

THE TRADITIONAL BUSINESS LETTER

A business letter has a more structured appearance than a social letter and follows some old-school standards. If you aren't using company letterhead, write your company name at the top left, followed by its address, with each line flush left. Two lines down, put the date. Two lines below that, put the recipient's name, then, on the next line down, the recipient's title or department, followed by the recipient's company name and address, each on a separate line below the title. The salutation begins two lines below the recipient's address. If it's a formal letter, use the recipient's title and last name; if it's a more familiar letter, you may use the person's first name. Always use "Dear" as the salutation.

The body of the letter is not indented, and a line space separates each paragraph. The closing is aligned left. Leave space below your closing to add your handwritten or digital signature. About two to four lines below the closing, print your name, then beneath it, put your title or department, followed by your phone number. The last line should be your email address. (See Sample Business Letter, page 119, for an example.)

BUSINESS NOTES YOU MIGHT WRITE

Here are some notes you are most likely to write in business. Notes are a bit less formal than letters, but that does not diminish their use in formal occasions—like a thank-you for a formal event, or a congratulatory note to a client. For examples, please see the Reference Guide, pages 120–121.

THANK-YOU NOTES

In a world of nearly infinite communication choices, the medium you choose to communicate your appreciation can be a part of the message itself. When you take the time to find someone's address, pick out stationery, handwrite a note, address and stamp an envelope, and get it in the mail, the effort *shows* some of that gratitude. You don't need a special occasion to write a thank-you note. The note can provide the occasion when you deploy it well, but there are four types of thanks for which we would recommend the handwritten note—none of them negate an in-person thank you, but all these scenarios benefit from a handwritten note.

1. When you have been interviewed for a job, position, or a major career opportunity.

2. When someone has given you a gift or done a favor for you and you have not had a chance to thank them in person.

3. When a colleague or professional acquaintance invites you to their home for a meal.

4. Because you appreciate someone and want to acknowledge it in a special way.

FOLD-OVER NOTE
AND ENVELOPE

MOSAIC

ANN ROBERTS

MANAGEMENT CONSULTANT
1 (612) 802 - 5079
ANN@MOSAIC.COM

BUSINESS CARD

MONARCH SHEET
AND ENVELOPE

N

CORRESPONDENCE CARD
AND ENVELOPE

FULL-PAGE
LETTER PAPER
AND ENVELOPE

PENS AND
POSTAGE

It is hard to overstate the good impression the handwritten thank-you creates. Research shows that people almost universally respond positively to receiving thank-you notes. People like to receive thanks in the mail, making them think well about the person who sent it. Let *that* sink in and be your motivation. This is something you can do that is guaranteed to make someone think positively about you.

For a note of thanks, try for three to five lines that consist of an opener, a thank you, a bit about what you appreciated, and a closing. You can add more—even a second thank-you before you close—but keep the focus on your gratitude and wishing the other person well rather than launching into a full catch-up of how you've been. You do not need to send a thank-you note for a thank-you note you received (the cycle would never end!). But you should send a thank-you note for a thank-you gift that you couldn't open in front of the giver. See the Reference Guide on page 72 for a sample thank-you note.

CONGRATULATORY NOTE

A congratulatory note might be very similar to a thank-you note in length and style, but it focuses on the achievement being celebrated instead. It can also be incredibly casual and brief, using only initials and a single congratulatory phrase ("L, Congrats on closing the deal!—R") Sometimes it's sent; other times it's given in person. Because this is business, it's dependent on the occasion whether you'd pair it with a congratulatory gift. Often, gifts are taken care of by the company or team as a whole, but there are occasions and working relationships where a congratulatory note with a gift from just you the individual would be appropriate. One guideline to remember about business gifting is to never gift up the chain unless a colleague you have a close working relationship with is retiring, or if it is a one-on-one working relationship and you know your boss very well. See page 120 in the Reference Guide for a sample congratulatory note.

APOLOGY NOTE

Formal but effective, an apology note focuses on the apology and making amends. It does not focus on reasons and excuses, no matter how tempting or fair. The point is to ensure the apology is clear and that forgiveness is requested, not expected. (See page 121 in the Reference Guide, for an example. Also see The Good Apology, page 139.)

ADDRESSING AND STUFFING ENVELOPES

In our increasingly digital world, many people aren't used to addressing mail. Below is the basic format for addressing a standard letter or envelope sent within the United States.

Name of Recipient	Susan Iverson	Susan Iverson
Name of Company	The Emily Post Institute	c/o The Emily Post Institute
Street Address 1	25 Cross Road	25 Crossroad St., Suite 2B
Street Address 2	Suite 2B	Waterbury, VT 05676
City, State Zip Code	Waterbury, VT 05676	

When addressing married people or those in long-established relationships who live together, put their names on one line with the word *and* between them. If their names are too long to fit the first line together, put the second person's name on the next line, indented and beginning with the word *and*.

> *Pierson Carmichael Sanderson, III*
> *and Geoffrey Maximillian Kent-Sanderson*
> *123 Church Street*
> *Greenwich, CT 06830*

Absent a ranking professional title, either name can go first, except when using only titles and one last name: in this case, the order is always Mr. and Mrs. Lastname. When using first names with a shared last name, using either partner first is fine. "Emily and Chival Russe" and "Chival and Emily Russe" are both correct (so long as they share a last name). The rule of not separating a man from his name no longer applies in this way.

If you don't know and cannot ask a married woman which title she uses, your best bet is to go with *Ms.* in business. Use *and* to indicate the marriage. *Ms. Emily Post and Mr. Chival Russe.* This is a good reminder to ask, when someone gets married, or when they join a company or organization, how they handle last names and titles, and then write it down somewhere so you can refer to it when needed.

When writing to a group of people who live together but are not in a relationship, list each recipient's name on a separate line:

> *Jacqueline LeChevre*
> *Sarah Diedrick*
> *Allison Jackson*
> *478 Carpenter Street*
> *San Antonio, TX 78212*

You might be tempted to put "and Guest" on the name line for an event where a guest would be given a plus-one, but this is best left for an inner envelope or as a note attached to an invitation inviting the guest to bring a plus-one. "And Guest" is not a resident at the address you're mailing the invitation to, and therefore it doesn't make sense to write it on the invitation's outer or only envelope:

OUTER ENVELOPE: Mr. David Coward

INNER ENVELOPE: Mr. David Coward & Guest

INCLUDED AS A NOTE: Dave, please bring a guest if you'd like. Please let us know when you RSVP if someone will be joining you.

STUFFING THE ENVELOPE

For letters, cards, notes, and invitations, you want to stuff the envelope so that when it is opened and the contents are pulled out, they will naturally be positioned in a way that makes it easy to open the card or letter and read without flipping over or around. Do not fold the the letter up into a square when the envelope is long or fold a letter so many times that it opens like an accordion.

For letters, fold the bottom third of the letter up and crease it, then fold the remaining top third down over the bottom third, and again crease it—your letter is now tri-folded. Stuff the letter into the envelope so that the folded bottom edge goes into the envelope first and the top of the letter (which is folded down and the part that would be lifted first to open the letter) is facing the opening (the back) of the envelope, not the front of the envelope where the names and address are. Seal it, and you're good to go.

TRI-FOLD: FOLD BOTTOM THIRD UP, THEN TOP THIRD DOWN

FOLD 1

FOLD 2

OPEN EDGE FIRST

STACK ENCLOSURES WITH AN INVITATION

Invitation · Enclosure · Enclosure

CASH OR CHECK INSIDE LETTER OR CARD

Cards and fold-over notes are stuffed so that the open edge is inserted first into the envelope, and the folded edge is at the open or top of the envelope. The card should be inserted so that the front or side with the writing faces the back of the envelope. This way, the card faces the person opening the envelope.

If there are any enclosures, you may stack them with the letter or invitation, usually putting the enclosures on top of the invitation itself. This helps you ensure that nothing gets left behind in the envelope. Sometimes, items are also tied together in a little bundle.

REFERENCE GUIDES

METHOD OF COMMUNICATION FORMALITY CHART

Think about what method works best for the type of message you need to convey.

LEAST FORMAL   **MOST FORMAL**

●————————●————————●————————●————————●————————●————————●————————●

DM	Text	DM on	Email	Phone	Video	In person	In person
or PM	message	in-office				at your	at *their*
on social		messaging				office	office
media		app					

TYPES OF STATIONERY

FOLD-OVER NOTES AND ENVELOPES

Style: Various

Purpose: Thanks, condolences, congratulations, special occasions

BUSINESS CARD

Your Name: Spelled exactly as it appears on your LinkedIn profile and email signature

Contact Information: Only put down the contact information that you feel comfortable sharing. Business cards are not necessarily kept private. Email is the most common, but is not used by everyone on their business card.

Company Name: The name of the company or organization you work for

Title/Position: The role you are in at your company or organization

Optional: Website, social media, QR code

CORRESPONDENCE CARDS AND ENVELOPES

Style: Engraved with name, monogram, or family crest, and optional border

Purpose: Quick notes, follow-ups, thanks, invitations

Size: 4½ by 7 inches or 6⅞ by 4¼ inches; 96-pound weight suggested; pair with envelope

NOTE OR MONARCH SHEETS AND ENVELOPES

Style: Name and/or address suggested (centered at top)

Purpose: Social letters

Size: Note 6⅞ by 8½ inches or Monarch 7¼ by 10½ inches; 32-pound weight suggested; pair with envelope

FULL-PAGE LETTER PAPER AND ENVELOPES

Style: Name and/or address suggested (centered at the top)

Purpose: Personal business letters

Size: 8½ by 11 inches; 32-pound weight suggested; pair with envelope

PENS AND POSTAGE

Keeping pens you like to write with and a variety of postage with your stationery makes writing easier and getting notes and letters into the mail much more likely to happen.

ACME Gift Co. *(your company and address, if not using letterhead)*
456 Eddington Drive
Tucson, AZ

January 2, 2021 *(the date)*

Liz Miller, *(recipient)*
Marketing Manager *(their title or department)*
ACME Stationery Co. *(their company name and address)*
123 Main Street
Eugene, OR 10000

Dear Ms. Miller, *(or if more personal, use Dear Liz,)*

The body of the letter is left-aligned (not indented) and each paragraph is separated by a full line space.

The closing is left-aligned and stacked, as is the heading. The sender's full name, without title, should be printed below the closing and then a space reserved for an actual handwritten signature followed by the position of the sender and their company name, followed by the company address and telephone number.

Sincerely,
[SIGNATURE]
Jefferson O'Neill
CEO
ACME Gift Co.
808-123-4567
ABigWig@AcmeGift.com

SAMPLE NOTES

FOLLOW-UP NOTE

January 31, 2026

Dear Peter,

I appreciated your taking the time to meet me for coffee last Thursday. I have been thinking about the story you told me about managing the gallery space. It was helpful to hear about the ups and downs you navigated while working with such creative people. It gave me a few really helpful insights on dealing with a project team that also has very creative personalities. I hope we can do it again sometime soon.

Sincerely,
Sam

THANK-YOU NOTE

June 30, 2026

Dear Johnathan,

I had such a fun time Friday afternoon. Thank you so much for hosting a little "promotion" party and giving me some time to say goodbye to the team. I appreciate your support as I head over to the Marketing Department; I'm really excited about it. But I am going to miss you all in PR, and that makes the party you threw for me all the more special. Thank you, again.

With gratitude,
Dezirae

CONGRATULATORY NOTE

January 27th, 2025

Dear T,

Congratulations on your big win! You did such a fantastic job leading the team to new heights. We are all so proud of you and we're all rooting for you and the team!

With great admiration,
T.S.

APOLOGY NOTE

September 22, 2025

Dear Julian,

I am writing to you with my sincerest apologies. I regret my actions and the impact they had on you and your team. I let emotion get the better of me and didn't think about the long-term consequences. I can only ask for your forgiveness. I am so sorry.

Sincerely,
Bill

VIDEO CALL CHECKLIST

☐ Technical setup—correct software and connection link, strong internet connection, camera mic and speaker

☐ Correct identification—account name, contact information, email

☐ Staging the call—camera position, lighting, background

☐ Start of the call—be on time, turn on camera, unmute to speak

SAMPLE EMAIL CHAIN

Dear Ms. Ketchum,

Thank you for giving me the week to think about your offer. I would like to formally accept. I am very grateful for the opportunity, and I look forward to hearing more about next steps. It has always been my dream to work for Ten Speed Press, and I am excited to be part of the team.

Sincerely,
Elizabeth Connolly

While you might have a client or boss you always address as Mx., Mr., Ms., or Mrs., you are often welcome to start using the person's first name once you see it in their signature.

A reply to the above might look like the following, with just a tad less formality. The honorifics have been removed, and the "Dear" is made friendlier with a "Good Morning." Note that the second word of a greeting should be capitalized, and when using To Whom It May Concern, you would always capitalize each word.

Good Morning, Elizabeth,

We are thrilled to hear the news, and may I be the first to welcome you to Ten Speed Press. We were so impressed during your interview, and we cannot wait to see what you do with the job.

Would you like to have lunch together on your first day? There is a lovely spot around the corner from the office. My treat.

Best,
Kaitlin

Editorial Director, Ten Speed Press
she/her
159 Main Street
Emeryville, CA
879-404-5678

Now that both parties have done proper greetings and closings, the email thread can start to resemble a conversation rather than a letter. (Note that the stock signature Kaitlin uses can communicate any work contact information you'd like.)

That is such a kind offer. I would really enjoy that, thank you!

Thank you again,
Liz

Great. We'll pick a time on Monday once you have a handle on your day.
—K

COMMUNICATION TURNAROUND TIMES

The quicker you can reply to any message, the better. Remember, time is money. However, there are also different expectations around the timeliness of replies for different communication mediums. Pay attention to the content of a message, the recipient, and how it was received to determine the most appropriate reply times. Here are some approximations of communication turnaround times based on methods.

METHOD	IDEAL RESPONSE TIMING	REALISTIC RESPONSE TIMING
LETTER	Within a month, weeks to months	Within a week, if you're awesome. Within a month, if you're responsible. Within a year, if you're normal.
EMAIL	Immediately to within a work week. Within 24 hours. No later than 24 to 48 hours. Days.	Immediately, if Netflix just bought your documentary. Within the day, if it moves business along. Within the week, if you're busy. Within two weeks with an apology for the delay, if you're normal.
PHONE	Within a business day.	Immediately if there's Not a Lot Going on Right Now. Within few minutes if you just missed someone. A day to a week or maybe even two if there's A Lot Going on Right Now.
TEXT	Within one business day. In minutes, maybe hours.	Immediately, if someone needs a verification code from you. Within the business day, if you can remember. Within the week, if you're normal.
MESSAGE APP	Within one business day.	Immediately if you're in conversation. Within the hour, if you're paying attention and not in meetings all day. Within the day, if you're normal.

CHAPTER 6

Conversation Skills at Work

How we speak to one another at work—not just the method we use, as discussed in chapter 5, but the tact we take with our conversation—is a huge part of how we are perceived at work by our colleagues and cultivate positive professional relationships. Even if we speak the same language, our different life experiences, ideals, perspectives, neuro-divergences, and emotions impact how we understand each other in conversation. Life is ripe for miscommunication, which can easily lead to misunderstandings, impacting relationships and the bottom line in business. However, we can use etiquette to bridge the gap when we encounter differences or difficulty.

One thing that can help us better understand others and be better understood is to adopt a curious, candid, and optimistic approach when speaking with others. We must take care and recognize the wholeness of others; part of doing that is keeping communication comfortable, clear, and effective. Reminding yourself that you don't know the entirety of someone's story or perspective leaves room to hear them and not just your assumptions. Treating others this way makes us more likely to be heard in return. We all have critical thoughts, assumptions, and more that can be our first instinct, or first response. Knowing and practicing that curious, candid, and optimistic approach helps you avoid acting on those thoughts.

Good conversation skills teach us to be thoughtful with our language and considerate and respectful when listening to others. Strong communication builds trust and relationships—which we know are the foundation of any good business. Let's look at conversation skills that can help us participate professionally.

YOUR PHYSICAL PRESENCE IN CONVERSATION

It's not just the words you say that create the experience of a conversation. Your posture, gestures, voice, eye contact, and facial expressions are all part of the conversation. Let's look at each, to help you hone your conversation skills.

POSTURE

To be polite in conversations, you want your posture to signal you are approachable and engaged, or at least at ease. Torso upright, with your shoulders relaxed. Direct your face (literally your attention) to the person speaking. This signals that you are paying attention and engaged with the speaker.

FACIAL EXPRESSIONS

A neutral, or even positive, expression while listening helps others express themselves without wondering what you're thinking. Relax your facial muscles while you listen. A raised brow, a clenched jaw, or pursed lips do not signal, "I'm liking what I'm hearing!" A blank or distracted stare can be just as unsettling. Even if you're hearing and thinking deeply about what someone is saying, you can come across as looking frustrated or concerned if your brow is furrowed and your arms are crossed. Being aware of your facial expressions (and how they are coupling with your posture) will give you a good sense of how you come across when you're in conversation.

PERSONAL SPACE

For most people in the United States, personal space means keeping about a foot and a half (half a meter) to three feet (a meter) between you and the other person. Avoid leaning in too far or being so enthralled that you're hanging off the other person. Keeping too far away can also be awkward, as it might signal that you are unwilling to enter the classic three-foot comfort zone. The other person might wonder if you think they are contagious, foul-smelling, or unpleasant in some way. Staying right around eighteen inches to three feet away is the goal.

VOICE

Serious, silly, kind, harsh, dismissive, arrogant, defiant, humorous, loving, patient, reassuring—we can strike many different tones. Still, when it comes to professional etiquette, it's all about getting good at using the tone you want when needed, the tone that matches and respects the moment.

While we might know what we sound like from regularly making videos of ourselves, we don't often focus on how we sound to others. Tone, emphasis, and volume are all aspects of our voice that we want to have good control over so we can adjust for certain circumstances. For gauging volume, try to speak loudly enough for someone two to three feet away to hear you and quietly enough so that someone six to eight feet away would not.

Avoid shouting when in professional settings. Whispering should be used only when speaking quietly to avoid disturbing others. It should rarely (if ever) be used to keep others from hearing what you're saying. If you can't say something in front of those present, wait to say it when you have a private moment.

We don't all speak the same way. Stutters and words that come to the speaker slowly are normal, and when it comes to conversation, you want to avoid "hurrying things along" or "helping" someone, especially if you've just met. It's not as assistive as you might think. Don't guess words for someone or suggest they *"relax."* While you may think it's helpful, those who experience it say it's not. Instead, be patient and focus on the words as they come.

GESTURE

Each of us has a unique gestural vocabulary. Often, these gestures are habitual and we are un-aware we're even making them. Take the time to think about and adjust your gestures to fit a situation. Quiet meeting? Dial it back. Telling a funny story at lunch? Let your expressions and hands punctuate the humor. There is no right or wrong answer regarding how animated to be when you speak. The trick is to match and adjust based on the situation you find yourself in. An excellent communicator uses gestures intentionally to layer more information into in-person conversations.

ACTIVE LISTENING

Good listening skills are paramount to good manners. Sure, you can talk, but can you listen? Can people tell you're listening? When you listen, do you *hear*? Listening (and/or paying close attention to nonverbal communication) allows us to participate well in conversations or meet-ings. How you behave while you listen and how you respond to the speaker will greatly impact the quality of the experience. If we are simply planning out exactly what brilliant, cutting, or hilarious thing we will say next, we aren't part of a conversation; we are just thinking about speaking. Getting comfortable with the idea that your brilliant remark or amazing idea could go unsaid is a wonderful skill to develop. The humbleness alone is impressive, but learning to have patience and recognize how much of the conversational pie you are entitled to when it comes to speaking versus how much of the pie is you listening will make you a great asset at work and a great conversationalist in life. Here are some traits of a good listener that can keep you actively listening:

- Keep your attention directed at the person speaking. Make eye contact when possible. Focusing on someone's mouth or the bridge of their nose is an alternative for those who cannot easily sustain or make eye contact.

- Nod and/or say "mmhmm," "yes," "uh-huh," "aha," "okay," and other short phrases and expressions that honestly fit the conversation to show that you are following along.

- Do not be distracted by looking at a phone, checking email, glancing at your smartwatch, or scanning the room.

- Respond with questions or comments: "You know, that reminds me of the Helping Hands farm project . . ." "Wait, had he already closed out the meeting when you did that?" or, "Wow, how did that make you feel?" Note that you don't want to always respond with stories or thoughts about your own life. A good listener and conversationalist will balance this, keeping most of the conversation focused on or relevant to the person speaking.

- Weigh what is important to respond to and what can be left unsaid, rather than responding with every thought you might have. In business especially, there are lots of times when patience and waiting for the right time to talk about something is key to moving things forward well.

RESPECTING THE GIFT OF ATTENTION

Have you ever been talking to someone and, *uhh*, you notice . . . *is she taking out her phone?* . . . that the other person is . . . *Okay, I'll wait until you're finished.* . . . Then they pop their head up from their phone and say, "Sorry, just needed to send that off." Don't be this person. It can be so frustrating to lose someone's attention in conversation. Whether they are typing at a computer, into a phone or tablet, sifting through papers on their desk, or looking for something in a drawer, this type of multitasking is rude and dismissive—potentially degrading—and usually completely unnecessary.

When we talk with others throughout the workday, it's important to stop what we are doing and give our full attention and focus to the person speaking to us. If you need to finish something, check on something, or answer an important call, acknowledge it: "Pardon me just a second while I finish this up so I can give you my full attention." People are more likely to understand an intrusion if you acknowledge it.

THE SKILLED TALKER

It can be difficult to pay attention to those listening to you when your brain is focused on what you're trying to say, but a "skilled talker" will notice the state of their audience while they speak. They can tell when their audience is enthralled and wanting more, interested in contributing a question or a thought, or bored and losing their attention. A skilled talker's radar will go off at the slightest stifled yawn, glazed or drifting eye, or the merely polite response. *ALERT ALERT— this person is losing interest in the conversation! Mayday, Mayday, we're going down!* Let's look at a few other aspects of being a skilled talker.

A skilled talker stays aware of their audience. Cultivate and listen to that radar. Don't panic when it goes off—there's nothing to be embarrassed about—and stop yourself if you need to: "I'm so sorry. I'm going on and on about my toddler. How was your trip to Ohio?" or, "I could go on, but I'd love to hear your perspective." At this point, you switch to your good listening skills or you realize the conversation is over. Ending a conversation is also an option: "Brittany, I've talked your ear off. Please don't let me hold you up any longer; I know you've got that deadline."

A skilled talker is inclusive and notices when a group conversation needs expansion. If the conversation seems to be turning into a ping-pong match, the skilled talker will quickly recognize when only one or two voices are dominating and will encourage others to engage by finding a time to interject and ask a question of someone else. "Jonathan, you work in D.C., what do you think?"

A skilled talker knows what they don't know and is comfortable saying so. "I'll be honest, Dietz, I'm not familiar enough with particle physics to venture a guess, but I'd love to hear more about your team's findings." A skilled talker does not speak of people familiarly to those who don't know them. They don't say, "Bob absolutely nailed it," when no one present knows Bob. Instead, they provide more context and information: "Bob, one of our coworkers pre-pandemic, absolutely nailed the pitch that year. It was flawless. Legendary!" Similarly, a skilled conversationalist is never *surprised* to learn something about anyone because that would mean they'd made assumptions about the person. Instead, they are interested or glad to find something out. "That's cool that you love engines" is much more polite than "I'm surprised you're an engine gal." In every conversation, tact is as essential as honesty.

Skilled talkers generally don't refer to someone in the third person, by pronouns alone, when they are present. If you've ever heard the phrase "Who's 'she,' the cat's mother?" this scenario is where it comes from. When someone is present, refer to them by name or address them directly, not by pronoun only. It's a courtesy of acknowledgment and engagement. When you, Travis, and Preeti are all chatting it up at the lunch table and you're telling Trav about how you and Preeti handled the negotiations in your latest business venture, you don't say to Trav, "She was awesome; she just came in super serious and silent and they didn't know what to do!" You say, "Preeti was awesome, she just came in super serious and silent and they didn't know what to do!"

A skilled talker is adept at working with an interpreter. Your eye contact and body language should address the person you are conversing with, not the interpreter. But a skilled talker always thanks the interpreter for their help after the conversation.

TAKE CARE WITH YOUR WORDS

The words we choose and how we say them are an aspect of ourselves that we should self-assess daily, if not moment to moment. You likely already do. Maybe one morning, you're short or a little rude in tone to your roommate, partner, or spouse, and you apologize after you hear how it sounds—that's self-assessing and taking responsibility—go you! That's the kind of self-reflection we're talking about here. The key to ensuring that your professional self is the best it can be is to self-assess and become aware of your voice, how you use it, and how the words you choose can come across. Doing this *before* a big meeting, pitch, or interview is worth the time. Doing it regularly is what can make you great.

When we are careless with words, it communicates that we don't care about making good impressions or maintaining the ones we've already made. It implies a careless attitude and perhaps careless work. Be intentional and deliberate with the words you choose. For example, do you mean *always,* or is it just the easiest, most common, or maybe most weighted word you could use? Taking the time to fine-tune your language not only means you're being considerate, respectful, and honest in your communications, but it can also help you strengthen your listening skills, patience, and awareness of others. Paying attention to a few language tweaks and finding ways to implement them can greatly affect how others receive and respond to you.

Here are some tips for improving your communication skills:

TRADE "YOU" FOR "I." Taking responsibility for your own behavior, perspective, or experience rather than putting the focus on others is a great way to improve the efficacy of your communications. Whenever possible, switch from "you" statements that highlight other people's negative behavior to "I" statements about how you are feeling or have been impacted by that behavior ("You don't listen" becomes "I don't feel heard"). You can also claim a personal perspective rather than declaring something as an absolute: "It's not what I would do" rather than "You're making a giant mistake."

TONE DOWN THE LANGUAGE. Deescalate difficult or angry conversations by toning down your language: "I don't think the mood board you made for our client aligns with their vision" instead of "I hate the work you've done." Or "You did great!" instead of "You murdered that!" Language that is based on violence, particularly physical violence, even if it is not meant to target anyone, can significantly negatively impact people. Whenever you remove it from the conversation, you help deescalate things.

SPEAK IN ACTUALITIES. Is it *every* time? Does someone *never* do XYZ? When we exaggerate, we leave ourselves less room to engage with subtlety and detail. Painting a fair, realistic picture of what you're experiencing is respectful to others involved and helps deescalate tense conversations. "It's not every time, but it has been too many times recently, and that's why I'm upset." This is an important form of honesty.

FLIP YOUR LANGUAGE. Don't focus on the negative. Try to start interactions with people on a positive foot. "Good morning" is a much nicer way to start the day than "Can you believe the way people drive in this city?" Rather than saying, "Here's what *you're* doing wrong," try "This is where you could improve," or "I'd like to see improvement here." Flipping a *don't* to a *do* can inspire growth and act as a healthy challenge. It's certainly a more motivational approach.

LEAVE ROOM TO BE WRONG. We can all get things wrong. Embracing this reality can make it easier to accept and move on when we do. Some mistakes require reparative action, and knowing everyone makes mistakes can make that easier to do. In business, being wrong can seem like the worst thing. But take it from CEOs the world over that being able to say "I was wrong" and definitely being able to say "I don't know" (more on that later) are keys to moving onward and upward. You can also be gracious and not burn bridges by allowing others the space to be wrong. It's true that some mistakes, some wrongs, could cost you your job. But better to be able to take responsibility for them than not. Your reputation is as much about how you handle yourself when things go wrong as it is about when things go well.

DECLINE AND ACCEPT REGRETS GRACIOUSLY. It is okay to say "No." Many of us feel bad when we decline a kind offer for a job or a request for help with a project. We know we feel disappointed when others say "No" to us, so we don't love having to put others in this position. However, when we graciously decline ("I'm sorry, I can't this time, but good luck!") we take the sting out of someone hearing our rejection. And since we've given them the benefit of a clear and honest answer, they'll likely be understanding in their response. "Sorry, I can't" can be responded to politely with "That's okay, thanks for letting me know" or "No worries. I'll figure it out." These are preferable to "What do you mean, no?" or "Seriously, I'd help you if the tables were turned." It's okay to be disappointed that someone turned you down, but that disappointment is for you to manage, not them. They may feel pressure from your *no,* but that's not your fault or responsibility. (Unless you are responsible for them.)

IT'S ALSO OKAY TO SAY "I DON'T KNOW." It's a bold and honest move to admit when you don't know something. It's not a sign of weakness, as some might think. In business, we aren't being tested the same way we are in school. We can use our resources to help us fill in the gaps. You can probably learn anything you don't know or turn to someone who knows the answer. This truth should make you feel more confident about admitting when you don't know something. When you are willing to learn or are unbothered by not knowing, you take a lot of the shame and embarrassment out of the situation immediately. It's pretty powerful. It's okay not to get a joke or not to know everything about a subject (or even that a subject existed). Admitting that you don't know something is far better than wading into a conversation when you're already lost. Most people will be willing, or even excited, to help you get acquainted with a topic. "I'm not familiar with that. Can you give me the basics?" You come across as self-aware and secure in yourself.

JOKE CULTURE

Good humor can bring a smile, draw people closer, keep days pleasant, and help make any task more bearable. But not all forms of humor are good for the workplace or professional interactions (and not all "humor" is funny), regardless of how it's delivered. The stand-up comedian may have audiences roaring, but the jokes are unfit for others to repeat, and certainly not without the permission of a planned performance. Humor can sometimes allow us to address taboo or verboten topics, but that is not desirable when work is to be done.

It is not up to anyone else to "get the joke" or "lighten up." Your delivery, your timing, your knowledge of your audience, and the joke itself have to deliver. *The onus is on you.* If it's not funny or understood, that's your fault, not your audience's. In the spirit of clarity of communication and to prevent mistakes that could be costly (even if they *are* well-intentioned), avoid humor that:

- Contains stereotypes based on gender, race, age, origin/nationality/culture, or economic background.

- Is overly sarcastic, ironic, or negative.

- Involves topics related to sex, violence, politics, and/or religion.

Think about how to keep laughing, winking, smiling, and grinning with each other *without* needing to trade in these areas, and you will be well on your way to finding a true wit that everyone can participate in and appreciate.

The more you assess and adjust language, the more it will become second nature. For more on conversation skills, see chapter 5, "Methods of Communication."

CAREFULLY COMMUNICATE CRITICISM AND FEEDBACK

We want to take great care with delivering negative feedback or criticism so that it is received and the desired outcome can be achieved next time. A time-tested strategy is the "compliment sandwich": give praise, then constructive criticism, followed by another positive comment. "Jade, the eye you're bringing to this month's launch is spot-on. I'd like you to bring that much attention to filling out your time slips on the project from here on out. I think the client is going to be thrilled."

Another technique is the "praise, concern, suggest" framework: start with a specific positive, bring up any issues or concerns, and then offer solutions. "Jade, the press release and social campaign you set up for the launch are fantastic. I have been concerned about getting your time slips for the project in. Would a reminder in your calendar to fill it out each day before you head out be helpful?"

Science suggests a three-to-one ratio of positive to negative feedback to help support an environment where people are likely to feel secure receiving feedback. Try to mention at least three positive things or have at least three positive interactions (such as a welcoming greeting at the start of the day) for every concern or negative issue you raise. This ratio ensures that the recipient of criticism stays emotionally available to receive the feedback and successfully implement it.

Working to ensure you have lots of positive interactions with your direct reports can be helpful when it comes time to offer feedback or give criticism. You've built bonds through positive greetings and exchanges, clear communication, praise, and sharing experiences together.

THE THREE TIERS OF CONVERSATION

In business where the stakes are higher, it's worth paying extra attention to what we say. Even in a world where it seems like every topic is fair game anywhere anytime, learning some conversation basics will help you decide what topics of conversation are okay to venture into under what scenarios. Although social media might indicate otherwise, we shouldn't speak to everyone we encounter about every thought or experience we have in life. We have casual conversations, we have private conversations, we have conversations about deeply personal topics around our beliefs and identity, and we have lighthearted conversations about common shared experiences. "Man, traffic today was brutal!"

A work colleague may not receive your full thoughts on opposing presidential candidates, but you might share your belief that voting is essential to being a good citizen. However, at home, among your closest family or friends, you might voice your political thoughts with all the candor and enthusiasm you have for the topic. Being familiar with which topics perform well in which scenarios can be highly beneficial to keeping your professional life professional. Let's look at the three tiers of conversation to help you know what topics to turn to when.

TIER I

Tier I topics are low stakes, easy to participate in, and safe for testing conversational waters anywhere in your professional life. They are the standard small-talk topics and include the weather (a classic), entertainment (music, books, podcasts, plays, performances, TV, movies), sports, hobbies, and shared experiences (such as the food, the event, the atmosphere, or the traffic that morning).

TIER II

Tier II topics are subjects that people can have very different and strong feelings about. These topics include religion, money, sex, romantic relationships, and politics. Conversations about these things aren't always welcome at work, and while some work friendships might forge bonds where these topics get discussed, it is often done on a break or off hours. Some professionals have personal boundaries around not discussing these topics with coworkers. The topics themselves have the potential to get personal or even offensive. When broaching Tier II topics, test the waters before getting too deep, and be willing to disengage. Be prepared for the other person to decline the conversation. There is also the chance that broaching these subjects could result in a rousing conversation with enthralling ideas, and the price of admission will be a willingness to listen to someone who sees things differently than you do. These Tier II topics are important, but work is a place where you should treat them with even more care.

Asking if it's all right to broach the subject will give your audience an out if they wish, which is thoughtful and polite and shows your care in approaching delicate topics. "I know it's not the safest subject, but did you catch last week's debate, I'm dying to talk with someone about it." "Oh, Graham, I did, but let let's talk about it after I get through my call this afternoon, I want to keep my focus."

TIER III

Tier III topics are only broached privately with close company: family or friends, or folks who know us well enough and whom we can trust with the shared information. This means they are topics that we rarely bring up at work or expect to hear about from others. Tier III topics include family, health, personal finances, and anything shared in confidence. Not everyone wants to hear about these topics, even when we are comfortable talking about them. Some people might make assumptions or take note of your ability to be discreet and your sense of personal privacy based on how you treat these topics.

Money is an interesting subject when you cross it with etiquette and business. Business is often about making money (or, in some cases, raising it), so money is on the table as a topic. However, it's still a delicate one, and there is a difference between talking about business and talking about an individual's finances. In business, it's best to be clear and direct about money, like offering a quote or giving someone a ballpark estimate. Shying away from the topic of money in business likely won't help you grow your business, but being thoughtful about how you talk about money will help your career throughout your working lifetime.

BEWARE THE TEMPTATION OF GOSSIP

Building rapport around sharing negative or salacious gossip can feel like a quick and seductive route to connecting with others, but the cost is simply too great to engage in this behavior. Ultimately, gossip undermines the relationship with the target, but it also calls into question the loyalty, discretion, motivation, and trustworthiness of the person spreading it. Be careful when talking about other people if they are not around to hear it, as this can end up being very damaging to your professional reputation and working relationships. As a self-check, ask yourself how you would feel if someone was talking about you in the same way. Or even better, ask yourself if you would be comfortable with the person you are talking about knowing what you said. Genuine criticism and even chitchat worthy of sharing will stand up to the test.

It's also important to note that using work colleagues as receptacles for venting about life outside of work is not time well spent on the clock. Sometimes, tackling a personal problem with a close colleague who doubles as a close friend or mentor can help you focus on the rest of your day. This type of individual support should only occur on a designated break and shouldn't take up more than ten or fifteen minutes. Because you're on the company's dime and have agreed to be there, the personal comes second unless it's an emergency. Even with today's emphasis on work-life balance, the consensus is that while at work, you should be focused on work, and if you can't focus, you've got to take personal time off.

THE MAGIC WORDS

We consider the magic words—*please, thank you, you're welcome, excuse me,* and *I'm sorry*—to be some of our most effective politeness tools. The effect these words can have on people and relationships is indeed magic. These words can express intent, show respect, indicate regret, and help to soften an exchange. They should be used everywhere and will always be considered appropriate when used well. It's equally important to use these words in a board meeting or speaking to a line cook in a kitchen. When used regularly and with a sincere and friendly delivery—not with attitude or through gritted teeth, or said so sweetly that they are intentionally insincere—these words show respect and consideration for those around you. To be cute about it, *the words themselves aren't magic; the magic is in you.*

MAGIC WORD/PHRASE	WHY IT'S MAGIC
Please	Changes a demand or command into a request. Welcomes or invites.
Thank you	Expresses or demonstrates appreciation and acknowledgment. Strengthens relationships.
You're welcome	Acknowledges appreciation. This is more important than people realize. Knowing your gratitude was heard and received is part of this exchange. If a thanks is warranted in return, it's not "Thank you" and "Thank *you*." It's "Thank you" and "You're welcome, and thank you too." "My pleasure." It is not arrogant to accept gratitude.
Excuse me	Acknowledges mistakes or impact on others. Whether you're squeezing by or excusing a rude behavior such as a burp, "excuse me" demonstrates an awareness of your impact on others.
I'm sorry	"I'm sorry" can be light for casual everyday moments like finishing the coffee and not making more, or bumping into someone. It can do heavy reparative work when needed and used well. It can express sympathy.

With each of these phrases, the magic really is in you. Any one of them could be said in a rude, sarcastic, or insincere tone that has no sense of professionalism and clearly signals that you do not mean to be polite. Protect your magic words, from pleases to apologies, it's important to use them genuinely. Doing so will help strengthen your relationships with your coworkers and clients.

CONVERSATIONS IN PASSING

In America, we regularly have micro-conversations in passing. For example, if you cross paths with your coworker Ralph in the hallway, you would just say, "Hi, Ralph, how's it going?" and keep walking. It doesn't matter if Ralph is walking in the other direction, standing, or seated. The expression, when it's issued on the go, is not meant to elicit a long response; it's meant as another form of "Hi." Other cultures might think we're weird, but it's a common part of American daily interactions. Do it too much, and you look like you're seeking attention; never do it, and you may come across as the office recluse. For those not accustomed to the practice, take note: beyond "Good, 'n' you?" there isn't much more of a reply that is expected. The question is more of a friendly verbal acknowledgment than a genuine inquiry; there is a different time and place for that.

SERIOUS CONVERSATIONS

For some people, the workday can quickly transition from normal to serious. There's a problem with a client, a lawsuit comes in, the approval didn't come through, and now you're shifting gears. While we've already discussed the tiers of conversation, here's how to demonstrate that you are paying attention and taking things seriously.

- Avoid being distracted (by your phone, kids/other people, pets, a podcast, or music). If anything plays in the background as you work, shut it off for the conversation.

- Direct your body, face, and attention to the person speaking and make eye contact (if possible).

- It's okay to ask questions, but do so thoughtfully. Ask yourself, *Is now the time to ask for these details?*

- Exercise patience. Before responding, let someone get through all or most of what they need to say.

- Don't fidget. Tapping a finger or foot, bouncing a leg, and clicking a pen are all classic examples you want to avoid when the conversation is serious.

- Offer your perspective rather than just giving it: "I'm happy to share my perspective if you'd like to hear it."

EXITING A CONVERSATION

There are many ways to deflect or redirect a conversation; even admitting that you "don't want to go there" is okay. When navigating conversation, especially with folks outside our innermost circles, doing so gently and with an easy tone can help keep things from getting awkward: "How's PT going?" "Oh, let's talk about anything else. It's good to get my mind off it." We can exit a conversation by ending it, or we can choose to redirect it. Either way, finessing this moment can help reduce the awkwardness between you and the others you're speaking to.

WHEN YOU DON'T NEED TO HIGHLIGHT WHY YOU'RE EXITING THE CONVERSATION: "It's been great chatting with you. I'm going to keep making the rounds." You might even add, "Take care. Maybe we can chat more later," if it feels right.

WHEN YOU'RE ONE-ON-ONE WITH SOMEONE AND NEED TO BE MORE DIRECT: "Pardon me, Sylas, before you get too far into this story, I should excuse myself; I have a hard time hearing anything about animals suffering, even during rescues." You don't have to apologize or give a reason for wanting to move on from a conversation. However, letting the other person know is better than sitting through something you can't tolerate or just walking off without any explanation.

For all of the thinking we do about how to start and conduct a conversation, it is equally important that we end or exit a conversation well. How we part ways will set the tone for our next interaction, and in business, we always want to set a good tone to keep the project or deal moving forward or the relationship's development on track. Most endings are clear and easy because there's a time constraint or an obvious reason for the conversation to end.

When it's less obvious that the ending point has been reached, we need to use our language and often a magic word or two to help ease any potential awkwardness. During these moments, we want to use either a clear and firm tone or a friendly and apologetic one, depending on what is warranted. We can also always offer the person we are talking to an out, which is a polite move.

DIRECT: "Sorry, I wish I could talk; however, I've got Marshall in ten minutes, and I still have to review the prospectus."

FRIENDLY: "Hey, great to see you, Maggie; I gotta run to prep for this call."

OFFER AN OUT: "If you need or want to go, please don't let me keep you."

TO CORRECT OR NOT TO CORRECT?

Unless you are responsible for teaching someone else, do not correct others, especially not in front of others. The exception is if someone has misidentified you (either by name, pronoun, social/professional title, or your job title). In these cases, the correction is important to make as soon as possible so that (a) the person getting the identity wrong doesn't repeat it, and (b) the person whose identity has been incorrectly used is respected.

While there are rules for our grammar and pronunciation, colloquial language is nuanced and no one version is perfectly correct. Today, we switch from casual to formal speech to operate in different environments and relationships. Correcting someone's grammar and speech in conversation is pompous and arrogant—even if you're right. It makes it seem like the corrector is somehow the editor of the conversation, a role they weren't asked to play.

THE GOOD APOLOGY

Accidents will happen, and mistakes will be made. How you handle them says a great deal about you, maybe even more than how you handle your successes. Being capable of delivering a genuine apology and taking responsibility is a huge asset and it will help you succeed in your professional relationships. Being humble enough to know that you will need to apologize to someone at some point is not a weakness—it's one of the biggest strengths you could ever display. It is *so easy* to go straight to our own defense because we know why we did what we did. Whether it was raising our voice or talking out of turn in a meeting, making a comment that was uncalled for, taking credit for work that we didn't do, or lying about hours or whereabouts during work time, when you are comfortable with apologizing and know why you're making an apology, you can begin repairing the damage. Stating the words "I am sorry" or "I apologize" and the infraction you're taking responsibility for is the best place to start. From there, you can identify the impact of your action (or lack of action) and how you will avoid it in the future.

Avoid the word *if* in an apology. It questions the offense or the other party and suggests that whatever you did or said might not have actually had the impact it did. It's a form of gaslighting inside an apology. Even if it's something small, allow the person impacted to be the one to dismiss the offense: "I'm sorry I was snippy yesterday during the meeting," rather than suggesting they might dismiss it for you: "I'm sure it wasn't an issue, but I'm sorry if I was snappy yesterday."

A good apology also avoids continuing with a *but* to explain your side. This doesn't mean you don't get represented; just don't use your side of the situation as a contrast. Rather than saying, "I'm sorry, but the deadline was on us, and I had to make a decision," try "I'm sorry that you feel dismissed. The deadline was approaching, and since it wasn't moveable, I had to act." This version validates the other person's feelings and states your facts without using them as a contrast (see Apology Note, page 114).

PROFANITY AND VULGARITY

Yes, swear words add range and emotion. Yes, profanity is realistically used in many workplaces. And yes, they can be cathartic and *appropriate* in some situations. But no, they will not work with every audience, and when you run afoul of someone by using foul language, it can damage a relationship. The safest advice to give when it comes to swearing in the workplace is to have a default setting that does not use curse words.

The damage profanity can do isn't worth the sense of bonding it can foster. These words are often used as exclamations of anger or frustration, with the delivery being loud and aggressive, which is not conducive to a productive and safe company culture.

Profanity is also a lazy way to communicate. When certain curse words can be used as almost anything (noun, adjective, verb . . .), it's easy to use them for everything. Don't let curse words replace good vocabulary or become filler or exclamatory language for you, taking the place of *ummm* and *wow*. When these words and phrases become embedded in your personal way of speaking, you might not be able to turn off using them when it's really necessary. Foul language is still one of the issues employers tell us they struggle with, and a survey on TheLadders.com found it to be in the top five fireable etiquette offenses.

From an etiquette perspective, vulgar and violent language has no place in a professional setting. "I'm gonna kill him" is just an expression, but it is violent and unnecessary. Hold your own as a professional and don't join in even if your boss swears or talks grossly about people. That isn't professional bonding; it will only exercise and perpetuate social skills that won't serve you well with others, whether at work or out socially. Language that is mean, violent, dismissive, or cruel might feel powerful or help you vent in the moment, but the hurt it can cause makes it truly profane and beyond the bounds of decent behavior.

Unfortunately, the vulgar use of disability and physical or mental conditions as casual, colloquial phrases is far too prevalent—to the point that people are unaware it's even an issue. Let us be clear: respectful, considerate, professional language never disparages others or their work, and it certainly doesn't use conditions or diagnoses as hyperbole. Saying things like, "I swear, she is bipolar today, so watch out," or "OMG, I have PTSD from how bad that meeting was," or "That is so *lame*. We totally should have gotten the account!" is always inappropriate. There are other ways to say these things that don't disparage entire communities of people and their experiences. Consider the colloquial phrases you use regularly and whether they might be offensive. Curbing this habit in yourself makes a huge difference to millions of people. Never use a known diagnosis or words that have historically been connected with a disability as hyperbole.

RESPECTING PRIVACY
AND USING DISCRETION

We respect privacy and use discretion in two distinct ways at work. For some, the general nature of our work may require discretion and privacy. But we also need to respect privacy and use discretion regarding what we know about our colleagues. Let's look at how to behave professionally regarding privacy and discretion.

REGARDING WORKPLACE, CLIENTS, OR CUSTOMERS

Millions of people work in industries that require them to carry the burden of confidential information they cannot share. Medical, legal, financial, and many other professions fall into this category, and the clients, patients, and customers these professionals interact with trust that their information will stay private and be handled with great care. Whatever the nature of the information in your care, take the responsibility seriously. The list of what is not okay to talk about outside of work should be something you could recite in your sleep, you know it so well. Equally important is knowing who within your organization is allowed to know this information so that you don't inadvertently share it with an employee who isn't entitled or required to know.

REGARDING COLLEAGUES

We often spend more hours per week at work than we do (awake) with our families or closest friends at home. Personal bonds can grow, and the relief of having even just one person at work know a little bit about your personal life is worth it for many. Some people and companies might have strict boundaries around any personal talk at work—the idea is that you are not being paid to discuss your personal life. Most companies today have realized that encouraging bonds, connection, and awareness of each other as whole people can lead to a happier, more productive workplace.

No matter the company policy, remember that any personal information you know about a colleague should not be repeated. Only the colleague should share their personal life. This includes telling a partner or roommate at home, since you never know when the two worlds might collide.

SOMEONE ASKS YOU A PERSONAL QUESTION YOU DON'T WANT TO ANSWER. Let's say that dating isn't a subject you're comfortable sharing with your coworkers. When Bob asks you in the office kitchen how your dating life is going or if you're married, single, or searching, it's okay to say something cheeky like "A secret I'll take to my grave, Bob, see ya later!" if you want to deflect, or you could try "Oh, I made a choice a while back to not discuss my love life at work. But I can tell you I had a great time hiking Mount Rainier this weekend." This is usually pretty well received given that workplaces have a history of keeping the focus on work and not on personal lives.

WHEN SOMEONE SHARES INFORMATION YOU'D RATHER NOT HEAR. This is harder to handle, but there are certainly times when it's okay just to listen politely if you have the time and the bandwidth and feel zero pressure to share a story in kind. But other times, you might need to politely disengage. With the other person sharing something personal, you want to be delicate. "Bryan, before you share any more, I should let you know that I'm not comfortable hearing about medical issues."

REFERENCE GUIDES

FOUL LANGUAGE ALTERNATIVES

- Cheese 'n' rice
- Snickers
- Heck
- Jerk
- Darn it or darn it all
- Shoot
- Aww, nuts

- Shut the front door
- Oh my goodness
- Rats!
- Dashitall (okay, a bit of a stretch)
- Fudge
- "Jeezum crow" (we joke that it's the Vermont state bird)

APOLOGIES

GOOD APOLOGIES	LACKLUSTER APOLOGIES
"I'm sorry my words were offensive and hurt you."	"I'm sorry if my words were offensive and hurt you."
"I'm sorry I missed the deadline."	"I'm sorry I may have missed the deadline."
"I'm sorry for the delay on my end."	"I'm sorry for any delay on my end."
"I'm sorry I created stress [worry, frustration] for you."	"I'm sorry if I created stress [worry, frustration] for you."
"I'm sorry for my part in this. I should not have done that."	"I'm sorry for my part in this, but you . . ."
"I'm sorry I was late."	"I'm sorry but there was traffic and school pickup and I just didn't happen to get here on time."

CONVERSATION TRANSITIONS

ENDING:
"Excuse me, I just noticed it's three o'clock. I need to go."

"It's been so great catching up, see you soon."

"Thanks so much for telling me. I'll get back to her later and let you know."

REDIRECTING:
"You don't say. That makes me wonder about something else I heard . . ."

"Paul, I really appreciate that, however right now I'd like to focus on . . ."

"Could we change direction and discuss XYZ . . . ?"

INTRODUCING A TOPIC:
"There is something that I've been curious about recently. Have you heard anything about . . . ?"

"Yesterday, Summer told me about the new building in town. Have you seen it yet?"

"I heard the funniest thing about the headshots they took at the event."

JOINING A GROUP:
Join first by making eye contact and listening to what's being said, then, if you have something to contribute, you can put it out there when there's a natural break in the conversation. "I couldn't but help but join in when I heard you talking about the show. I went on October 18th in Miami and it was life-changing!"

MAKING A SELF-INTRODUCTION:
"Hi, I'm Daniel Post Senning from the Emily Post Institute. It's a pleasure to meet you."

CHAPTER 7

Civility at Work

The same way our professional selves are a slightly more formalized version of our casual relaxed selves, workplace civility is a slightly more formal version of our general everyday etiquette. Practicing civility at work can positively affect so many aspects of our day-to-day work lives. It's everything from how we behave within our physical workspace or our availability when working remotely to how we interact with others on various teams and within the hierarchy of our organization. How clean do you keep your workspace? How do you manage your calendar? How do you treat shared office spaces such as the kitchen, restrooms, and conference areas? How do people engage everyone from the receptionist to the owner or founder? From an etiquette perspective, we can build better business skills and create a culture of civility at work by looking at our own behavior and our impact on colleagues and our work environment. As always, etiquette is used best for self-assessment and setting standards for personal accountability. Let's see how we can use etiquette effectively in the workplace.

YOUR WORK ATMOSPHERE

Common courtesies at work aren't so much about chivalry, like holding doors and coats. They're about being aware of your impact on the people and the environment around you. Being aware that there is a shared atmosphere, culture, and even group dynamics at play, whether you're a one-man shift (with people coming before and after you) or part of a 500-person company with a corporate campus, will help you look for and identify aspects of your company's shared culture. Look for ways to improve how you participate in this shared culture so that you can be more effective at work and hopefully enjoy your time there.

Work atmosphere and group social dynamics often make or break a professional experience. A company with great workers in a terrible atmosphere will never see its full potential. Uncivil work environments lead to higher turnover rates, less productivity, and even intentionally destructive behaviors. Let's look at some ways to help contribute to a positive and productive professional atmosphere.

COMPANY CULTURE

Your company may have goals for establishing and maintaining a certain type of culture. If your company offers these, it's smart to read over any HR materials about the mission or values statement and culture expectations. It has been our experience that etiquette standards support these statements as many are built on concepts such as trust, respect, community, and consideration—very similar to our etiquette principles of consideration, respect, and honesty.

Reviews, accountability, celebrations, support of educational and career advancement opportunities, awards, and team-building exercises are just a few of the ways you might see your company putting those goals into action. There are two particular aspects of company culture that we'd like to highlight as we begin, because when put into action, we think they make a huge difference to work atmosphere: gratitude and acknowledgment.

THE IMPORTANCE OF GRATITUDE AND RECOGNITION

Gratitude binds both parties together through a shared positive experience. The person expressing gratitude gets to acknowledge the support or generosity that has come their way, and the person receiving gratitude feels appreciated and acknowledged. In both cases, the exchange boosts serotonin in the system. The more you express gratitude, the easier it gets to find opportunities to do it again. Expressing your gratitude is crucial to your business relationships.

Acknowledging the quality of the work done is really important. Praise or admiration of our peers or from a supervisor is one of the most fundamentally satisfying things we can experience at work. It's great for morale. We need to work together, and being recognized for the value we bring to others and our organization is not only satisfying but inspiring, and sometimes even relieving, if we feel unsure if others see our efforts. Whether we admit it to ourselves or not, giving and receiving appreciation supports cooperation and personal growth. That's a big win-win, if you think about it.

Appreciation is something you can be generous with. It doesn't cost a thing, and it inspires, rewards, motivates, and supports the people we extend it to. We want people to do what they should be doing: by acknowledging their good work and expressing your gratitude, you encourage that and set the stage for them to do it well. Just because it's a regular part of their job doesn't mean it's unappreciated or thankless. Even with the direction to thank and thank often, don't let it become rote, meaningless, or preemptive. Protect the power of your thanks by meaning it when you offer it. Stay connected to the other person and the act when you issue it. See chapter 5, "Methods of Communication," for how to write a thank-you note.

PRO TIP: Personalize your thank-you by using the person's name and mentioning something specific.

PERSONAL PROFESSIONAL STANDARDS

Regardless of your company's cultural goals, you can set your own personal standards for how you work with others and contribute to the overall workplace experience. Your participation in creating a productive work environment will be noticeable and impactful, and when the whole team or company operates this way, things really start to soar!

SHOW UP WITH WORK AS YOUR MAIN PRIORITY. Yes, emergencies happen, and days get derailed, but in general, showing up to your job with an attitude that you are here and ready to be focused on the task at hand is essential to helping create a sense of productivity and purpose at work.

BE ACCOUNTABLE AND TIMELY. Show up on time for the day, the meeting, the call, the client dinner—whatever it is, if it's work-related, being on time and accountable is imperative. Follow through on tasks assigned or work you've agreed to do. Reply directly to queries and communication in the format they arrive in. Ask for help clearly when needed. Acknowledge when you fall short, and take responsibility.

RECOGNIZE YOUR COWORKERS AS MULTIFACETED PEOPLE. Keeping work as the priority doesn't mean you have to ignore the reality that everyone has a life outside of work. Gone are the days when the only way to interact at work was about work. Building a bit of camaraderie with others humanizes us. We don't treat one another as worker robots. Heck, we don't even advise that you treat robots like robots. We think saying please and thank you to your AI devices is worth the added words—if anything, it's great practice. By greeting others, inquiring about their well-being, sharing a little about ourselves to build rapport, appreciating good work done, and being fair and considerate when offering feedback, we can support those around us as individuals who are all part of a team. (See chapter 6, "Conversation Skills at Work.")

RESPECT THE SPACES YOU WORK IN. By "respecting the spaces that we work in," we don't just mean that you should clean up after yourself (although this is crucial!). We also mean that you read the room. Pay close attention as you move through the spaces in your workplace, and you'll be able to get a sense of how you should behave and contribute to the atmosphere well. Is your reception area quiet and tranquil? Coming in waving and shouting to Becky at the desk, "Morning, Becky!" probably isn't the right move. A head nod and midlevel volume "Morning, Becky" with a pleasant smile will do just fine. If two coworkers work together at an open desk in a nook, sitting down to take a FaceTime call nearby will likely be disruptive. As you move through spaces at work, think: *How can I disturb others the least? What would the minimum impact look or sound like here?*

BRING A POSITIVE TEAM-PLAYER ATTITUDE. When we think of ourselves as part of a whole, we can feel a sense of obligation to that whole, a sense of responsibility to pull our weight and do our share. When we think about this obligation positively, we can become an effective example for our entire team or organization. Positivity is a choice. And yes, bad days and bad moments happen. But overall, approaching work with a positive attitude contributes greatly to the atmosphere. How do you cultivate a positive attitude? Start small. Set the tone for the day by making sure your morning greeting sounds bright and appropriate for the environment, or bring an open and encouraging mindset to your 10:00 A.M. meeting. Much like cultivating a sense of gratitude, the more you do it over time, the bigger an impact it will have and the easier it will become. What starts as one small positive goal can build to become an overall mindset that helps you see the world around you more positively. And you don't have to turn into Mary Sunshine to make a good impact.

SHARE WITH OTHERS. Cooperation looks different in different lines of work, but it is almost always a component of a successful business. *My way or the highway* thinking can help in the short term, but most often, success comes from people working together with a sense of give and take. Learning to share resources, accolades, information, and accountability is critical to teamwork. It both makes people feel good and facilitates working together.

OFFER TO HELP. One of the best ways to start building a supportive relationship with colleagues and coworkers is to offer help. Make it a daily or weekly routine to find someone and offer to help them with something. That's some gold-star, employee-of-the-month behavior right there, whether they take you up on it or not. Even if they don't, you get the credit for the offer, your coworkers know you are there for them even if they don't need it, and you didn't have to do much to reap those rewards.

GIVE GOOD FEEDBACK. Learning how to critique work in a helpful way is a real art. No matter the profession, nearly everyone will need to give and receive feedback. Find the right time and place. Consider the relative dosage of positive and critical feedback; too much criticism shuts people down, making them less likely to hear, understand, and make the necessary changes. Be direct and clear about problems and difficulties if you bring them up, but balance them with things this person is doing well. Be ready to listen to the reply and contribute solutions if it will help (see Carefully Communicate Criticism and Feedback, page 133).

CHECK YOUR BAD BEHAVIOR AT THE DOOR. It seems like common sense that things you know better than to do in your personal life with family, friends, and even acquaintances should be avoided at work, too. But all too often, whether it is stressful environments, bad mentoring, or just a lack of thought, work brings out the worst in people. Avoid the following behaviors and you'll help contribute to a more positive work atmosphere: demeaning yourself or others, gossiping or trash-talking colleagues, claiming credit or assigning blame where it doesn't belong, and ignoring and dismissing others. Sometimes, it is the thing you *don't* do that is the best thing you do all day.

LEAD WITH CIVILITY. Whether you are in a leadership position or joining the lowest level of an organization (but particularly if you are in leadership), your behavior helps set a standard for those around you. We are social creatures who learn from and adapt to each other automatically. Good feelings inspire more good feelings. Negative behaviors inspire negative reactions and stress. Building a culture of civility and respect requires time, effort, awareness, and thoughtfulness. Anyone can lead with civility by treating those around them well. In fact, it is the only way.

FOR FORMAL VISITS AND MEETINGS

Board meetings and visits from clients are just a couple of examples of times when our everyday work atmosphere might get stepped up to a formal level. While the conference room might be the same one you use for your weekly Monday staff meeting, our demeanor changes when we enter a formal atmosphere. We stand or sit up straight. We give our full attention to those we are present with, facing them, making eye contact if we can, and using our best listening skills. We wait to speak until we are certain someone is finished, or perhaps, in some cases, only when we are addressed or invited to speak.

This is different from our everyday interactions, and the additional investment of attention and care recognizes and simultaneously helps create formality.

ACKNOWLEDGING
OTHERS AT WORK

Acknowledgment is an important part of building relationships and creating a positive atmosphere at work. Without it, people often feel invisible—quite literally unseen. Whether in front of the building or as you make your way through the lobby, hallways, stairwells, elevators, the kitchen, and yes, even the restrooms, we want to make sure that we acknowledge the presence of others when we are around them.

When addressing others, we want to get identities right and that we aren't unnecessarily greeting people—like shouting from afar or interrupting a clearly private conversation to get a greeting in. Let's look at some of the fundamental aspects of addressing others well in a professional setting so that we can help contribute to smooth, simple interactions in the workplace.

IDENTITY: NAMES, SUFFIXES, AND PRONOUNS

Names, titles, suffixes, post-nominals, and pronouns are *all* part of our identity, and it's important to pay attention and to get them right. It's the first step in building a good professional relationship with someone and making a good impression on them. Imagine how annoying it would be if most people got your name wrong upon hearing it, and how much worse or degrading it would be when someone who knows you well or knows better does it. A person's identity is deeply precious to their sense of self. We handle identities in etiquette like we handle fine china, a glass ornament, or anything else that is precious—respectfully and carefully.

In Emily's day, it wasn't uncommon to remain on a last-name basis with someone long into a business relationship. The standard of the early twentieth century was to address others with their title and last name only and wait for an invitation to call them by their first name. Today, people are more likely to introduce themselves or be introduced with just their first and last name in business. The expectation is that you use their first name when addressing them unless they have only been presented to you with a title and last name. This is a big change in etiquette over the last forty years. Even though there are still places where titles and last names are used, it's less common. Never use a nickname until you've been invited. "Robert, it's a pleasure to meet you." "Please, call me Rob." "Rob it is, then." But don't call him Robbie or Bobby unless he invites you to do so.

> **PRO TIP**: When in doubt, use titles and last names. It never hurts and will demonstrate that you know and understand the formality, even if it's not expected.

SUFFIXES

Suffixes are used to distinguish individuals who have exactly the same name but are of different generations in a family. William Goadby Post Senior and William Goadby Post Junior would appear as William Goadby Post, Sr and William Goadby Post Jr. (use either a comma or the period for abbreviation, but not both). When indicating a Roman numeral (the third, the fourth, etc.) use no comma—William Goadby Post III. Once a senior dies, a junior is no longer a junior.

PRONOUNS

The pronouns we use are an important part of our identity, and as such, it's polite to get them right when we speak about each other and when making introductions. You might think someone's pronouns are easy enough to tell just by looking at them or reading their name, but this isn't always true. While typically used as a plural pronoun, *they/them* is now regularly used as a singular pronoun. There is no one right way or time to present your pronouns. When making introductions, pronouns can be elegantly stated in a follow-up piece of information or directly announced. "Bryce, I'd like to introduce Riley Wilson. They manage our art department." From this, you can gather that Riley's pronouns are *they/them*; now you know to use *them* when talking about or introducing Riley.

If you need to make an introduction and aren't sure of someone's pronouns, ask. "Joan, what pronouns do you use?" Note that you don't ask what pronouns Joan "prefers"—a common but incorrect construction for this question. The idea that certain pronouns are "preferred" is offensive to many people. While preference can play a part for people who use multiple pronouns, that shouldn't be how you frame the question. For ease of sharing the information, pronouns can be included in email signatures (see Your Signature, page 88).

WHEN SOMEONE GETS IT WRONG

The choice to make a correction or not is entirely up to the person who was misidentified. The moment and the mishap will determine what you decide to do, but remember that it's normal to get things wrong from time to time. Knowing how to issue a proper correction, whether you're the offender or the offended, can help smooth over the awkwardness.

IF YOU MISIDENTIFY SOMEONE ELSE AND THEY SPEAK UP: Keep your response kind and concerned, and keep the fault on *you,* not the other person. Let's say you mispronounce a name; upon receiving a correction, say the name correctly and thank the person for the correction. "I'm sorry; thank you for the correction, Deborah [pronounced as the person has pronounced it]."

IF SOMEONE INCORRECTLY IDENTIFIES YOU: You may choose whether to correct them in the moment ("Sorry, it's Deb-ohr-ah," or "Pardon me, my name is pronounced Deb-OHR-ah") or later on ("I didn't mention it during the introduction, but I should let you know that my name is Deborah, instead of Debra"). "Instead of" is softer language than "not Debra." Small tweaks can make a big difference in how corrections are received.

DON'T LET IT GO TOO LONG: If you have a colleague or work acquaintance whose name you repeatedly get wrong, it's time to set aside the excuses and learn how to say it right. Find examples of the correct pronunciation, write the name down phonetically, and/or rhyme it with something to help remind you. Above all, practice until it feels comfortable and sounds right. It is the height of politeness, and it is necessary to respecting this person.

FORGETTING A NAME

It happens to all of us at some point. If you do, admit it with an apology to recognize your mistake: "I'm so sorry. I should remember, but your name isn't coming to me. Do you mind telling me again?" Then, say thank you when they do.

PRO TIP: If your name is difficult for people to hear or pronounce, it's helpful to have a "sounds like" example to help people you meet.

USING SIR, MA'AM, MISS, AND MX AT WORK

American etiquette and the US military have a long tradition of using the terms "sir," "ma'am," and "miss" to show respect when addressing someone, whether you know them or not: "Good morning, sir," or "Yes, ma'am." For many, these terms are respectful, useful, honorable, and comforting. Forty-four percent of Americans say that they appreciate their use. However, 13 percent of Americans say they do not appreciate these terms being used—that's slightly more than one in ten. For the latter folks, these terms don't create a respectful sense of formality, but instead create an unwelcoming and artificial distance or authority when used in casual relationships or everyday encounters. Another 42 percent of the population says using these forms of address does not matter to them.

This creates a conundrum. What's a person who's trying to be respectful and considerate to their fellow people to do when a "Good evening, miss" or a "Yes, sir" could be either appreciated or offensive? And in business, where there are sometimes hierarchies yet also a sense of togetherness that test this judgment call, how do you know what's appreciated without asking? You do your best with what you know. When addressing the boss or department manager, do other employees say "sir" or "ma'am"? Are you in a region where these forms of address are used frequently, such as the South or Midwest? Based on the numbers, it's safer to lean toward using them in everyday interactions until someone suggests you don't. If you aren't in a position to know, and you guess wrong and you see the other person is upset, or they say so, apologize and do your best not to repeat the error. "My apologies, yes, ma'am" or "My apologies, Frank, thank you for letting me know." It's the best you can do in the moment.

If someone makes a mistake, be patient and forgiving. Of course, you can gently correct if the situation warrants: "Craig, do you have a second? I know 'sir' is often said as a sign of respect, but it makes me feel old. Please, call me Darren."

ADDRESSING A GROUP OR CROWD

Traditionally, it was common to address a crowd or group as "ladies and gentlemen," "boys and girls," or "guys and gals." Today, unless you know the gender identities of those in the crowd, you should use more inclusive and less gendered terms such as "My dear colleagues," "Good people of _____," "Hello, class," "Welcome, patrons," "Attention, everyone," or "Welcome guests, we are so pleased . . ." and simply leave gender out of it. It should also be noted that even though the term *guys* is considered to be gender-neutral, some don't identify with it and may be offended by it, as it traditionally referred to men.

TITLES

Titles, or honorifics, have long been used to help acknowledge or communicate gender, seniority, credentials, and marital status (as in the case of "Mrs."). They are a sign of respect and impart formality when addressing others. They can also indicate an awareness of social distance that is acceptable and even preferred in business. Not everyone you meet professionally is, nor should they be, your BFF or even just your F simply because you've been introduced. Professionally, even though many people use first names right off the bat, it's good to be familiar with titles and their use so that when the occasion arises that someone does go by Ms. Formal, Mr. Traditional, or Mx. Oldschool, you're prepared to use their titles with ease. Always wait for your boss and any client to invite you to call them by their first name. This might happen when you first meet them, but if it doesn't, it's best to wait until the invitation is issued.

SOCIAL TITLES

Ms., Mr., Mrs., and *Mx.* are the most commonly used titles for adults today. *Ms.* and *Mx.* are the two most recent titles, having been added to the list in the last century. These additions prove that titles can and should continue to change to reflect American society. Here's a brief rundown of adult social titles.

Ms.—An adult woman, no relationship status indicated (this is often the default title for women if you don't know what title a woman uses, especially in business).

Mrs.—An adult woman, married, widowed, or divorced.

Mr.—An adult man, no relationship status indicated.

Mx.—An adult of any gender; nonspecific, gender fluid, gender nonbinary, gender nonconforming, male or female, cis or trans, no relationship status indicated.

If you have to introduce a married couple at a work event, asking them how they would like to be introduced beforehand is best. It's hard to know if a woman uses "*Mrs.*" or "*Ms.*" and whether the members of a couple share a last name or have different last names. Some women use one last name professionally and one last name socially. With so many factors at play, the smart move to make things smooth for yourself when it counts is to ask ahead of time. "At tomorrow night's event, how would you and Lisa like to be introduced? And do you go by Ms. or Mrs.?"

PROFESSIONAL TITLES

Within a professional field, or when someone is acting in a professional capacity, professional titles are to be observed, used, and treated with the utmost respect. Some professions, such as medical doctors, carry a tradition of their titles being used in social situations, while other professions use their titles only within their field, as many lawyers and veterinarians do. Professions for which titles are used in both professional and social situations include physician, judge, elected official or diplomat, professor or person with a doctorate (depending on personal preference), and military officer.

The title holder will decide when it is used, and their choice should be respected. Dr. William Lindley, a professor of English, could be "Dr. William Lindley" or "Prof. William Lindley," both professionally and socially. Either is technically correct (although traditionally academics don't use *Doctor* socially) and a person will often base their decision on the occasion and their own personal views. However, having a title doesn't entitle you to be rude about enforcing its use. A snippy or even confidently delivered "It's *Dr.* Lindley" is not pleasant nor polite, while a kind and gentle "I prefer to use my professional title. Please call me Dr. Lindley" feels more like a gentle correction and an invitation.

GREETINGS AND PARTINGS

It is hard to overstate the importance of greeting the people you work with daily. Almost as important, and often overlooked, is the importance of the goodbye when the day is done. Acknowledging our own comings and goings and registering the ins and outs of those we work with are the most basic forms of social accounting. Transition moments are great times to log a few considerate interactions with others, and they are times when these simple manners demonstrate their importance.

These simple, respectful interactions bookend and ground whatever workday trials and triumphs will occur between them. It might not feel like a big deal, but remove greetings and partings, and the workday becomes less connected and complete. Think of the heartwarming story of the powerful CEO who knows the name of the janitor she passes in the lobby each morning on her way to the elevator at 6:00 A.M. sharp and makes time to greet them. It is a noble virtue because basic manners can easily cross power, pay, and experience boundaries. Every person is worth our consideration. Make the expected courtesies of actively greeting and parting with coworkers and site staff a habit. Missing it won't be the end of the world, but doing it regularly fortifies a foundation for the rest of the time you spend together at work.

This doesn't mean you must greet someone whenever you see them again throughout the day. Think of it as a daily reset, and once you have logged in, you can move on to the more efficient acknowledgment of each other with eye contact, a wave, or nod of the head. And at the end of the day, you can say goodbye. "Have a great night, Gladys!" "See you tomorrow, Thomasina." See more expressions of parting on page 160.

EXPRESSIONS OF GREETING

Around the office and in different scenarios with clients or vendors, you may use a range of greetings. What's important is to match the formality of the moment with the formality of the greeting.

CASUAL	INFORMAL	FORMAL
Hi,	Hello,	How do you do?;
Hey,	Hi,	greeting plus name or title, such as:
Yo,	Morning,	Hello, Mrs. Smith;
'Sup,	Good morning,	Good morning, Mr. Shelley;
What's up?,	Afternoon,	Good afternoon, Madam President;
Hiya,	Good afternoon,	Good evening, sir/ma'am/mx/miss
Howdy,	Evening,	
Hey y'all,	Good evening	
How's it going?,		
Mornin',		
Afternoon,		
Evenin'		

WHO GREETS WHOM?

Who greets whom? We frequently hear different versions of this question. For example, what is the obligation of coworkers to greet each other upon first seeing one another? Does the person in the room greet the person entering the room, or does the person entering the space greet the person already in it? Does a senior ranking member first greet an entry-level employee, or does the employee ensure they greet and address the senior ranking member first when they meet in the elevator? What if you don't intend to interact and just pass one another? Do you have to greet people every time you cross paths with them? We call this etiquette-ing yourself into a corner: when you can see so many ways to tackle a situation that you don't know which is the right one. Here are some tips to help you determine what to do:

- Anyone can greet anyone when we are talking about small passing-by moments, whether in the hallway, the elevator, the lobby, the kitchen, or any other communal space.

- Generally, if you're the one entering the space, it's nice to say hi and make eye contact or even just nod to the people already in the space, should you notice one another.

- Avoid calling out to someone from afar to greet them. In business, it disrupts the space when people are trying to work. Eye contact, if you can, and a friendly smile can be useful in this situation to acknowledge someone without disrupting the space or startling others.

THE HANDSHAKE

The handshake is the American default for a respectful gesture of greeting. It is a gesture with deep symbolic roots and says any of the following: I come in friendship, I mean you well, I have no weapon, please take my hand, you can trust me. It is an offer to touch—a rare occurrence among strangers, acquaintances, and colleagues. It is kept brief and contained within a simple gesture, and even so, the act of making human contact means so much. When social distancing during the Covid-19 pandemic pulled us apart, one of the biggest questions people asked about etiquette was whether the handshake was dead. Let us assure you, it is as important now as ever.

It's very difficult to refuse when someone reaches out for a handshake. There are five elements to a good handshake: eye contact (or the direction of your attention if you can't make eye contact), a smile or friendly expression, a good grip, the right amount of pressure and movement, and disengaging at the right time.

1. **EYE CONTACT.** If you can stand and make eye contact, do so. If you cannot stand, don't worry about it, but ensure your attention is squarely directed at the other person. If you cannot make eye contact, direct your attention to the other person's face as best you can; sometimes, focusing on the mouth or the bridge of the nose can help.

2. **SMILE.** Have a friendly, relaxed, or respectful expression on your face.

3. **GRIP.** Extend your right hand toward the other person, keeping your fingers together and your wrist turned so your palm faces left. Clasp the other person's hand, the crook of your thumb to the crook of their thumb. Close your hand around theirs, and they'll close their hand around yours. Use the same degree of pressure you would apply to turn a doorknob—no limp fish or bone crusher grips. And do not place your left hand over your

clasped hands or on the other person's upper arm, shoulder, or hip. Those gestures are unnecessary at best and inappropriate in many cases. Leave your other hand at your side, out of the equation entirely.

4. **THE SHAKE.** Move your hand up and down one to three times. It's not a big or vigorous movement, but active enough to feel a connection with the other person.

5. **LET GO.** While letting go too quickly can seem abrupt and unfriendly, holding on too long is awkward and leaves the other person wondering if they will get their hand back. They'll focus on how awkwardly long this handshake is and not on anything you say during the greeting or introduction.

Seize every opportunity for a handshake, no matter the hand offered or the grasp needed to shake it. An outstretched hand is a sign of respect and a chance to connect. Likewise, if you can, reach out to initiate a handshake. If someone cannot shake your hand due to ability, health, religious, or other reasons, they'll let you know. Then, rely on your words and expressions to create a pleasant greeting. A respectful wave or nod is appropriate when greeting someone who clearly cannot use their hands or arms. If you don't ever or are currently choosing not to shake hands, it's best to clarify for others: "Please pardon me, I don't/can't shake hands, but I'm so pleased to meet you."

YOUR SMILE

For every hello, hi, and how are you, the nods, handshakes, and waves, a smile is probably the best greeting of all and can accompany all of these gestures. No matter what your teeth look like or the shape of your lips, when a natural smile—even the tiniest one—spreads across your face, there is no mistaking the genuine warmth and pleasure expressed. It may be the simplest and most universal greeting to use. Emily Post wrote in 1922, "A ready smile is more valuable in life than a ready wit; the latter may sometimes bring enemies, but the former always brings friends."

EXPRESSIONS FOR PARTING

For all the time and effort we spend getting started on the right foot, it is equally important to end well. The last impression can linger in the same way a first impression can set a mood. Your introduction sets you up for success; your goodbye gives you a chance to shape, flavor, or color the impression that remains after you are gone and can set the tone for the next interaction.

Here are some of the expressions you can use when saying goodbye and the level of formality they impart.

CASUAL	INFORMAL	FORMAL
Bye,	Take care,	I wish you well;
G'bye,	I'm headed out,	Good evening;
See ya,	Goodbye,	Good night, sir/ma'am;
any non-English version of goodbye such as Ciao or Adios,	See you tomorrow,	Goodbye;
	Have a good night/evening,	I bid you farewell;
Later,	Good evening	I'll be leaving shortly, is there anything else . . .
G'night,		
See you soon,		
Buh-bye		

WORKSPACES

Office, sales floor, construction site, kitchen, hospital, truck, cooperative workspace—wherever you spend most of your workday, understanding the etiquette of the space will help you navigate it confidently and successfully. Common courtesies such as timeliness, cleanliness, friendliness, and thoughtfulness all contribute to building cohesion, reducing stress, keeping focus, and creating and maintaining a shared workplace culture that people can work in effectively and enjoy.

So much of what contributes to and creates great places to work are skills that many of us learn in preschool or at home at a young age: share, be kind, pick up after yourself, and join in on group activities. The same basic principles apply to adults at work, and it can be a comfort to lean on their familiarity, especially when you're new to a job.

What this looks like at work is as simple as greeting and saying goodbye at the start and end of the day, not keeping people waiting, cleaning up after yourself, and pitching in when needed. It can also look like taking care of others; for example, effectively asking a coworker to keep private calls quiet at a shared desk or apologizing for a mistake you have made. Let's take a deeper look at courtesy in the workplace.

THE OFFICE

Dunder Mifflin? *Dilbert*? *Mad Men*? Whatever image you conjure when you hear the word *office,* there is no denying that there is something iconic, even archetypal, about the place we go to work. Big or small, new or old, quaint or modern, shared or private, strange or familiar, the office is a special place that deserves special attention and has its own manners.

VISITING OR PASSING THROUGH

Treat an office you do not work in daily with respect, even if you're familiar with the space and the people working there. When you are visiting, or even if you work at the company but not in the office and are passing through, schedule or coordinate your visit with your office manager (or a person in a similar role) so people know why you are coming in. Call or email (and wait to get a confirmation response) if you hope to get something specific done or if your visit is not part of a regular routine or scheduled appointment.

When you arrive, if you're not a frequent visitor, greet the receptionist, introduce yourself, and state your purpose or appointment: "Good afternoon, Karen Sheedy, here to see Rip Trawling for our ten o'clock appointment." If the building has security, you'll likely need to show ID and might even be given a visitor pass. Always display and use the pass as instructed. As you move through the office, a friendly smile and confident eye contact, if you're able, will help put others at ease. Try to minimize your impact and the potential distraction you may present to the people who are working. Don't linger after your business is done unless invited. While it's best to leave personal calls until afterward, if you need to handle something immediately, keep it to a minimum and the volume low, seeking out a private space to talk if possible. Remember to thank your hosts, anyone you may have chitchatted with whom you'll see on your way out, and, of course, the receptionist as you exit.

YOUR DESK

Your desk is *your* desk; in many ways, it reflects you and how you approach your work. It is part of your professional image. Set up and maintain your desk to facilitate getting your job done. You'll want to check in with HR about any expectations around how it is kept. Keep a pen or pencil and paper handy, no matter how much of your work is digital. It's better to be ready than not.

Reduce clutter that impedes your focus or ability to accomplish tasks. Recognize that some decoration, or even the way you organize your desk (or don't), could distract others. This line will be different for different people and offices. Maybe pictures of your kids or the vacation home of your dreams motivate you to keep at that repetitive task, or maybe they just give you daydream material that takes you away from your work. Be honest with yourself.

Some companies have *Clean Desk* policies that require employees not to leave certain materials unattended, and desks to be completely cleared at the end of the day. Others take a more creative approach, encouraging fun distractions and imaginative play at work and allowing private spaces such as desks to be kept at the worker's discretion. Know your company and your supervisor. Keep your workspace in a condition that reflects the values of your team or organization and yourself.

OPEN OFFICE ENVIRONMENT

Cubicles and open offices have their own courtesies and standards. A cubicle's partial privacy can be both a blessing and a curse. The biggest mistake people make in these environments is not respecting focus. Just because a cubicle has no door doesn't mean you can walk right in, call out to someone, or pop over the divider. When someone is at their desk, whether it's an open environment, a cubicle, or an office with an open door, it is important to ask for their attention. *Don't just interrupt without acknowledging it.* Ask, "Hi, Sue, do you have a minute?" Think of it as a verbal knock at the door.

The second biggest mistake people make in these environments is thinking that more privacy is afforded than there is. Keep phone calls, music, podcasts, or other noises in earbuds and headphones (not coming out of your speaker). Don't use loud ringtones, alerts, alarms, or notifications. Whether it is talking too loudly on the phone, to each other, or about topics that are not public, watch the volume in these spaces and take the truly private conversation somewhere safe.

PRIVATE OFFICE

The dream of dreams, your own personal office space, where you can close out the busy greater world and focus on your own work. You might even get to decorate it as you see fit—with a budget to boot! With such a work luxury comes great responsibility. Believe it or not, your door has a language all its own—a bit limited, but it speaks volumes. The "open office door" has become a metaphor for availability precisely because it physically establishes it. Here are the translations you need to know and respect.

DOOR POSITION	TRANSLATION
Open Door	Come on by. I'm likely available, and it's okay to ask!
Door Ajar	Give a light knock first, but nothing you're interrupting is too private or important.
Closed Door	I'm busy. Come back later or try to schedule an appointment. Knock if you have to interrupt me.

Remember what a closed door means to others. While, yes, they can reach out to you via messaging apps, text, or email, or even try buzzing you on the intercom, if you're available again, reopen your door so that it's clear to others.

THE HOME OFFICE

Thanks to efforts to get broadband internet services to more communities, the home office is more common than ever before. Social distancing restrictions and work-from-home mandates during the Covid-19 pandemic rapidly accelerated this shift. Now, remote and distributed workforces are commonplace and here to stay.

Whether it is your family, housemates, a partner, or a pet, those you share your home office with also share some of your work life and have an impact on it. Identify the time and space your work requires and communicate it with those you live with. Work courtesy in these situations means coordinating your work and personal life so the latter doesn't overly impact or influence the former.

Try to simulate or reproduce the experience your colleagues would have with you in the office. Continue to be considerate of the quality of calls or video meetings, background noise, response times on all correspondence, accountability to deadlines, creative collaboration with teammates, and opportunities to volunteer for new work or help colleagues with problems. Great home office manners facilitate the work getting done no matter the location.

If possible, create a permanent home workspace, whether a room or a desk space, which you can regularly return to and don't have to put away during non-work time. Build efficient routines and keep your work materials and supplies handy and organized. Establish a well-lit space and background for video and voice calls that is professional and free from clutter and noise—it's worth the effort.

The effort you make to set yourself up well for working from home *is* the first courtesy of working remotely.

SHARED SPACES

There are many common spaces at work that we occupy and use to interact with colleagues in between working hours. We don't have ownership over these spaces, but there are still responsibilities and expectations for behavior, which means they can be hotbeds of frustration and missed manners opportunities.

THE KITCHEN

The office kitchen needs to be a clean, comfortable space for people to prepare and sometimes eat food in. Here are some of our top considerations when using the office kitchen; the first two are the two we hear the most about.

1. **ONLY EAT YOUR OWN FOOD.** If someone has given you open permission to help yourself to their food, that's very generous of them; beyond that, ask first, always.

2. **CLEAN UP.** The kitchen should be a "leave no trace" space in the office. Whether you're pouring a cup of coffee, heating something up, or cooking up a whole meal from scratch, you should never leave a mess in the kitchen. Dishware and utensils need to be clean and readily accessible. Ensure you meet your company's standards. If there isn't a standard, ask for one to be implemented. We found "wipe every drip and drop, and ensure that food is not stuck to the plates once they've been washed" to be effective.

3. **AVOID ODOROUS FOODS.** Avoiding foods that are known to have pungent aromas is a courtesy in the world of shared kitchens. Delicious as they are, fish, bananas, (by Emily Post's personal standards, oranges), onions, garlic, cruciferous vegetables such as cabbage, broccoli, Brussels sprouts, and more can all have lingering or strong odors that can easily impact others. These items are best saved for meals outside of the office. By the way, pungent doesn't mean gross. It just means strong. There's no reason to yuck someone's yum, but being careful with strong-smelling foods will stand you in good stead with your colleagues.

4. **STORAGE SPACE.** Different offices have different policies on how much and where you can store your own food. Pay attention. Taking up more space than you are allotted is not good workplace etiquette And neither is leaving your leftovers. One of the cardinal rules of the office kitchen is to remove your food when you're finished with it. The mold-art that can ensue isn't worth it, nor is it nice for anyone to be around.

5. **COMMUNAL FOOD.** Some companies supply snacks, or breakfast or lunch items, and sometimes they even offer entire meals and on-site chefs for employees. Engage to the degree you want, and be mindful of rules such as only taking your portion or volunteering to help clean up if you participate in a large, shared meal. The expectations on shared food will vary greatly depending on what is offered. If you aren't sure what you're allowed to take or what might be considered "taking advantage of" supplied food at work, ask.

6. **LITTLE NOTES.** The word *etiquette* means "ticket" or "tag" in French. Putting little notes in the office kitchen as reminders, requests, or name tags can be helpful, but be careful of wearing out your welcome. Little notes that are passive-aggressive or unnecessary will irritate people quickly.

THE RESTROOMS

It feels like telling you water is wet to say that bathrooms are private, but that is our biggest etiquette around the office restroom. It's a space where we need and want to respect each other's privacy. Here are simple things you can do to make sure you're using the office restroom appropriately.

- Give others the respect and consideration of privacy. No calling, filming, or recording should happen here—in fact, pay people the respect of not making them wonder by keeping your phone out of your hand and putting it away for visits to shared restrooms.

- Avoid having lengthy conversations in the restroom. Depending on the bathroom style, the restroom can often become a default gossip or private conversation space. Resist the urge. Maybe that's a futile suggestion, but when thinking of business etiquette and trying to be our best professional selves, we highly recommend letting the bathroom be a place for grooming, hygiene practices such as brushing your teeth and applying deodorant, and, of course, well . . . you know.

- Know what's flushable and what's not. Safest bet: toilet paper and human waste only. Everything else goes in the bin.

- Tidy up after yourself, wipe up splashes, get trash into the bin—not just near it—and don't leave spots on the mirror.

HALLWAYS, LOBBIES, SNACK BARS, AND OPEN SPACES

Interactions in hallways, lobbies, atriums, and at snack bars or carts are a part of work courtesy, even if they are not intended as places to get work done. Interactions in these public spaces mirror briefly running into a colleague at the market or a weekend ballgame. People who know each other can acknowledge one another with a greeting or nod, but there is no social obligation to stop and talk unless there is a mutual desire.

You can likely make or take calls in these spaces, but you should also be conscious that you are not disturbing anyone or preventing others from using or moving through the space comfortably. These are great places to practice the kind of public courtesies that work well out and about around town: offer to hold a door, give up a seat to someone who needs it, exchange pleasantries with an acquaintance. Bringing these common social courtesies into these workspaces is a rich opportunity to contribute to a pleasant workplace.

THE OFFICE GYM

Like any other gym, you want to follow the rules at the office gym. Always look for the posted rules or guidelines for using the space so that you know sign-up policies, time limits, and the expectations around taking care of the equipment and cleaning up after yourself. Outside of those rules, here are a few tips that are helpful when exercising around others:

- Greet others, but don't expect anyone to be available to converse while they work out.

- Wear headphones or earbuds so that others don't hear the show, music, or other entertainment you're listening to while you exercise.

- Clean up, especially when using mats, free weights, resistance bands, rollers, and other gym equipment.

- Remember, it is still the gym *at work*. Yes, you can step outside your usual work attire and work rules, but these are still your colleagues, employees, and superiors, and you will want to dress and behave in ways that feel professional.

CELLPHONES IN THE WORKPLACE

How you use your phone at work will be unique to your company and its rules around personal cellphone use, your work environment, and your own personal phone use policies. Some companies have strict *no personal phone use* policies, and the good etiquette is to comply. When personal phone use is allowed, or at least not banned, you have to be responsible for yourself and hold yourself accountable to keeping your use to an appropriate level.

- Prioritize the people you are present with. Don't be controlled by your phone, responding to it automatically. Keep your focus and attention on the people you are with, and excuse yourself when you take your attention away and give it to your device.

- Limit the use of cellphones in meetings. Meetings can sometimes be completely phone-free zones, though this is less common today than twenty years ago, so monitor your use carefully and try to minimize any distractions you would cause.

- Using your speakerphone is only okay if you're conducting a meeting with the others present in the room who should be on the call, or when you have your own phone booth or private office and can shut the door.

- Most people keep their phones on silent or vibrate while at work, even if their personal phone doubles as their work line. No one wants to hear twenty different ringtones throughout the day. On the plus side, this quiets the overall noise level of an office space; on the downside, it's easier to miss calls.

- Use designated cellphone areas. Some companies have rules such as taking your phone outside the office for personal calls, or to a designated phone use area, like a lobby or even a particular floor or part of a building.

DIGITAL WORKSPACES

The idea of bringing us to the work, rather than passing the work around, is nothing short of revolutionary. And it has changed our working format forever (until the next thing—hello, holograms!). Whether it's the G Suite, Microsoft OneDrive, iCloud, Canva, Adobe Creative Cloud, or any other platform-based word processor, spreadsheet, design application, or shared digital workspace, there are courtesies to making the digital workspace work well for everyone who uses it. (See Messaging and Work Management Apps, page 106.)

STANDARDS Your company or team should have a comprehensive set of established standards for working in these spaces. Follow them. No specific rules? Keep it simple if you are trying to figure it out independently. Don't use all of the resources; only take your share, whether it is a number of downloads, meeting invites, products in a store, or unique requests of the AI assistant. If every photo uploaded to your Dropbox account is supposed to have a caption that will become the alt text, then you must put that alt text in the comment section for each image you use or create. Your company's rules, guidelines, and standards aren't just there to give you something to do. They are about the deeper communication networks and workflow efficiency the organization has deemed necessary.

YOUR IMPACT Don't change or delete unrecoverable work done by others unless you've been asked to do so. Clean up after yourself and remove partial drafts, unnecessary files, and anything extra or irrelevant to the shared work. Don't disturb or change an existing organization system without permission or collaboration with those who built it. Do thoughtfully label, tag, store, and categorize information so that others, as well as yourself, will have access to it and understand it.

Whether you're making edits or starting from scratch, using the system thoughtfully and correctly will make a difference to others who use the space.

RESPONDING TO LIFE EVENTS

While some folks choose to separate their professional and personal lives, big life events are often shared with coworkers with whom you've developed rapport or even friendly or meaningful personal relationships. It's okay to let your team know about major events in your personal life. There may be times when coworkers are even included in our personal life events. Responding appropriately in these moments can positively affect work relationships.

COWORKER'S/EMPLOYER'S WEDDING

Today, it is more than appropriate to say "Congratulations!" to either member of a couple who has just gotten engaged or married. The old tradition was congratulating the groom and offering best wishes to the bride. Those days are long gone. Don't expect an invitation, though; many guest lists have cutoff points, and *coworker* is often a category where couples draw a line.

If the office decides to host a shower for the happy couple, know that this may be done regardless of whether coworkers are invited to the wedding. It's one of the few exceptions to the rule of *only inviting shower guests who are also invited to the wedding,* the reason being that many colleagues know that a couple can't manage to host all of their coworkers at their wedding, but they are close enough and want to celebrate and honor the occasion. If the coworkers decide on their own to host this party, it is considered polite. The honoree may accept and attend the shower graciously without worrying about inviting them to the wedding.

If you receive a wedding invitation, it's entirely up to you if you can or want to go to the wedding. However, whatever you decide, RSVPing on time and in the requested fashion and sending a gift are still important etiquette boxes to check.

If you attend the wedding, be sure to bring your best self and remember that even though you are at a social function together, you're still connected to the couple through work. Keeping these three principles (consideration, respect, and honesty) in mind will help you bridge that business-social divide.

COWORKER/EMPLOYER WELCOMES A NEW CHILD

Anytime a child is welcomed into someone's life, it's a big deal. There is some etiquette to communicating with those at work about the new arrival and possibly entertaining a shower to honor the occasion. The office does not have to host a shower, but if they offer, it's okay for the parent(s) to accept if they wish to.

Offering congratulations and asking about how things are going since the new arrival are welcome as the news spreads. Because pregnancy and birth are incredibly personal, it's best to pay acute attention to whether the new parent or parent-to-be wants to discuss or share any additional aspects or details at work, including photos.

NEW PARENT: "It's official: Jarrod and I are going to be dads! Our baby girl is due in October."
COWORKER: "Frank, that's wonderful news! Congratulations!"

COWORKER: "Alexis! Welcome back! How are you and the little one doing?"
NEW PARENT: "Geordie and I are exhausted, but she's amazing! Would you like to see a few pictures?"

COWORKER'S OR BOSS'S RETIREMENT

Retirements, or "rewirements" as we once heard it called, can be a mixture of sadness and joy. Retirement is personal to each person; therefore, you want to try to strike a balance between sentiments of how you will miss someone and encouragement that this "next phase" in life is something to be joyous about. Paying attention to how the person retiring handles things is usually a good indicator of which direction to take. Congratulations is what most people will offer a retiree. If the retiree seems happy about the retirement, asking how they plan to spend their time will likely be welcome.

Most companies, departments, or teams will at the least host an in-office party for the retiree. It's a chance to gather, eat a little cake, and share good wishes for this milestone. Some companies, or sometimes a family member of the retiree, will organize a larger or more formal retirement party. If you are invited, it's best to be prompt and responsible with your RSVP. The host is likely putting a lot into organizing, and there's the added stress of hosting a large number of colleagues collected over the course of a long career.

Follow these steps to play the great guest role to the best of your ability.

1. RSVP.

2. Pay attention to the event's formality.

3. Dress accordingly.

4. Participate well as a guest.

5. Congratulate the honoree.

6. Thank the host.

7. A follow-up note would be appropriate and likely appreciated in this particular case.

FOLLOW-UP TO THE HOST

Sept. 15, 2027

Dear Michah,

It was such a pleasure to meet you on Saturday evening. Thank you for hosting such a wonderful send-off for McKayla. She has been such an invaluable part of the team at Shadwick Wrenfield. We are really going to miss her while we cheer her on as she embarks on this new chapter in life. Thank you again for a wonderful party.

All my best,
Kevin Applebaum

FOLLOW-UP TO THE HONOREE

Sept. 15, 2027

Dear McKayla,

How bittersweet it is to wish you congratulations on your retirement. You have been such an instrumental part of our lives at Shadwick Wrenfield; it almost feels impossible to think of you not being there daily. I am grateful for your kindness when I joined the team. I wish you the best as you enter this next chapter of life and hope to see you from time to time around town.

Enjoy retirement, and congratulations again!

All my best,
Kevin A.

[Or no initial if you're the only Kevin at the company.]

COWORKER/BOSS FALLS ON HARD TIMES

While there are many companies where the expectation is that non-work problems are not discussed or considered while you're on the company clock or dime, the reality is that many of us create a sense of camaraderie with our colleagues. We want to reach out with compassion and sympathy when something tragic or difficult happens. As long as your coworker is the one who has shared with you about the hard time that they are experiencing, it's okay for you to offer your sympathy.

COWORKER: "Yeah, I was in Los Angeles last weekend, sadly, because a friend passed."
RESPONSE: "Oh my gosh, Jay, I'm so sorry. That's just terrible. How are you doing?"

Or

COWORKER: "The car hit at about 40 mph, and now Jayden is in the hospital."
RESPONSE: "Oh that's awful, I'm so sorry."

Whether you can offer help, support, or even a listening ear will greatly depend on when you're informed of the news, how close you are to the person, and your availability. It can be tempting to immediately start setting up meal trains, offering to visit at the hospital or home, or even offering to help out financially. Any and all of these can be great and thoughtful, but they aren't required from an etiquette perspective. It might even be overwhelming for the person to have lots of suggestions or offers come at them at once. Keeping your response to just sympathy at first can still leave room for talking about ways to help when the time is right. It also allows the news and the sympathy to have their moment before you jump into support and help mode.

A thoughtful note can make a big impact in difficult times. Never discredit the amount of solace and support someone can find in the kind words offered by a friend or colleague.

SYMPATHY WITHOUT OFFERING HELP

May 31, 2026

Dear Kaia,

I was so sorry to hear about your accident. I hope that now that you are home and recuperating, things are looking up. We really miss you here at work and are wishing you the smoothest of recoveries. We have everything covered here; you don't have to worry about a thing except healing.

Wishing you the very best and lots of comfort right now.

All my best,
Jeremy

SYMPATHY WITH OFFER OF HELP

May 31, 2026

Dear Kaia,

I was so sorry to hear about your accident. I hope that now that you are home and recuperating, things are looking up. We really miss you here at work and are wishing you the smoothest of recoveries. We have everything covered here; you don't have to worry about anything except healing. We have a meal train ready to go if that sounds appealing to you, and I'm also happy to come by one evening after work to help with cleaning or any other household tasks that are difficult for you as you heal if that'd be helpful.

Wishing you the very best and lots of comfort right now.

All my best,
Jeremy

REFERENCE GUIDES

TOP TIPS FOR RESPECTING IDENTITY

The best advice around names, nicknames, and pronouns that we can offer from an etiquette perspective is this:

- Listen when someone says their name; ask them to repeat the pronunciation if you are unsure. "Lovely to meet you both. I want to get your name right. Is it KIERsten or KERsten?"

- Refrain from immediately commenting on someone's name or asking, "Where is your name from?" While appreciation or curiosity might inspire you to ask the other person, it can feel othering.

- Pay attention to identity markers such as pronouns, social titles, and suffixes. Pronouns, in particular, are good to look out for as they aren't always obvious from name or looks alone.

- Ask for clarification if you didn't catch someone's suffix, title, or pronoun.

- Wait to be invited to call someone by a nickname.

- If you make a mistake and mispronounce a name, apologize, and do your best to listen to the correct pronunciation and repeat it correctly.

- Always apologize if you get an aspect of someone's identity wrong. We all have moments where we make mistakes, but an apology is key to being considerate about repairing the mistake.

TOP EIGHT DAILY OFFICE COURTESIES

1. Show up ready for the day or your shift.

2. Acknowledge others and greet them with a smile.

3. If you can, make eye contact when speaking with others (for video calls, turn on your camera and face the lens).

4. Use the magic words in all your interactions, both verbal and digital.

5. Use shared spaces appropriately, never leaving a mess or taking more than your share.

6. Decline to participate in office gossip.

7. Offer help to others or check in to see how their work is coming along.

8. Say goodbye to colleagues on your way out the door for the day.

SAMPLE WEDDING RSVPS

Today, it is common to be invited to a coworker's or even your boss's wedding. If such an invitation should arrive at your door—or be dropped off on your desk—here is how to fill out the reply card if it isn't digital.

Use the big M to lead off with your social title (if you have a professional title that you use socially, you can strike out the M and write "Dr.," for example).

> **M**s. Delphine Post
>
> ☐ Accepts with pleasure.
> ☐ Regrets being unable to attend.

Then select "accepts" or "regrets."

You may choose what you wish if there is a place to select a meal. Unless you have a severe allergy, it's best not to include extra detail or requests here. "I eat fish but only shellfish, so if the fish is salmon, I'd rather have the beef" is too much. Just choose the beef. If you're responding on behalf of yourself and a partner or plus-one, indicate which person is having which menu option if you're choosing different items.

SAMPLE CONGRATULATORY NOTE

Honor your colleague's achievements both in and outside of work with notes of congratulations. You can send one for getting engaged or married, welcoming a new child, getting a promotion, retiring, and more.

June 24, 2027

Congratulations, Beth-Anne!

I was so happy to hear about your promotion! You have worked so hard and done so much to really whip things into shape on the Franklin account. I'm really excited for you, and I think you will be great in this new position.

Cheers to you, Beth-Anne!

Kindest regards,
Alexi

CHAPTER 8

Meetings

Meetings are a big deal. They are where and when our natural expectations of each other at work are heightened. If timeliness matters in business, it matters even more for meetings. If behavior matters in the office, it matters even more at meetings. Where clarity of communication matters in business, it matters even more in meetings. Respecting hierarchies matters in business; it matters even more in meetings. We connect in meetings, making our social skills and ability to interact well matter even more. The limited time you have in a meeting to accomplish what needs to be accomplished places a premium on our behavior at the meeting. And depending on the type of meeting, it could be life-changing.

We experience so many different types of meetings at work. A meeting could be about getting to know each other, generating ideas, reporting on progress, or solving a problem. Whatever the purpose, it will be best served by paying attention to how the meeting has been arranged, your role, and who the others present will be. Let's look at how to be our most professional regarding meetings.

ORGANIZER RESPONSIBILITIES

When organizing or hosting a meeting, you should have a clear sense of who is being invited, the time and location or method of connection, and the agenda. These are the essential meeting details to get right from the start. Provide attendees with enough information so that someone who knew nothing about the meeting or its topic could understand the plan.

ORGANIZING AND INVITING

An executive assistant or administrative assistant (or even a virtual assistant) might be used to organize the meeting. If you are organizing but not hosting, make sure this is clear so attendees know your role in case they need help. This can be accomplished by saying something like, "I'm reaching out on behalf of ____ to set up a meeting for next week" or, "[meeting details] I'm happy to answer any scheduling questions you have. Mr. Anderson will provide the necessary materials and can answer any questions you have about the meeting agenda." Some assistants will have deep knowledge of the content to be covered in a meeting, and others will only have the logistical details.

SENDING A MEETING REQUEST

Like any invitation, it should include the date, time, location, and method of connection, links or phone numbers to call in to, a topic/agenda, and any relevant content. The information should be enough for invitees to learn anything they need to know to participate well, including whether cameras need to be on if this is a video meeting, and any considerations regarding confidentiality. Send the invitation early enough that attendees can prepare. Attendees should know what they're committing to when they RSVP.

Always include a point of contact (phone or similar) in the meeting invitation, encouraging people to get in touch if something comes up and they will be late or unable to join. Be clear that this is for communication around attendance and not to call in to the meeting.

See chapter 5 for the difference between asking for a meeting, offering a meeting, and telling someone there will be a meeting. This will help you issue an invitation that matches the tone of the meeting.

SETTING UP FOR IN-PERSON MEETINGS

As the organizer, you may or may not be responsible for prepping the meeting room. Depending on the nature of the meeting, this prep could include providing or setting up AV equipment, prepping and placing name placards, making a reservation, confirming accessibility and making the necessary arrangements, arranging materials, and gathering note-taking supplies. You might also need to ensure refreshments are available. Each seat usually has a glass of water on a coaster, with a water pitcher nearby. If you're not hosting, check with the host to be sure you're checking all the boxes in the hospitality department for in-person meetings.

Seating is a big consideration for some meetings, and different meetings will require different arrangements. In business, unlike in social or business-social settings (like a dinner party at your boss's house), we seat by order of precedence. Often the head of the company is in the center of the long side of the table and in the seat with the best view, with the next highest ranking person from their team to the right, and the next highest to the left of the highest ranking and so on, alternating sides down the table. If there is an honoree, this person will be seated to the host's right and in the "best" seat. The best seat has the best view or the best view of any "action" such as a speaker, presenter, or performer.

Regardless of the type of meeting, and if there is any presentation or entertainment, accessibility supersedes the importance of roles. A person with a wheelchair needs the easiest access to and from exits, and possibly a podium or stage if they are speaking. A person relying on an ASL interpreter needs to be able to see the interpreter easily. Let's look at a few specific examples.

BOARD MEETING

Attendees are seated by precedence of their role or title on the board.

For a rectangular table, the order is as follows, with the top role seated in the middle of the long side of the table:

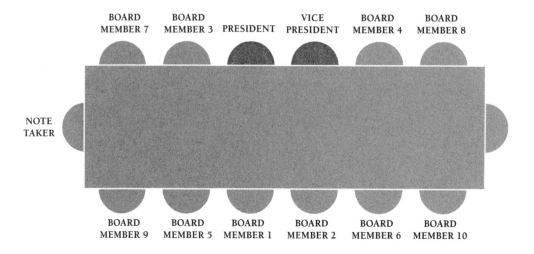

For a round table, the president is seated in the position with the best view:

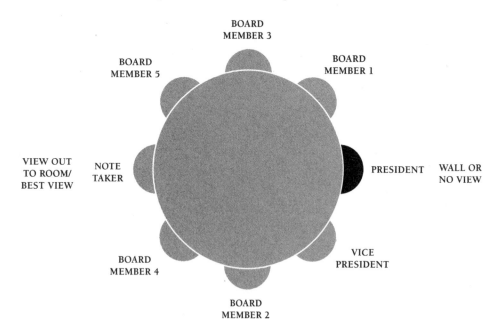

BUSINESS-CLIENT/PROSPECT MEETING

The hosting business is on one long side of the table, and the client or prospect organization who is visiting is on the opposite side. (The heads of each company are in the middle, with their ranking team members sitting to the right and left of them in order of importance.)

HC—Hosting Company, V—Visitor

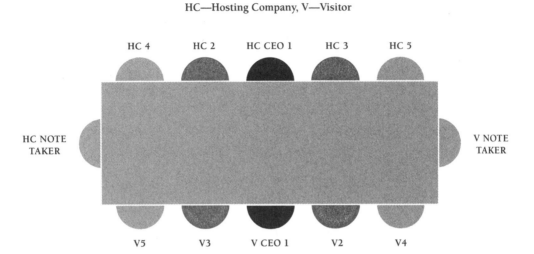

FORMAL INTERNAL BUSINESS MEETING

For a formal internal meeting, ask the host or leader of the meeting where they'd like to sit, they can be at the head of the table or the side (really, any seat they wish). From there, seat everyone else by rank, alternating sides of the table.

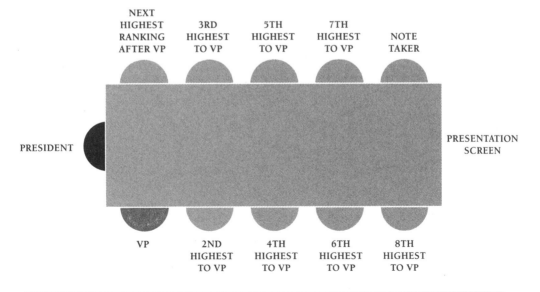

CONSIDERATIONS FOR ALL MEETINGS

ACCESSIBILITY ACCOMMODATIONS Accessibility and safety supersede protocol. A person in a wheelchair needs to be able to easily—and quickly—access the exit should they need to. Hearing and visibility concerns must be addressed as well, and not just when a presentation is happening. Hearing aids and seating arrangements can help in both cases to ensure folks will be able to participate fully in the meeting.

CULTURAL DIFFERENCES If you are hosting a company or organization, look up the visiting organization's culture and see if there are any considerations regarding meetings, introductions, gifts, and expressing gratitude that might help you adjust your preparations and make your guests more comfortable.

TAKE CARE WITH LANGUAGE AROUND TIME Triple-check that you have listed the call's correct date, day, time, and time zone. This includes the duration or end-time information as well. When confirming the time, don't use "tomorrow"; based on when you send the message and when the recipient reads it, your "tomorrow" may not be the same as theirs.

SCREEN OR PROJECTOR If these items will be used, you'll want to ensure that the most important people receiving the presentation can see it easily and comfortably. From there, the ranks descend from the next most important down.

SPEAKERS AND MCS Seat speakers and those leading ceremonies or meetings with easy access to the podium or front of the room.

IDEAL TABLES FOR SEATING

- Rectangle or U shape for business meetings

- Classroom style or auditorium for large meetings/presentations

- Round for social settings and group work

HOST RESPONSIBILITIES

The host will be responsible for starting the meeting on time and leading the meeting, whether they were the one who organized the meeting or not. A good host knows which meetings need to begin sharply and which can allow for a grace period—five minutes (phone/video call) or ten minutes (in-person meeting). Once everyone has gathered or arrived, the host welcomes everyone to the meeting. Some meetings will require introductions, which can be made at this point. If the meeting doesn't require introductions, the next best step is to review the meeting agenda and timeframe. The host should moderate the meeting, keeping an eye on the time, agenda, and conversation. The host will also conclude the meeting and ensure that follow-ups happen. Let's look at these responsibilities more closely.

GREETINGS AND INTRODUCTIONS

As the host, you'll start every meeting by greeting the others present and making any necessary introductions or announcements (like that the meeting is being recorded or the room is reserved for an hour only). Do not forget this business etiquette step. While getting right to work saves time, the niceties of greetings and introductions should not be skipped. "Thank you all for being here today; I'm Kurt Vaughn, and I'll take the lead on this campaign and run the Satelite Media Tour remotely. I'd like to introduce my colleagues Kim Alvarez, she'll be on the ground with you in Chicago, and Alison Keaths, they'll be working content development throughout . . ."

AI COURTESIES

Today, with AI transcribing, notetaking, and processing capabilities, meeting follow-up has never been easier. The courtesy is to let attendees know at the start of the meeting if you're using an AI app. You can take it a step further by distributing or offering to distribute a range of outputs from an AI meeting application, depending on how your company uses these services. We are particularly fond of summaries, highlights, and entire transcripts or videos that can be distributed. Not all meetings will be via video, but when they are, these are handy tools—and they will only keep getting better.

AGENDA

A well-conceived and presented agenda is a thing of beauty and efficiency. The best practice is to share it beforehand, allowing everyone to use it to prepare. At the meeting, the agenda is a great aid to keep both the host and the group on task and coordinated. A good host will guide their attendees through a meeting smoothly, keeping an eye on any time constraints. That agenda has a purpose, and while it's okay to go off it if a moment warrants, a good host will keep bringing the focus back to the agenda. See the Reference Guide (page 191) for a sample meeting agenda.

> **PRO TIP**: If you need to table something to get back to the agenda, follow up on it appropriately. Good meeting notes, whether handwritten or AI-generated, can be very helpful for this task.

MODERATION

While not every meeting will require *Robert's Rules of Order,* all meetings require some form of moderation. Moderation does not mean you dictate and rule over the meeting. But it does mean that you will be the person who keeps the conversation on track. If you're meeting about the annual budget for a particular service your company offers and the conversation starts going into theme options for an upcoming annual event, it's time as the host to reel things back in. "I agree that we'll want to nail down the theme for this year's conference soon, but I'd like to table that or set up a separate meeting to discuss it. Right now let's work on finalizing the budget." Validate the importance of the conversation and table it for later.

If you have an attendee who interrupts the meeting too frequently, whether with valuable ideas or distracting comments, it's best to nip this in the bud by asking for questions or comments to be held for the end of the meeting or after the meeting if time constraints don't allow for Q&A. "Julio, I appreciate the thoughts; however, right now, I'd like to save comments until after we've completed the agenda items."

CLOSING, FOLLOW-UPS, AND TAKEAWAYS

Almost as crucial as opening the meeting well is closing it, which is another job of the host. As the time approaches, give attendees a warning: "We are ten minutes away from our hard stop. So let's see if we can get through the next . . ." You are responsible for offering a concluding statement or a brief summary and thanking everyone for attending or contributing. This acknowledgment and thanks serve as a natural signal that the meeting is over. But your job is not over quite yet . . .

A host or an organizer could be responsible for distributing follow-ups and takeaways from a meeting. Follow-up can include notes, thank-yous, summaries, assignments, reports, minutes, transcripts, and more. Be sure to include task deadlines and be clear about who takes responsibility. Meetings without appropriate follow-up can leave coworkers feeling like they were a waste of time, and leave those who couldn't attend out of the loop. A meeting is only as good as the work that comes out of it.

If you are an organizer who did not attend the meeting, get clear directions from your host on handling follow-up.

ATTENDEE RESPONSIBILITIES

As the invited attendee of a meeting, you are, in many ways, a guest. Like any good guest, you want to be on your best behavior when someone else is hosting. Whether it's a colleague, a manager, an owner, a client, a vendor, or even a subordinate who has called the meeting, your role is to respond to the invitation, show up to the meeting ready to listen, and, if need be, participate. We suggest familiarizing yourself with *Robert's Rules of Order*. Even if your organization doesn't use them, you'll gain a sense of and get to understand an example of ordered participation and fairness in discussion.

REPLY TO THE REQUEST

If you think we hammer home the point of RSVPing to social events, prepare for the Wilton Sledgehammer version for meetings. The etiquette here is finite: respond to meeting requests or schedule propositions in a timely manner. Meetings are so integral to moving business forward that RSVPs for professional meetings are some of the most important to pay attention to and take care with.

ARRIVE ON TIME

Showing up on time is crucial to demonstrating respect and consideration for those you are meeting with. It also demonstrates your professionalism and communicates that you understand the importance of punctuality and respect people's time.

If you are going to be late, *as soon as you know you'll be late*, text, call, or email the organizer and/or the host of the meeting so that the message gets received that you will be late. Whether this results in the rest of the attendees waiting for you will depend on the context of the meeting and the players involved. If the meeting was set up well, you'll know who's involved and how they could be impacted by your lateness. No matter what, your notification must come with a sincere apology. Do not make excuses. "José, I am so sorry I will be fifteen minutes late for the meeting. I understand if you need to start without me. Please extend my apologies to everyone."

When arriving on time, greet the host, followed by the other attendees. There might be a few minutes to chitchat while folks assemble, and this would also be a good time to pour yourself a cup of coffee or grab a bite if any refreshments are being offered. Remember, though, that the focus of this time is the meeting and not the food or chitchat. Be ready to sit down and focus when the host indicates it's time.

If you're unsure of where to sit or if certain seats are being reserved, it's best to ask your host. "Flavia, where would you like us to sit?" If there's no one to ask and you're unsure as an attendee, avoid the seat that looks like it's the "head of the table." This is likely where the host will sit. For a long table, it will be one of the two heads or short ends of the table. It's also a good idea to avoid those two middle seats on the long end of the table, as in business these are where the most important players sit. Of course, you can always wait for more important players to arrive.

If you're late, try to minimize the distraction of your arrival. Come in as quietly as possible and take a seat. The host will either welcome and introduce you or politely ignore your late entrance and continue the meeting.

> **PRO TIP**: After the meeting, apologize to the host for being late. "Flavia, I just wanted to say I am so sorry I was late."

PARTICIPATION

Your participation in meetings will vary from being a fly on the wall to speaking up frequently or presenting. Finding a balance between sharing your thoughts, asking questions, and simply being an active and good listener is the work of honing your participation skills. Here are a few things to focus on.

FOLLOWING ALONG

There will be many meetings where you will simply follow along and may not have any questions or information, comments, or suggestions to contribute. This is not a time to fidget by tapping your pen, finger, or foot (see Distracting Habits, page 33). It doesn't mean you aren't doing anything, it's simply a time to listen and absorb the information you're hearing.

If you get lost during a meeting, you'll want to assess whether you should peek at a neighbor to see where you are or if you can simply speak up or interrupt with a "Satya, I'm sorry, I'm a bit lost. What page of the prospectus are we on?" Saying something like "You've lost me; where are we?" places the burden and blame on the presenter, which isn't right, given that you were the one who lost focus.

ASKING QUESTIONS AND MAKING COMMENTS

In school we raise a hand to indicate that we'd like a turn to talk or ask a question, but it's not always the preferred method in business. More commonly, we regularly meet with teams that we know well, and raising a hand is completely unnecessary. That said, in a larger meeting, it might still be the preferred method. Rather than shooting your hand up high, keep it low, raising your arm from the elbow with a relaxed but upright hand. A nod of the head and eye contact can also help get a leader's attention. In any case, wait until open discussion is invited or you're called upon to speak.

SAVING FOR LATER AND WRITING THINGS DOWN

Tactics that often are chosen during the five-step process (see chapter 2) and that will help you listen and focus during a meeting are to write down things you'd like to ask or say and evaluate whether there's an opportunity to address them later. When urgency starts to feel real, writing something down can help to de-stress the moment and allow you to behave well as an attendee. This doesn't mean you can never say something midmeeting, but not all meetings make it easy. Think carefully about whether you can easily and respectfully speak up, and if you can't, write it down and wait until later or after the meeting.

EATING AND DRINKING DURING MEETINGS

Meetings over meals are enjoyable but present some tough challenges. Eating and talking do not go well together, even though we pair them constantly. No matter the style of meal being served, do your best to contain the mess and never speak with food in your mouth. A beverage such as water, coffee, or tea is fine. But don't plan to eat during a meeting or even bring a snack unless you have checked with the host or you know everyone else will be doing the same.

EXCUSING YOURSELF

For regular meetings with those you know well, you can excuse yourself at any point that feels right to use the restroom or refill a coffee. Outside of that, you want to avoid leaving the meeting. No, this doesn't mean sweating bullets because you need to use the restroom, but it does mean considering the time and the content being discussed and seeing if you can wait.

If the meeting is interrupted and you are called elsewhere, apologize for the interruption and excuse yourself. "I'm sorry, please excuse me. I'll be right back. Something came up that I need to handle." Follow up with your host as soon as possible to find out what you missed. If you need to suggest that a portion of the meeting be covered once you're back, do so. "I can report on the Solomon numbers once I'm back. Feel free to skip forward to the Jefferson account."

DISTRACTIONS

Whether it's the window, the buzzing phone in your pocket, another attendee, or something else in the office or room, distractions can get the best of us, even in meetings where we really want to be present. Catch yourself and refocus. Do your best to eliminate distractions from the start by turning off your devices if you can and keeping your attention on whoever is speaking.

FOLLOW THROUGH

Following through on decisions, tasks, and deadlines that emerge from meetings is crucial to moving business forward. Good business etiquette has us focused on clarifying expectations at the conclusion and rising to the tasks and deadlines that have been assigned.

PRO TIP: If a meeting wraps up and you don't have a follow-up task or next step, offer to help someone else or take on a support role.

VIDEO MEETINGS AND CONFERENCE CALLS

The same rules that govern in-person meetings inform the etiquette for conference and video calls, with a few new courtesies particular to these types of meetings.

AS THE HOST

SET UP YOUR CALL WELL, much like you would an in-person meeting. Once everyone has been invited, your next job is to get the call up and running on time. A test run ahead of time is ideal, particularly if there is anything new or unfamiliar about the equipment or software you are using. Leave enough time ahead of the scheduled start to get through log-ins, load and update software, make connections, and configure settings. Be clear about whether you need cameras to be on during the meeting.

GREET EVERYONE AS THEY JOIN THE CALL. Once the group is present, greet everyone again. If you're requiring cameras to be on, now's a good time to invite attendees to do so. "Once you're settled, please turn your camera on." Then review the agenda and proceed as discussed above.

PAY MORE ATTENTION TO THE ATTENDEES. With video, basic communication cues are easier to miss or could be overshadowed by glitches. Keep an eye not just on participants onscreen but also on the group chat for any messages people might send you during the meeting. Do your best to move through your agenda in a timely manner, remembering that you can also agree to follow up later on anything you don't know the answer to.

TONE. As long as it's appropriate for the nature of the meeting, it never hurts to smile, have an upbeat tone, and encourage those you're on the call with to participate. Video calls can have a stale quality, and while you don't need to make a show of it (forcing a smile the whole time), keeping a friendly demeanor, looking into your camera, and having an active and engaged attitude can go a long way toward keeping your attendees' attention.

THE HOST OR ORGANIZER ENDS THE CALL. As with any good meeting, it's best to open it up at the end for any questions or thoughts, if appropriate. Give a warning and try to finish on time. Remember, you can always agree to discuss a topic further at another time if needed. Make sure everyone has had a chance to say their goodbyes before you hang up or end the call. A message after the call thanking everyone for their participation and detailing any actions to be followed up on is thoughtful.

> **PRO TIP**: Factor in time for a staggered start or a bit of social time at the beginning of a call. Also, leave time for transitions between major topics and speakers. This is not wasted time. It is realistic, and some social engagement can help establish the tone of the meeting, and facilitating this is a part of hosting.

AS A PARTICIPANT

SET YOURSELF UP WELL. Use a quiet location. If you cannot, be sure to use mute and maybe even use noise-canceling headphones, microphones, and backgrounds to remove distractions for those on the call. Always be courteous to your office mates. If you have a shared office space, either relocate or communicate ahead of time so that they can find workaround solutions while you're on the call.

> **PRO TIP**: Like keeping a jacket or change of clothes at the office, have a few of your grooming essentials (a hairbrush, a mirror, a little makeup, if you wear it) right near your desk so you can always do a quick check and touch up if needed.

SHOW UP ON TIME OR EARLY. This gives you time to handle connection issues and be ready to be on camera. Bring whatever you need for the meeting. Don't think you need to bring anything? Bring a pen and notepad just in case—even with AI note-taking apps, it's helpful and shows you're ready to be engaged.

PAY ATTENTION TO ANY REQUESTS FROM THE HOSTS. Whether about how to prepare for the meeting—bringing certain materials, or being ready to present on a topic yourself. Or about the format of the meeting, like turning your camera on, or speaking in a certain order or for a certain length of time.

KEEP YOUR ATTENTION ON THE CALL. Try to look into the camera lens and avoid an angle that faces you away from it, which gives the appearance that you are not "looking at" others on the call.

BE PATIENT. Whether you are dealing with spotty connections that freeze the screen or audio or are waiting to participate, don't let impatience get the better of you. For most work video calls, you can find a way to bring up your point, add your thoughts, or ask a question; even if it doesn't happen in the moment, it can happen at the end of the meeting, or in a follow-up email or conversation after the meeting. Take comfort in knowing that. It will help you de-stress. If it's a technical problem that persists, let the host or organizer know that you are having tech issues and will be delayed, need help, or will reschedule, depending on the problem.

ALWAYS SAY THANK YOU BEFORE YOUR GOODBYES. And check that you know about any follow-up tasks that come from the meeting. You may leave once you've said your goodbyes to the group and have heard the host say goodbye.

USE VIDEO CALL FEATURES. On large calls, keep an eye on the chat space. In less formal meetings, use features such as applause, hearts, or raised hands to acknowledge others or get the attention of the host if you'd like to speak or ask a question.

CONFERENCE CALL MEETINGS

Conference calls between three or more people have become a staple in business. A well-managed call is appreciated by all. Here are some tips specific to a good conference call:

- Without visual cues, it's easier to interrupt. Wait for a clear pause or to be addressed before speaking.

- Use a quiet space or if you cannot, use headphones to avoid or eliminate background noise.

- You should not eat unless you are very close business partners and have an understanding—and even then, never on a call with a client, vendor, supplier, or prospect.

- Also, tempting though it may be, avoid multitasking. If you're not muted, the dishes you're washing can be heard, the traffic on your walk has an irregular rhythm that will be noticed, and the email you're typing on your keyboard can be heard. You might try muting yourself, but your delay or lack of reply or attention will be apparent at some point.

- If you use the mute button, ensure it works before you rely on it. Test if it's on by saying another participant's name. They'll answer you if they can hear you, which is better than them hearing whatever it is you're muting for and alerting *you* to it.

REFERENCE GUIDES

SAMPLE EMAILED MEETING INVITATION

Hi Paul,

Thanks for agreeing to meet with Dan and me; we're excited to hear more about PartyClick! I've posted a link below for a Zoom meeting with both of us on Monday at 1:00 pm PT. I look forward to speaking with you then.

Best,
Lizzie

Link—ex.zoom.com/this-will-be-the-best-meeting-ever

SAMPLE MEETING AGENDA

- Greetings, introductions, review agenda

- Announcements

- Prospective client lists (Jeremy presenting)

- Return customer revenue expectations (Jen and Katie)

- Divvying of tasks for Q3

- Questions and discussion

- Assignment review/closing remarks

HOST MEETING PREP CHECKLIST

☐ Invitation: the correct date, day, time, and time zone

☐ All attendees were issued an invitation

☐ The correct link or call-in number was issued

☐ Contact information to use in case attendees have a last-minute cancellation or need to get in touch due to being late or having technical difficulties

☐ Send necessary prep materials, or request them from attendees

☐ Check whether the in-person room has been set up appropriately given the nature of the meeting

☐ Send an email reminder with any necessary log-in information

☐ Prep presentations

ATTENDEE MEETING PREP CHECKLIST

☐ Participate in scheduling if necessary

☐ RSVP once a date and time have been sent and an invitation issued

☐ Double-check that it's on your calendar correctly and that any log-in information is accessible

☐ Review the agenda and any meeting documents well before the meeting

☐ Bring any requested materials or information to the meeting

☐ Have pen and paper handy before the meeting

TIPS FOR BUSINESS VIDEO CALLS

BE ON TIME Video (and phone) meetings usually have a grace period of five minutes.

WEAR APPROPRIATE ATTIRE Seize the opportunity to be seen and the chance to make a good impression. Consider the purpose of the meeting and who will attend, and dress accordingly.

SHOW YOUR FACE Always assume you'll need to be on camera for a video call so that you can be prepared—even if there are occasions when it's okay for your camera to be off.

KNOW THE INTERFACE Once you log in, familiarize yourself with where the mute button, raise hand, and chat features are.

EATING, DRINKING, AND SMOKING OR VAPING ON CAMERA Eat only if you've been invited to on the call. A glass of water or a cup of coffee is fine, but no slurping, gulping, chugging noises, or upending your glass. While you may be alone in your own home, avoid lighting up or hitting a vape pen during a call.

BEWARE BAD MEETING TRAPS

Despite the best planning and earnestly engaged participation, things can go badly. Watch out for these things that can trip up a good meeting.

- Disagreements
- Disorganization
- Time waste
- No work done or decisions made
- Too many meetings
- Bad tech, dropped call

- Distractions
- Complaining
- Interpersonal issues
- Lack of preparation
- The work could have been done individually

CHAPTER 9

Business Social

Sometimes, work is work, and there is no time or room for anything but the task at hand. But often, social life and business mix. Some work-social events are for working, and others are for relaxing and bonding. Some occur on company property, like the Friday afternoon cake and punch for Amanda's birthday, and others take us halfway across the globe, like the annual company retreat or holiday.

There are times when we enter a social event and it turns into a business opportunity spontaneously. There is a lot to figure out regarding how we want to conduct ourselves professionally in social settings. Let's start by looking at our roles as hosts and guests while working on the social side of business.

BUSINESS INTRODUCTIONS

In business we make introductions often when clients visit the office, when we meet a team from another company, or when we meet a new coworker. Relationships begin with introductions. They are an essential part of business etiquette and professionalism.

Business introductions are often more formal than social introductions. In business, it's almost always the relationship (client, vendor, supplier, prospect) or rank that determines who is introduced to whom and how. Introduce honored guests and visitors first, then respect organizational hierarchy. "Mr. Client, may I present Carys Flemming, our CEO." Let's take a closer look.

FORMAL BUSINESS INTRODUCTIONS

The formal business introduction is phrased as a question: "May I present ____?" (pronounced "pre-zent," not "prez-ent" like a gift), instead of declaring or offering the introduction "I'm pleased to/Let me introduce . . ." In the most formal situations, the introduction will be made in one direction with the idea that you are presenting one person to another and not back the other way. Address the "more important" person or higher-ranking person first. (Note: A client often outranks a boss, but you can always check with your boss before an introduction. "Should I address you or the head of Sitwell first in the introductions?") With this level of formality, people might shake hands or they might smile, make eye contact, and give a friendly but respectful nod. Shaking hands is still recommended when possible, especially for Western business interactions.

FORMAL INTERNAL INTRODUCTION

PERSON MAKING INTRODUCTION: "Ms. Sheera Bigtime, may I present Mr. Junior Newbie?"

SHEERA BIGTIME: "How do you do, Mr. Newbie? Are you enjoying your new position with us here at Global?"

JUNIOR NEWBIE: "I am, thank you. And please, call me Junior. I am so grateful to be working with such a great team."

FORMAL INTRODUCTION WITH GUEST

PERSON MAKING INTRODUCTION: "Ms. Client, may I present Ms. Sheera Bigtime, our CEO, and Mr. Junior Newbie, a new hire on the Helping Hands project?"

In this case, Mr. Junior Newbie should let Ms. Sheera Bigtime speak first once Ms. Client has replied, since she is of higher ranking.

RESPONDING TO A FORMAL INTRODUCTION

For the person receiving the introduction, "How do you do?" is the most formal and traditional response. It functions more like saying "pleased to meet you" than asking about one's well-being, which is why Ms. Bigtime is following up with a question above. As the person receiving the introduction, make the person you are meeting feel comfortable by being gracious and welcoming. As the person being introduced, you have it easy: answer whatever question is posed to you. For both parties, smile and engage, whether you're moving forward with business or using small talk to get to know one another. Now, even though "How do you do?" is the most formal response, even in formal situations today you will hear people respond to a formal introduction with "It's a pleasure to meet you, Ms. Bigtime."

SEMIFORMAL AND CASUAL INTRODUCTIONS AT WORK

Semiformal and casual introductions will happen all the time among team members, peers, and some folks outside the office. While you want to have a formal introduction ready for some business contacts (VIP clients for instance), the majority will warrant and be comfortable with a semiformal introduction. With semiformal and casual introductions, we drop the one-sided structure and formal language. It's okay to say, "May I introduce/Let me introduce . . ." Or the casual version, "Sheera, this is Junior Newbie. Junior, this is Sheera Bigtime."

Note that even though the business casual introduction is much simpler than the formal introduction, we still use last names. While socially, casual introductions often use first names only, in business, where last names and titles are more likely to be important we still think it's important to include last names, no matter the level of formality.

SEMIFORMAL INTRODUCTION

"Ms. Sheera Bigtime, may I introduce Mr. Junior Newbie? He started with us this year on the Helping Hands farm project we sponsor." Or, "Ms. Sheera Bigtime, this is Mr. Junior Newbie. He started with us this year on the Helping Hands farm project we are sponsoring." Or, "Sheera Bigtime, I'd like to introduce Junior Newbie, a new hire on our Helping Hands project, to you."

PRO TIP: The "to you" at the end of the casual introduction sentence preserves the order of the introduction.

CASUAL INTRODUCTION

Even for a casual introduction at work, it's still smart to include last names and offer some information about who each of these people are at the company. "Sheera, this is Junior Newbie, our new hire on the Helping Hands project. Junior, this is Sheera Bigtime, our CEO." Or, "Sheera, I'd like to introduce you to Junior Newbie, our new hire on the Helping Hands project. Junior, this is Sheera Bigtime, our CEO." And yes, you *can* have a casual introduction with a CEO at some companies.

WHAT TO AVOID WHEN INTRODUCING OTHERS

Acknowledgment matters. When we are with others, a manner that has stood the test of time is to introduce people who may not know each other so that they become acquainted and can comfortably engage with each other. Let's look at a few points to avoid.

- Ignoring the introduction altogether—this is the worst offense.

- Remaining seated when you are easily capable of standing.

- Not making eye contact when you can.

- Shouting the introduction (unless you're in a loud location that requires it).

- Dropping an introduction on someone and then walking away, which will come across as having dumped the person being introduced like a problem to be dealt with by someone else.

- Saying things like "You two simply had to meet. You will get along so well!" It places pressure on the two being introduced, and it's awkward if you're wrong.

- Making mistakes with people's names, titles, or pronouns.

If someone corrects you regarding a mistake in an introduction, apologize, thank them for the correction, and then move on using the correct name, title, or pronoun. Be confident that receiving a correction allows you to get it right in the future, and that's a good thing.

THE SELF-INTRODUCTION

The person who can self-introduce confidently and smoothly can approach and engage anyone. In business, this ability is priceless. There are plenty of times when you'll need or want to make a self-introduction, such as at conferences, while traveling for work, or when soliciting business. Having made it this far in life, you've likely already introduced yourself more times than you can count. Let's ensure you hit all the etiquette marks for your next professional self-introduction.

Many people get nervous about introducing themselves, even if they've been doing it for years. It's a mild type of social anxiety, and it's normal. A good, confident, well-structured self-introduction will go a long way toward starting off any relationship on the right foot, and it can make a fantastic impression. Here's how to nail it.

READ THE ROOM As that CEO you've always admired steps into the elevator (and isn't in discussion with anyone or paying attention to her phone), you could say, "Excuse me? Pardon the interruption, my name is Elizabeth Allen. I work in the design department. I just wanted to let you know that I admire you as a CEO and the work you've done here." Or if you're introducing yourself to someone outside the company, "Pardon me, may I introduce myself?" "Sure." "I'm Elizabeth Allen, a designer at Ten Speed, and I was hoping to . . ."

PRESENT YOURSELF WELL Stand up straight or sit up as straight as you can if you're in a wheelchair or unable to stand, lift your head, make eye contact if you can, smile, and give a nod, a light wave, or offer a handshake. Say your name clearly and offer any business-related information that feels right given the circumstances or the objective of the introduction: job title or position, experience, pronouns, or where you're from if this would be helpful or pertinent. For example, when going around in a group offering self-introductions, you might go with "Hi, I'm Pete, a surveyor at Founding Rock in Alabama; I use *he/him* pronouns." Or when approaching someone at an event, "Hi, I'm Pete, from Founding Rock in Alabama, I'd love to ask you about your new development if you have some time."

Do not be shy with your self-introductions in business. There is no time for Hamlet to wrestle with self-doubt in this moment. Know yourself. Know where you are from and what you do. Know what your goal is when approaching someone else. Presenting yourself clearly says to others, "I know who I am. I know where I'm from. And I know what I'm doing." A real go-getter is often first identified by their ability to introduce themselves confidently.

BUSINESS CARDS IN INTRODUCTIONS

The presentation of or exchange of business cards requires care. It's an extension of someone's identity and deserves respect. Let's look at both formal and informal exchanges.

FORMAL EXCHANGE As the presenter, ask permission to give your card. "May I offer you my business card?" This question might follow an introduction or be part of a goodbye. To up the formality, invoke international manners and present your card with two hands, with your name facing the recipient so they can read it. As the recipient, carefully receive the card with two hands, take a moment to read it in front of the presenter, and remark on the design and quality. Once the card has been appreciated, place it in a cardholder, with the rest of your important materials, or on the table in front of you—not stuffed into a pocket. Now, offer a card in return.

INFORMAL EXCHANGE As the presenter, offer your card by saying "May I offer you my card?" Or "Here, please take my card." Hand it to the recipient with your name facing them. As the recipient, check that you can read the important information when you receive it. You can place the card in a jacket pocket, purse, desk, or cardholder,. You can offer a card in return.

> **PRO TIP**: For occasions where you expect to exchange several cards, it is smart to carry a cardholder or have a designated place for them.

NETWORKING

Now that you've been introduced, networking is how you turn these connections into strong business relationships. Being willing to talk about your work and listen to what others do will allow you to forge new business relationships in all kinds of situations. For managing food and drink while networking, see chapter 10.

HOW TO APPROACH A PERSON OR A GROUP

When you're at a networking or mix-and-mingle-type event, it can feel bold to approach a group and join in, but if the event is intentionally for networking, you should be able to do just this. Catching someone's eye, seeing a space in the grouping, and catching a moment of transition are all things to look for if you approach a group in conversation. Once you're within talking range and can hear what's being said without appearing to eavesdrop, you can decide if you'll jump right into the conversation because you have something to contribute to the topic, or if you should introduce yourself first. The response from the people you approach and the type of event you're at will likely determine your course of action. Just like with conversation, there are times when you try this and it's just simply hard to break into the group. Don't fret. It happens to everyone. While approaching a group or being in a large group might feel like a desired goal, larger groups can build from smaller conversations. Look for opportunities to have an exchange with one or two people about the shared experience; it's a great icebreaker. After a slight back and forth, it affords you a great manners moment to introduce yourself. "Wow, this venue is fantastic; what a view, right?" "I was excited when I heard it would be held here." "I'm Debbie, Debbie Kingston." "Laura Ronson, I'm here with the team from Brentwood."

WHEN TO TALK BUSINESS

So when should you start talking business if you're not "on the clock" or at a professional networking event? The reality is that many different moments could become business-social moments. On a train headed to a friend's place for the weekend, you and another passenger might get to talking and discover potential business opportunity together. Your sister-in-law's engagement party might involve a business conversation you can participate in. It's not just big work mixers where business mingling and chitchat occur. The lunch counter could be one of your best places to acquire new leads or even hear a thought to improve your work efficiency. You just never know! And this is why it's so good and so important to find your own confidence with small talk. Why? It gets the ball rolling and the conversation started. Through small talk, you can discover if there's potential there or not.

Now, let us be clear. Etiquette does not suggest that every moment is ripe for a potential business deal, lead, or conversation. However, conversation allows you to discover if there is any business potential in the social interaction. When the event or situation is not explicitly business-related (like your sister-in-law's engagement party or that lunch-counter conversation), you'll want to be delicate about venturing into business conversation. Spend time chatting about the shared experience (the event, the day, the environment you're in) or other conversation basics such as hobbies or interests, sports, movies, music, and shows. Once you've established some rapport, or they have mentioned something work related, *then* you can ask someone what they do. If the person responds and seems interested in talking about work, maybe even asking for more details or batting a few ideas around, you should probably table the work talk and offer to get back in touch later. Yup. Once you know there's a potential for business between you, offer to get in touch during work hours to talk more about it. This allows for an exchange of contact information and solidifies an opportunity for a second interaction to develop the connection further. And you can get back to focusing on the moment at hand. It's an A+ move. You've piqued someone's interest and shown that you: (a) don't have to make everything about business, and (b) know how to prioritize a moment properly.

If you're at a business meal, wait until your host brings up the business or until after the meal (the main course) to discuss business. See more in chapter 10.

> **PRO TIP**: Practice, practice, practice. Practice small talk with those you encounter. You're exercising the muscles of mingling and making connections when you do, and it will make you more confident and comfortable networking.

Regardless of whether the event is more business-focused or more socially focused, you can use the three tiers of conversation from chapter 6 to help you determine what conversational waters to wade into and which ones you should avoid—or at least approach with caution and an "out" for the other party should they not want to discuss it.

For more formal and structured business-social events, it is a good idea to do a bit of research about the hosts, important guests who may be featured as attending, the businesses represented, and any details about the purpose of the event. Be curious about the people and organizations attending and why they are attending. It will set you up to up your conversation game. "Hi, Meredith, I was so moved to hear about CIP's work with the King Street Youth Center. Do you have plans to do this internship program again next summer?"

> **PRO TIP**: Don't forget to listen, listen, listen. It's the best skill to demonstrate in conversation.

CONTACT EXCHANGE AND FOLLOW-UP

Getting to the point of exchanging contacts with a promise of a follow-up can feel like a win; it could be game-changing. However, knowing exactly how to ask for or offer your contact information and how to follow up appropriately is key to getting a new business relationship off on the right foot.

If you're making the ask, you should initiate the exchange and do the initial follow-up work. "Would you mind if I followed up with you in a few days?" "What's the best way for me to reach you?" Once deals, partnerships, and work have begun, both parties are equally responsible for their own work. Remember, if you are seeking a business relationship with someone, you are responsible for getting the ball rolling and managing the inertia of the relationship.

KNOWING WHEN IT'S A NO

In social business situations, there will be times when a business conversation or connection is declined by the other person, and that's okay. While it might be disappointing, the most respectful thing you can do to move forward well in that moment is to accept the rejection and engage in a more socially focused conversation. A direct decline is something you can respond to with "Okay. Thank you for letting me know," and then if you are in a good position to continue a conversation, change the subject to something such as the shared experience or a topic you know they enjoy. An indirect decline is a little harder. If you've tried once or twice to direct the conversation to business and the other person keeps changing the subject, take that as your cue to follow them. This *is* their "soft no."

EVENTS

Some jobs involve many work-related social events, while others involve virtually none. Work events can be anything from conferences and symposiums to showcases and unveilings to gallery shows and awards banquets to the annual dinner at the boss's house. Any event you are invited to through work will require that you not only know your host/guest role but also bring your professional A-game, regardless of whether the event is heavy or light on the business side. To nail a work event, you'll want to RSVP appropriately, dress according to your role and the event specifics, bring any items you need to be prepared and participate well, and follow up with thanks afterward.

HOST AND GUEST ROLES

The ideal guest is an equally ideal hostess; the principle of both is the same. A ready smile, a quick sympathy, a happy outlook, consideration for others . . .

—EMILY POST

While hosts and guests exhibit many of the same traits, each role has its own expectations. Ask yourself which one you are most closely playing in a given situation. Is an important client visiting your office for the first time? Even if they are there to meet your boss, you are technically a host or at least a part of the "hosting team." Later that day, after the meeting goes great and your boss invites you and the team to dinner to celebrate, you become a guest. As the boss, and as the person inviting you, they are the host. Let's look at what defines the host and guest roles so that as you find yourself in each, you know how to be your professional best.

A GREAT HOST

Hosts take care of their guests. They operate on their home turf in some way, knowing the layout of the location or the people involved, making the arrangements, issuing the invitations, and providing some direction or guidance for guests or attendees throughout the event. Hosts get to make choices about timing, location, participants and their roles, and the guest list—they are likely also paying for the event, although your company often foots the bill (kind of a silent cohost who is always present). It's a lot to manage, and anytime you find yourself in the hosting role, do your best to rise to the occasion and meet all of the above criteria. For a list of great hosting manners, see A Great Host Checklist in the Reference Guide, page 214.

A GREAT GUEST

Guests bring their best selves to their host's event. Being a great guest begins before you arrive. RSVPing appropriately to the event starts everything off on the right foot. From there, show up on time, appropriately dressed, and with any people or items you were invited or requested to bring. Great guests look to their hosts for cues and follow the host's lead for the event, participating whenever possible with curiosity and goodwill. And every good guest will follow up and express their appreciation for their host's effort on their behalf. For a list of great guest manners, see A Great Guest Checklist in the Reference Guide, page 215.

MANNERS TIPS FOR NETWORKING AT AN EVENT

These tips will serve you well as you network at any business event, especially cocktail-style mixers.

- Place name tags and badges on the right side of your chest. When reaching to shake hands, the badge is visible and in the line of sight for someone looking from your extended hand up to your eyes. Lapel pins and remembrance badges are worn on the left side, close to the heart.

- When entering a midsized or small event, find your host first to greet them, if they were not at the door to welcome you. At larger events, it's up to you where you head to first, but locating colleagues or whoever you're supposed to be joining is a good first move.

- Keep your right hand dry by holding cold beverages in your left hand so that when you shake with your right hand, it isn't cold, wet, and clammy. This can take a bit of getting used to, so practice it.

- If you won't be drinking alcohol, it is always okay to politely decline. There is no need to offer an explanation or comment.

- If you drink alcohol, we recommend you stick to just one alcoholic beverage for the event. If you don't like that advice, please know your limits and stick to them. Be aware of your body. (How tired and well-fed are you? What is the altitude like if you're traveling?) Don't try to impress others with being able to consume a lot. This goes for cannabis as well in states where it is legalized.

- Politely participate in hors d'oeuvres:

  - Take one item from a passed tray at a time.

  - Don't hunt servers down to get a particular item.

  - Take the cocktail napkin (and maybe a spare); it can be useful.

  - Avoid overloading a small buffet plate—you can always return for more, just take a new plate when you do.

  - Do not double dip. It's a germ spreader for sure. And no, you can't turn the carrot around and dip the other side in the shared dip.

- Engage accordingly. If it's a mixer, commit to meeting three new people and exchanging business cards. If it's a celebratory or team bonding event, focus on relaxing with or getting to know your colleagues better.

- Take advantage of opportunities to connect with people at different levels of an organization. Work events can be opportunities to meet with higher-ups or develop relationships with rising talent and backbone employees.

- Say goodbye to your host when you leave and thank your host or the organizer afterward.

INVITATIONS

Inviting well means the recipient should know exactly who is hosting, who is being invited, the date and time of the event, and the purpose of the gathering. If your event needs an RSVP, you'll want to include it, along with an attire designation if needed. See the Reference Guide for sample invitations and sample RSVPs, page 217. As a host, inquire about accessibility needs and any dietary restrictions. "Please let me/us know of any accessibility needs or dietary restrictions we should be aware of" is thankfully becoming more standard on invitations. Remember, as the host, to ensure that your invitation's formality matches the event's formality. An emailed invitation that is poorly designed—or worse, not designed at all, but is just an actual email or comes with advertisements—will not convey a formal event. And vice versa: an extravagantly formal invitation to a casual work get-together will send mixed messages.

INVITATION STRUCTURE

For formal invitations, the hosts *request the pleasure of someone's company*. Month, day of the month, year, and time of day are spelled out (without using *and*). (Saturday, the second of July, two thousand twenty-five at seven o'clock.) Numbers in street addresses are spelled out up to twenty (Eleven Oak Street); then use numerals (24 Oak Street). No abbreviations are used, except for Mr., Mrs., Ms., Mx., Jr., and Sr. If an RSVP (with or without a deadline date) is being used, it is left-aligned and placed at the bottom of the invitation. Traditionally, only black or white tie attire suggestions were included, but today, it's not uncommon to see more than just these two attire designations. Attire information is placed on or below the same line as the RSVP but is right-aligned.

Formal invitations may be handwritten, printed, or done by a calligrapher. Casual invitations come in so many forms: via text, email, phone, fill-in cards, party-link, or printed or handwritten. The format is more general for a casual invitation: *Join us, Come celebrate,* or *You're invited!* Numerals and abbreviations are okay for casual invitations. On the rare occasions when it is used, the *No gifts, please* line is placed under the RSVP and left-aligned.

Offer to include anyone participating as a host (remember, to be a host, you don't all have to contribute in the same ways). You can also describe yourselves as a group (the Physics Department, or The Partners at Gravel and Shea, the Welcoming Committee) or list the hosts alphabetically.

Anything beyond what's listed above (for written invitations) should be included in an insert, sent separately, or discussed separately.

ACCEPTANCE OR REGRET: THE ART OF THE RSVP

The RSVP—répondez s'il vous plaît, meaning the pleasure of your reply is requested—*is not optional*. As a guest, your first job is to reply to the invitation. Formal invitations, with RSVP dates and suggested methods, should be adhered to. For casual invitations, assume a reply is appreciated. If there is no RSVP date, no matter the medium of delivery you want to respond soon after you receive the invitation. While some events, like a coworker texting you the same day for beers after work, can warrant a last-minute reply, dinner parties and other more planned events necessitate a quick reply so your host can plan.

Failing to respond to an invitation is a big mistake. Responding with a "no" is just as important as delivering a "yes." The biggest challenge for a host is a "?" on the guest list. Head counts impact every aspect of entertaining—food, beverage, security, seating, lineup—and for larger work events, hosts are really on the hook. Don't be that question mark on their list; get your host a response as soon as possible.

When you see an RSVP listed, your host has included it to ensure they can plan well for the event. Ignoring it or making your own adjustments to it is not helpful or polite. A considerate guest responds as requested and by the date listed if one has been given, or sooner if you have an answer when the invitation arrives. If the manner is not specified, match the medium: a call for a phone call, a text for a text, and so on. For RSVPs requiring you to register for an event, be prompt with your registration. Replying "yes" but then not registering for an event isn't helpful. If your RSVP requires you to add additional information, be sure to include it!

> **PRO TIP**: Be a hero to your HR or internal event coordinator by replying to invitations to company events. In a world of "no replies," you will stand out quickly in the best way by consistently replying to invitations.

ACCESSIBILITY AND DIETARY RESTRICTIONS

When you do RSVP, that is the time to ask about accessibility, offer to bring a dish to meet your dietary needs, or inquire about gifts that might be part of the event, or anything else important for you to know. Always be prepared to accept what your host suggests in response to your question, knowing that you can decline the invitation if it doesn't meet your needs. "Oh, I'm sorry to hear that. Unfortunately, I won't be able to come this time, but I appreciate the invitation."

TYPES OF
BUSINESS-SOCIAL EVENTS

Each work event will have its own set of social standards based on your industry, the people involved and the level of formality; and, by paying attention, you can determine what to wear and how to behave in these social-professional settings. Use the Attire Guide on page 50 for details about what to wear for events.

BEERS AFTER WORK

Okay, so it doesn't have to be beer, but it's not uncommon for colleagues to meet up at the end of the day and grab a drink together before heading home. Whether it's a drink after work, a bite to eat, or just walking together to the subway, saying yes to these casual colleague meet-ups is a great way to build relationships with coworkers. You don't have to say yes to every casual invitation from colleagues, but joining in when possible is worth it.

ACTIVITIES WITH COWORKERS AND CLIENTS

Golf or yoga, anyone? The classic round of golf, tennis, 3-on-3 hoops, or that monthly poker game can be fun to engage in with coworkers and even clients. The etiquette here is to know what you're getting into and ensure you can truly participate. Of course, Don Draper can outfit himself with clubs and win the round, having never played golf, but the rest of us are not so fictional. If you can't play or don't know how, you should state this rather than try to fake it. The person inviting you will encourage you to come anyway or say something like "Maybe another time." This doesn't mean you've blown your only shot at bonding, but it's better than having promised something you can't back up. When you say yes to these invitations, it's important to show up on time and be ready to engage in the activity.

Sky boxes, courtside seats, homecoming, UFC, heck, even being a spectator at a golf tournament "GET IN THE HOLE!!!"—can get rowdy and when one of these events is mixed with your professional reputation, you want to make sure you're walking the line. Let the boss or the client be the one who yells the most. Keeping your outbursts to cheers not jeers will go a long way to maintaining a good impression.

THE IN-OFFICE CASUAL OFFICE PARTY

The in-office party, a favorite in days of olde at the Emily Post Institute, whether for someone's birthday, a company or life milestone, or because y'all just need a social moment with one another, is often a welcome break in a typical workday. We get many *Awesome Etiquette* podcast questions regarding participation and food consumption at these events. Each situation will be different, but we will always suggest that participation is good. It's genuinely important to bond with your team or colleagues and these small breaks are a great opportunity to do so. And while, yes, the work you do matters, and there can be real deadlines at stake that prevent you from joining, any office that takes the time to schedule an in-office party is supportive of colleague bonding, and the party itself is their encouragement for you to take the time for it. Join in when you can.

While this isn't a time to break out the lampshades and go wild or start doing impressions of your boss, it is a time to step away from the desk, the workbench, or the job site and enjoy a bit of refreshment and conversation with your coworkers.

THE COMPANY PICNIC

Whether it's actually a company picnic or a casual gathering at the boss's house, when we're invited to a casual event outside of the office, and, in some cases, we have been given plus-ones for a partner, date, friend, or our family to attend with us, we are straddling the work-life balance. If that picnic's at a beach or a pool party at a colleague's house, will you wear your swimsuit? Trunks or Speedo? Bikini, tankini, one-piece swimsuit? The divide between casual and professional and personal and professional can get blurry at these times, and having a good sense of what you are comfortable with is important. If you don't mix work and your personal life, you might choose to attend the event solo, and that's okay. (Though you should be prepared for people to ask where your partner or family are if they know you have one. "Just me today, they've got other plans" would be a fine answer.)

Bring with you anything that has been suggested or requested. If you're headed to a colleague's home, it's thoughtful to arrive with some flowers or a small hosting gift—especially if you've never been there—but it shouldn't be expected. Hosts invite guests for the pleasure of their company, not a potential hosting gift.

Allow yourself to enjoy the refreshments and participate in activities or games when you can. Your host, whether a colleague or your boss, hopes for you to enjoy yourself. It might feel like the work pressure is all around because these are your workmates, and you're used to having your professional self operating around them, but this is one of those times when it truly is okay to relax a little bit. You can always look to your host for inspiration if you're unsure how casually to relax into the event.

THE COMPANY TRIP

Some companies host their employees on vacations or holidays. The whole company (branch or team) is invited to and treated to time away. Think of yourself as a house guest of your boss or manager on this occasion. While the trip is meant for you to enjoy, you don't want to let go of yourself so much that you forget these are professional connections. Few bosses want to find out or, worse, witness firsthand spring break–esque behavior on the company dime. These trips are a big deal. Your company may bring in billions, but coordinating a large-scale vacation means that a lot of time, effort, and cost have been put in, and you want to show that you are grateful for and respectful of that time and effort. Be sure to thank the coordinators and hosts of the trip. This is one of those times when a handwritten thank-you note to the organizer and the head of the company would be a great way to show your appreciation. Remember that bonding can happen without jeopardizing your professional integrity, no matter how much you're encouraged to let loose. You will all still be back in the office next Monday.

DINNER WITH THE BOSS/CLIENT

We'll explore the ins and outs of a business meal in chapter 10, but it's worth mentioning here that a business meal, whether with a boss or client, is a time to shine. For some, it only happens once or twice in a lifetime; for others, it is a regular part of their business dealings. Feeling comfortable and confident that your dining skills are dialed in enough that all focus will be directed at the conversation and not your table manners is one of the keys to success in this classic business scenario. Please see chapter 10, "Business Meals," for specifics.

FORMAL OFFICE PARTY/CELEBRATION

Sometimes, the boss goes big. When your office holds a formal party or celebration, whether it's solely internal or clients and guests are included, you want to be at your best. This means knowing the attire required and who the other guests will be—not each specific guest, but will clients and their families be there? Will there be other branches of the firm attending? Are there prospects who have been invited to attend? Knowing what to expect can help you know what level of formality to strike in terms of your attire, behavior, and goal. Honoring a colleague? Then focus on the colleague, don't do anything that would take attention from them, and be sure to spend time congratulating them on their great success. Celebrating a great year? Bring your cheer, and take the time to comment on the great work folks did to help make such a banner achievement possible. Courting new clients? You'll want to come ready with business cards and a few pitches in your back pocket so that you're prepared if the conversation turns to potentially working together. If this function is black tie, you'll want to ensure your wardrobe is up to snuff. Thank goodness rental companies keep the latest styles in stock. See Black Tie, page 44.

CHIVALRY TODAY

Many people think of chivalry as a set of manners for how men should treat women or, more specifically, how gentlemen should treat ladies. Applying an idea like chivalry presents a challenge, particularly because there are elements of the tradition that are admirable and deserving of emulation, but business-social standards should never be dependent on or determined by gender. An element of chivalry is about recognizing a power difference and placing the responsibility of respect and consideration in the relationship on the person who holds more power—a powerful lesson for higher-ups to consider. Let's take a deeper look at this tradition and how it functions in business today.

TRADITIONAL VERSUS MODERN-DAY CHIVALRY

Today, we have the opportunity to adjust and apply gendered courtesies for business in new ways. If these courtesies were not on your radar, take note, as some traditionalists appreciate them greatly.

OLD CHIVALRY: Offer your seat to a lady.
NEW CHIVALRY: Offer your seat to someone who could use it more than you.

OLD CHIVALRY: Stand when a lady approaches or leaves the table.
NEW CHIVALRY: Stand when anyone joins or leaves your table in more formal situations.

OLD CHIVALRY: The man pays the bill.
NEW CHIVALRY: If you would like to pay, make a clear invitation or offer before the start of the meal to pay for the others so you assume the role of host.

OLD CHIVALRY: A gentleman helps a lady with her coat.
NEW CHIVALRY: Anyone may offer to help someone with a coat.

OLD CHIVALRY: A man orders for a lady.
NEW CHIVALRY: When appropriate, the host orders for the table.

OLD CHIVALRY: The man walks on the street side of the sidewalk.
NEW CHIVALRY: Walk where it feels natural and secure and lend an arm to anyone who is unstable.

OLD CHIVALRY: The man goes first into elevators and through heavy revolving doors.

NEW CHIVALRY: Anyone can offer to help with a door or, in the case of a revolving door, offer to get it moving.

If traditional gendered courtesies matter greatly to you, or you sense they matter greatly to someone you are interacting with, *offering* to perform the courtesy is the way to go. "May I hold your chair for you?" instead of "I'll get that for you" or just performing the gesture. This allows the other person to retain the agency. "Why, thank you so much, yes" or "That's okay, I've got it. Thank you, though."

TOASTING AND SPEECH GIVING

Toasts are commonly offered or heard at celebratory occasions. They are typically given at the start of a meal once everyone is seated, but can happen at any point (although smack in the middle of a course is a little odd). However, it's never inconsiderate to let folks tuck in for a bit or even wait for a moment between courses—the transition to dessert is another ideal option. You may toast with any beverage in your glass—just as long as it isn't empty! Ginger ale and sparkling cider make nice substitutions for Champagne, a classic formal toasting drink. Water is also perfectly acceptable. We don't advise you to issue a toast if you're new to a company or lower down in the company hierarchy. It's not that you can't. *Anyone* can give a toast, but often, the host or other manager and CEO-level employees are either prepared to do so or not prepared for *you* to do so, and thus your toast might come as a surprise. If it's not your event, consider the act thoughtfully, observing who is there, how your toast may impact them, and whether they've had the opportunity to issue their own toast before you take the opportunity. If there's any question in your mind, ask the host before grabbing the mic.

When offering a toast, stand if you can, raise your glass, and say what you wish. The very best toasts are short and, let's face it, often sentimental or thoughtful. In longer toasts, you might tell a story or make a certain point. Always stay focused on the honoree or close to the objective of the toast. Remember, people may be waiting to eat, so don't prolong it too much. At the end, raise your glass and say, "To _____!" (good work, longevity, family, success, a specific person, the company . . .) and then take a sip. Do not drain your glass. And do not slam the glass down afterward.

If someone is toasting you, do not drink to the toast. (It was traditionally considered conceited.) Nod or smile in thanks. You may offer a toast of thanks in return and drink to that. "A toast to you and your generosity!" Or you may simply raise your glass in thanks after everyone has had a sip in your honor, and then after you've raised your glass in thanks, take a sip yourself.

If you mistakenly drink to a toast, even though it is technically wrong, rest assured that this is unlikely to be noticed or considered conceited today.

VALET

Suppose the event you attend has a valet service set up. In that case, you'll give your key to the valet (if you have valuables in your car, you can lock them away in the truck or the console and give the valet key, which will only let the valet operate the vehicle and not unlock the trunk, console, or glove box). Avoid saying anything cheeky, like "Don't scratch it." Valets are usually top-notch, and you want to give them the benefit of the doubt. Your valet will give you a ticket; keep it. When you pick the car back up at the end of the event is the time to tip. We tip to reward good service, not to bribe people for it. Depending on the venue and your budget, $5 or more will be appropriate.

EXITING AND EVENT FOLLOW-UP

As you exit an event, you always want to say goodbye to your host if you can, and if not, be sure to say goodbye to your team and other colleagues who also attended. If you aren't at an event with lots of your coworkers, then you'll want to gauge whether it's necessary to find folks with whom you've spoken during the event to issue a goodbye, based on the conversations you've had and the potential for follow-up. If you really want Brenda's business, finding her before you leave and saying something like, "I'm headed out, but I really wanted to let you know how much I enjoyed speaking with you this evening. I'll be following up next week" is well worth the extra few minutes it takes.

After the event, you'll want to do two types of follow-up. The first is a thank-you to the organizers or, if you were someone's guest, a thank-you note to them for bringing you. The second is to follow up with anyone who gave you their card or with whom you said there was more to discuss or work to do together. If you don't, just think of all that networking effort you've made throughout the event going *poof!* The follow-up is key to making the networking you've just done count.

Dear Werner,

Thank you for a great event on Friday; I enjoyed attending, and I hope there will be more opportunities like this in the future. You and your team did a wonderful job.
I really appreciate what you and the Chamber of Commerce do to connect local businesses.

Sincerely,
Serge

Dear Sierra,

It was a pleasure meeting you at the Chamber of Commerce mixer on Friday. I was very impressed to hear what Beta is up to with vertical takeoff, and I know our investors would be keen to learn more. If you're still interested in speaking further, I'd love to schedule a call sometime this month to discuss details and determine the right time to bring everyone together.
So glad to have met you, and I'm looking forward to speaking with you again soon.

Best,
Elsbeth

We can hear some of you thinking *overkill* with a good ol' eye roll on that thank-you note. That note of thanks is a worthwhile act. Even if it seems simple and Pollyanna-like, you'd be surprised at how easy it is for you and its positive impact on the host who put in so much work.

REFERENCE GUIDES

A GREAT HOST CHECKLIST

Hosts take care of their guests from start to finish when it comes to an event.

- ☐ Invite well—the formality and details should match the intended event exactly. See Invitations, page 205, for more details.

- ☐ Prepare, prepare, prepare—from prepping well to being ready with contingency plans. It's also good to prepare for guests' needs by asking them about any accommodations, such as accessibility or dietary restrictions.

- ☐ Your mood sets the tone. Be sure that you're striking the tone you intend.

- ☐ Greet your guests at the door or, if you have someone greeting at the door, greet each guest as they enter the party space.

- ☐ Make introductions when guests don't know each other. See Business Introductions, page 196.

- ☐ Check in. Circulate the event to see how your guests are doing.

- ☐ Lead your guests, especially for transitional moments and dinner table conversation. Guests will look to you for cues, so don't hesitate to guide them through the event without micromanaging their experience.

- ☐ Spend equal time with your guests. While there may be a few guests of honor, or those you want to treat with extra attention, no guest should feel like they didn't get to spend time with their host (unless the event is huge and the guest list too big to spend time with everyone).

- ☐ Be flexible. Accidents will happen, and mistakes will be made. Handle them with poise and, if possible, good humor; they won't be a focal point of the event.

- ☐ Bid your guests goodbye and thank them for coming and any contributions on their way out.

A GREAT GUEST CHECKLIST

Guests bring their best selves to the party. Here's how to be the best guest.

- ☐ Respond promptly and in full to the invitation; avoid waffling on a response.

- ☐ Show up on time, dressed appropriately. There is no "fashionably late" in business. Do not show up with uninvited guests in tow.

- ☐ Participate well, whether listening, dancing, talking, watching, dining, or doing something else. Engage with others, bring your full attention to the gathering, and join in.

- ☐ Don't take advantage. Your host is doing their best to take care of you and be generous. Don't take more than your share or more than is reasonable, whether of food, resources, or someone's time.

- ☐ Thank your host. A genuine expression of gratitude is a must at the end of the event. Find your host to say your thank-yous and goodbyes. You might not be able to for a large bash, and that's okay, but for smaller affairs, don't just skip out without speaking with them.

- ☐ Follow up with a thank-you note appropriate to the occasion.

BEST PRACTICES FOR BUSINESS-SOCIAL EVENTS

Here are some of the most important things to aim for when attending a business-social event.

1. Set social goals beforehand. For example: Commit to introducing yourself to at least three people or discovering something new about a colleague or client.

2. Branch out from your colleagues and mingle. It's the best place to find new opportunities.

3. Only take your share of food and drink and know your own limits when it comes to alcohol.

4. Don't talk with your mouth full or chew with your mouth open.

5. Be generous with your time and attention. When you see someone approaching, make eye contact and make space for them to join the group.

6. Avoid negative gossip, airing dirty laundry, or discussing controversial topics. It can reflect poorly on you.

7. Follow up in a timely and professional manner when appropriate. If you made a connection, this is an opportunity to build on it.

WHEN IT'S TIME TO EXIT

Magic words can help you escape difficult, uncomfortable, and awkward situations. The next time you find yourself thinking, *How will I extract myself from this situation?*, look for an opportunity to deploy *excuse me*, or *pardon me*, or *I'm sorry, but . . .* and see if that starts to get things moving in the right direction—politely. Keep your tone of voice easy and relaxed.

When . . .
. . . someone is monopolizing your time:
"Pardon me, I've lost track of time, I should really mingle with some other guests."

. . . the conversation needs redirecting:
"I'm sorry, I know this is out of left field, but I'd love to hear your thoughts on XYZ."

. . . someone is speaking inappropriately to you or about someone else:
"Please, you'll have to excuse me. Take care." While literally leaving the conversation space.

. . . you are pressed for time:
"I'm so sorry, I've just noticed the time and I have to end it here. It's been lovely speaking with you . . ." or whatever is appropriate if there is follow-up to be done.

TOP BUSINESS TRAVEL TIPS

1. Know your itinerary and the goal of the trip.

2. You are responsible for getting yourself to every engagement on time, whether that's a flight, a meeting, or an event. Communicate with your hosts, colleagues, or others if you will be absent or late.

3. Consider your actions, attire, and words as representative of your organization from when you leave your home to when you return.

4. Bring business cards and have a designated place, like a cardholder to put the ones you may receive.

5. Know your company's travel policies regarding tipping, incidentals, and other expenses related to the trip.

6. Keep business as the focus of the trip.

SAMPLE INVITATIONS WITH RSVP REQUEST

CASUAL DINNER INVITATION

Please come for dinner
on Friday, April 20th
at 7 pm
34 Fuller Street
Edgartown

RSVP: Emily
233-659-1547

FORMAL DINNER INVITATION

Mr. and Mrs. Chival Russ
request the pleasure of
Mr. and Mrs. Colin Bailey's
company at dinner
on Friday, the twenty-second of July
at seven o'clock
34 Fuller Street
Edgartown

RSVP: 233-659-1547

CHAPTER 10

Business Meals

A well-choreographed meal is a thing of beauty indeed, and it certainly facilitates the bonding and business at hand when it comes to a business meal. Being able to participate well and confidently in one? Well, that's another matter and table manners really are the key. Why do table manners even exist? Because people find eating a bit gross unless it's carefully contained. This isn't about being prissy. It's about being practical and finding ways to keep the focus on the conversation and not how you're getting food and drink into your mouth.

Sauce on your cheek or a unique grip on your utensils can create distractions for people to have to ignore in order to focus on you and the conversation. This is why, to enjoy one another's company or to have a productive meeting over a meal, we need table manners to smooth the way. Table manners are an elegantly mechanical part of the meal that allows us to focus on and engage in the important conversation at hand. It is not worth losing someone's attention at a business meal because of distracting behavior at the table. Even if you end up securing the deal despite some less than stellar table manners, you want to be remembered for your brilliant ideas and business sense, not as the person who stabbed the steak as if she'd just hunted it down.

The table has long been a place where business has been conducted. And while today we customarily wait until dessert to discuss business topics, we have coupled food and drink with business for millennia. There are legendary stories of industry giants testing potential new executives by evaluating their table manners. Think what you might think about choosing to test someone this way during an interview, but the simplicity of it is pretty impressive. Manners matter, not because some stuffy, elitist person says they do, but because they are often rooted in practicality and serve us well. They are meant to help us *be* our best selves, not just *present* our best selves.

Whether you dine in Michelin-starred restaurants or the next dinner with a client is your first multicourse meal ever, we want you to feel confident and comfortable navigating the business meal experience. By honing our table manners skills, we ensure we don't fork our careers over dinner.

THE ONE THING

Right from the get-go, we want you to understand the most important table manner in the world of dining etiquette:

DO NOT OPEN YOUR MOUTH IF THERE IS FOOD (OR DRINK) IN IT.

This one can easily be a dealbreaker. We hear it not just from business owners but also from employees, clients, and customers. Repeatedly, they tell us they will write someone off for chewing with their mouth open or talking with their mouth full at a business meal. Showing or—even worse—showering people with the food that you are masticating is gross and can create too big a hurdle for someone to ignore. If you can keep your lips closed as you chew and drink, do.

If someone asks you a question while your mouth is full, signal with your index finger that you'll be just a moment while you chew and swallow. In more casual settings, you might cover your mouth with your hand or napkin and say (carefully, without releasing any food) "Pardon me" or "One sec."

The exception: if you are not physically able to chew with your mouth closed, do your best to use your napkin to obscure what you can, and just like with those who can close their mouths all the way, wait to talk until you've finished chewing and have swallowed your bite. No one should ever grimace or wince at someone who *cannot* close their mouth while chewing; doing so is just plain rude.

CASUAL BUSINESS DINING

There will be many moments when you dine with your colleagues casually. Grabbing Chipotle, Al's French Fries (sorry, we couldn't resist a Vermont shout-out), phở, or a sandwich was a regular occurrence around the Emily Post Institute before we switched to remote work. In other offices, it's the company cafeteria, the cart out front or in the lobby, or the diner down the road. Your table manners will still matter in these casual settings, but they don't have to be formal. You're not hosting a client and, unless your boss joins you, you're having a relaxing moment of camaraderie on your home turf.

Your willingness to eat alongside your coworkers can be a huge boon to your relationships with them. It is a way to build a network within your own company. If you want to get to know your coworkers, use meals and breaks during the workday as a time to connect. "Hey, want to eat together? I was thinking of having lunch around one thirty today."

Three things in particular to remember when dining casually with coworkers, whether you're out to eat or on-site during the workday:

1. **DON'T GROSS OTHERS OUT.** Just because it's casual doesn't mean you want to cross into being gross. If you can, keep your mouth closed when food or beverage is in it. Use a paper towel or napkin to quickly take care of any sauce or juices that have dripped on your face or hands, which can look gross to others. And be mindful of any food that gets on the surface you're eating at.

2. **KEEP IT CLEAN.** The office kitchen, eating areas, and even your desk should all be left clean. Clean up any mess that was created while prepping your food before you sit down to eat. And of course, clean up after yourself when you're finished eating, leaving the space as it was or nicer.

3. **MIND YOUR MANNERS.** Saying "excuse me" and asking for things to be passed—or moving around someone rather than reaching over them or their food—are two great manners to be used frequently in casual workday dining situations.

EATING AND DRINKING
WHILE STANDING AND TALKING

The cocktail hour and mixer events present us with a balancing act for sure. Drinks, small plates, finger food, napkins, cellphones, and business cards. It can be tempting to gather refreshments and park yourself at a high-top table for the duration, but that's not what this work event is for. Here are some tips to help you stay engaged and be polite with the food and drink you enjoy.

- Get a napkin and a spare when you get food from the buffet or a passed tray.

- Don't overload your little buffet plate. You can always go back again; just remember to use a new plate each time.

- Keep your right hand free so you can easily entertain a handshake—holding a drink in your left hand keeps your right from getting wet and cold from an iced beverage.

- If you have multiple items, look for a high-top or other table to set some items down.

- Do not double dip—this includes turning that carrot around.

- Do not leave a mess. If you've been gathered around a high-top table, avoid leaving napkins, toothpicks, straws, and other garbage items on the table. Find a trash can or a clearing tray where items are being collected.

TAKING YOUR SEAT

Always sit at your host's invitation and never before. In a home, wait for your invitation to the table before taking your seat; at a restaurant, wait for the host to bring you to the table. If you are meeting someone or a group, wait for them or at least one other person to arrive before taking a seat or asking to be seated. If you are serving yourself from a buffet at someone's home or an event, take your seat as soon as you've filled your plate (but wait to begin eating; more on that soon). In the most formal situations, everyone sits down simultaneously at the host's invitation.

If place cards aren't set, ask your host: "Where would you like me/us to sit?" In business, we often remove gendered courtesies such as the tradition of standing for a lady when she approaches or rises from the table. To recognize everyone on even playing ground, we advise either standing for anyone who approaches or rises from the table or not performing the gesture for anyone.

SEATING ARRANGEMENTS

Where you sit and whether it matters depends on the purpose of the gathering, the formality of the meal at hand, and whether there is a host present. This section focuses on business meals where the meal and the socializing are more important than the business.

WITHOUT A HOST, CASUAL SETTING

Informally, with no host, like when grabbing lunch with some colleagues, there is no rule to follow. Sit where you like. You don't have to, but *letting* someone else go first and have the comfy seat or the best view is a classy option. Any opportunity to offer others the best seat is an opportunity to show consideration and care for them.

WITH A HOST, CASUAL TO FORMAL SETTINGS

When there is a host, they determine the seating arrangement. The host takes the head of a rectangular table or the seat to the left of the "best seat" at a round or square table and places their guest of honor to their right. The best seat at a table is the seat with a good view or one that affords the most privacy and minimizes distractions while dining. Definitely not a seat that would be easily bumped by waitstaff or patrons.

When more than six people are expected, place cards can guide guests to the correct seat. Place cards should never be rearranged by guests. If no place cards are used, a host should offer directions individually or invite guests to sit where they choose. Unless a specific protocol is observed, guests are not organized by rank for business-social meals. While the head of the visiting organization will be seated in the guest-of-honor seat, after that, a host may choose where each guest sits, again, unless protocol dictates otherwise. Business meals that include spouses, partners, or plus-ones usually fall on the social side of business, and seating follows social protocols, mixing up guests who came together to provide a dynamic social environment. Take note, couples, your host will likely choose to split you up for the meal.

HOLDING A CHAIR FOR SOMEONE

Holding a chair for someone is a classic manner and shows care for fellow dinners. Traditionally, this was a gendered courtesy you would not use in most professional situations. If you are with a traditionalist who might appreciate the gesture, simply ask permission to perform the courtesy: "May I get your chair for you?"

To hold a chair for someone, stand behind it and pull it back from the table. As the person slides in and sits down, you may gently slide the chair forward, not hitting the back of their legs, while they sit.

PRO TIP: A waiter may offer to slide a table away from a wall or bench seat to allow a diner to sit, then slide it back once they are seated. Other patrons should not attempt this. Leave it to the restaurant staff.

POSTURE MATTERS

No elbows on the table? Wellllllllllllllll, that's not entirely true. Emily Post thought it painted a flattering picture to lean into polite conversation when you weren't actually eating. The bigger issue that the rule against elbows on the table is meant to address is bad posture at the table. The kinds of elbows on the table that should be avoided are those used to prop up a collapsing posture, as a pillow, or to anchor down the forearm while using a utensil. Avoid these at all costs.

To the fullest extent that anyone can, sitting upright at the table while dining with others is the goal. No, not ramrod stiff, but aligning your head over your shoulders and shoulders over your hips will align the spine and activate the eyes. Not only does it make eating easier, freeing the mouth, jaw, neck, shoulders, and arms to do the complicated work of cutting, scooping, carrying, chewing, swallowing, and talking, but it also draws you forward and into the shared social space you occupy with other diners.

PRO TIP: Keep your back off the chair's back when eating and talking at the table. In the Victorian era, this was the rule at the dinner table. The change in posture will be visible to those you are dining and speaking with.

ON NAPKINS

When you take your seat, place your napkin in your lap. In more formal situations, wait for your host to do so and follow suit. Linen napkins should be draped over the lap and folded in half, either in a rectangle or a triangle. Place the folded edge against your belt line. The napkin should provide coverage for your clothes and a place to wipe your fingers and face as needed. See Napkin Manners in the Reference Guide, page 240.

> **PRO TIP**: With the napkin draped over your lap, peel back the top layer from the edge and use the inside portion to wipe your hands and fingers. This keeps the outside of the napkin clean, both looking good and protecting your clothes from any mess on the napkin.

If you leave the table, lay your napkin loosely gathered or naturally folded to the left of your place setting. Use "LLL" to remember "leaving loosely left." Do not leave your napkin on the back of your chair or on the seat of your chair. It could result in staining an upholstered dining chair and possibly transferring any mess from the napkin to your clothing when you take your seat again. Despite what you may have heard, leaving your napkin on the back of your chair does not signal that you are returning to the table.

NAVIGATING THE SETTING

The American table setting is well-established. By applying some basic knowledge, you should be able to confidently set or navigate any place setting. Here are the standard features of the American place setting.

1. You are provided only the utensils you will need for the meal.

2. Each group of utensils will be placed in the order they are to be used, arranged from the outside of the setting in toward the plate.

3. Except for the oyster fork, dessert fork, and dessert spoon, forks are always on the left and knives and spoons are grouped together on the right. Knives are placed next to the plate, the blade facing in, with spoons to their right.

4. The bread and butter plate is always on the top left.

5. Drinks are always on the top right of the setting.

6. Special utensils, such as escargot tongs for holding snail shells, grapefruit spoons with serrated edges for citrus, lobster and crab crackers, and picks used for specific foods will either be at your setting or brought out for the appropriate course.

7. Favors might be at the top of your setting at a special meal. If it's a dessert item, like chocolate or candies, wait to open it until after the dessert has been served and eaten. If it's something fun, like a crackers or a game, save playing with it for after the dessert has been eaten. You may also take these favors with you when you leave. Leave yours at the top of your setting if you don't want it.

See Reference Guide, page 239, for easy ways to help you remember how to navigate your setting. It's important to know that utensils have their designated place, purpose, and order of use. Please see *Emily Post's Etiquette, The Centennial Edition* for full descriptions of the most commonly used utensils and hosting advice on how to set the table.

HOLDING AND USING UTENSILS

When we are dining with others, smooth, even, and dexterous movements will paint a picture of confidence and ease. These kinds of movements are why we believe there is a proper way to hold your utensils, one that will give you the best control over both your implements and the food you're eating. This method allows you to be controlled and precise, and it has been well-tested over time. The following grips on your utensils will allow you to function well at the table and to take part in a tradition dating back thousands of years with grace and elegance.

YOUR GRIP WHEN CUTTING Hold your knife in your dominant hand, with the blade facing down. Because it is the most dangerous utensil, you want full control over it. Close your middle, ring, and pinky fingers around the knife's handle. Use your thumb to grasp the knife securely. Place your index finger on the back of the handle, just above where the blade and handle join.

Hold the fork—tines down—with the handle in the palm of your hand. Close your middle, ring, and pinky fingers around the fork's handle. Place your index finger on the back of the handle, just above where the head and handle join. Use your thumb to secure your grasp of the fork.

CUTTING Use the fork to hold the item in place and the knife to cut or slice it. Always keep your elbows in while cutting—you don't want to bump your neighbor, and having your elbows out looks like you need to gain leverage on the food, which is less elegant and can draw attention. The advantage of the grip suggested is that it allows you to exert precise pressure with your knife and fork without needing elbow leverage.

YOUR GRIP WHEN SCOOPING When not using a knife, hold the fork or spoon in your dominant hand with the tines or bowl facing up. The handle rests on top of the purlicue of your hand (the curved space between your thumb and index finger). Your middle finger supports from underneath by resting against the neck of the spoon (where the bowl and handle join). Your index finger rests on top of this same spot and the thumb rests naturally on the side or top of the spoon's handle to balance. The ring and pinky fingers support the middle finger by resting under it. It's a similar grip to how many people hold a pen or pencil.

SCOOPING OR LIFTING FOOD WITH YOUR FORK OR SPOON When using the fork or spoon to scoop, scoop up and under the item and away from yourself. This helps prevent any sauce or oil splashes from hitting you. Don't scoop too big a bite. Getting into a balancing act with the food on your fork or spoon will rarely end well, especially if you rush to catch a falling bite. The side of your fork may also be used to cut or slice something such as a soft lasagna or a scalloped potato dish. But nothing that would require effort—that would mean using a knife.

RESTING POSITION BETWEEN BITES It's a classic table manner to always set your knife down with the blade facing the center of the plate (or toward you) in the resting position when you are not using it for cutting. For a right-handed diner, this would be the top right side of your plate. Once a utensil has been used, it is never placed on the table, always on your plate.

**AMERICAN
RESTING POSITION**

**EUROPEAN/CONTINENTAL
RESTING POSITION**

EUROPEAN VERSUS AMERICAN DINING

For both European (Continental) and American dining styles, when cutting, you hold the knife in your dominant hand and the fork in your other hand. Either the American or Continental eating style may be used, and you might even choose to switch between the two during the same course in a hybridized style. While you should not switch styles when visiting Europe, it would go unnoticed at most American tables.

AMERICAN-STYLE EATING

After you cut a piece of food, lay your knife across the top right "corner" of your plate, with the blade facing you. Then, transfer your fork to your dominant hand turned tines up so you can eat the piece you cut. When it's time to cut again, you transfer your fork back to your other hand, tines down, and pick up your knife in your dominant hand. Generally, you keep your fork in your dominant hand to pierce or scoop food when not cutting. To rest your utensils, leave your knife across the top of your plate with its handle to the right. Rest your fork with the handle at the four and the tines up, pointing toward the ten. This tells a server you aren't finished yet.

CONTINENTAL-STYLE (EUROPEAN-STYLE) EATING

When using a knife and fork Continental style, your knife remains in your dominant hand, and your fork, in the other, tines down throughout the meal. You pierce each bite of food with your fork and bring it to your mouth with the tines pointing down, or, in the case of something like mashed potatoes, use your knife to push a small portion onto the back of your fork. To rest your utensils, in the Continental style, place the fork (tines up) and knife (blade facing you) on the upper left and right sides of the plate with their handles angled out.

OTHER DINING DETAILS

- You can use your knife as a "pusher" to help transfer a bite onto your fork. Should you need to pierce something round and roll-y, like a cherry tomato or olive, use your knife to brace the item and then pierce it carefully with your fork, going against the pressure of the knife to keep the item from rolling. Once pierced, a cherry tomato can be tamed by slicing it in half before eating it, ensuring that no seeds go squirting out of your lips.

- Never pierce anything with the tip of your knife or eat from your knife.

- Avoid gesturing with your utensils. Set them down to gesture with your hands in conversation.

- Do not scrape or lick food off your utensils—and certainly not off the plate, even if you use your finger. If you want to get every last morsel of flavor, you can use a piece of bread to sop up the last of the sauce. Break off a piece, spear it with your fork, and use it to soak up the last bits of deliciousness.

- Don't scrape your teeth on utensils; the sound can irritate fellow diners and it's not good for your teeth.

- When you remove the utensil from your mouth, close your lips around it to contain the food.

FINISHED POSITION

When you are finished eating a course, set your utensils down so that the fork and knife handles are pointed at the four if your plate were a clock face with the fork (tines up) and knife tip (sharp edge of the blade toward you, not the diners across from you) pointing to the ten. A spoon is placed on the right side of the underplate when you're finished using it. If there is no underplate, leave it in the bowl, the handle pointed at the four if the bowl were a clock face. This tells your server or host you are finished with the course and makes it easy for them to clear your plate from the right side (which is traditional) while securing your utensils so they don't fall.

**FINISHED
POSITION**

DRINKING PROPERLY

Sipping is the name of the game when dining with others for a business meal or when attending a mixer event for work. Slamming your drink back can be satisfying, but it's inappropriate for a business function.

TAKE SMALL SIPS. Small sips allow you to avoid college-kegger vibes and can help you engage in conversation more effectively. You won't be trying to recover from a giant gulp when that brilliant thought strikes and you have something to say or when someone asks you a question. If your drink contains alcohol, small sips also allow you to pace yourself.

NEVER UPEND YOUR GLASS. Tilting your head back to drain every last drop is inappropriate in business situations.

AVOID USING YOUR BEVERAGE TO WASH DOWN FOOD. Chew, swallow, and then take a sip. And in a business (or any semiformal or formal) environment, do not use your beverage to swish out food stuck in your teeth. Go to the restroom to take care of it.

AVOID MAKING LOUD NOISES WHEN USING A STRAW. As you reach the end of your drink, resist the temptation to suck down your beverage in one long, slow draw, never letting the straw leave your lips. Instead, take small sips and engage in conversation in between. It's not a race.

POUR YOUR DRINK INTO A GLASS. Do not drink from the bottle, whether beer, soda, or juice. Use a glass.

USE A COASTER. When you're having cocktails in someone's home or a club environment, always look for a coaster or cocktail napkin to put under your drink when you set it down. If you don't see one, ask if the host has any.

DO NOT PUT YOUR PINKY OUT LIKE A LITTLE FLAG. (We see you, Drew Bledsoe.) It is the biggest misconception in the world of etiquette that affectations like this are proper. They can look simultaneously affectatious, arrogant, and prissy. And no, you do not need your pinky out to "balance the cup" when drinking from a handled teacup. Hold the handle and tuck your fingers under it.

ALCOHOLIC DRINKS

When alcohol and work come together, we advise the "One-Drink Rule." Stick to one alcoholic drink, if any, when business is involved. There are many factors that can influence how alcohol impacts you on any given day—sleep, what you've eaten that day, altitude, and medications. Since you never can tell how it will impact you, the safe choice is to stick to one drink—and yes, we mean one drink throughout the event. For a meal where you might be served several courses paired with several alcoholic beverages throughout, it's okay to take a few small sips from each pairing, or you may choose to engage one and politely decline the rest. The idea is to keep the overall consumption throughout the event to roughly one drink's worth.

If you're asked to order the wine, ask people what their preferences are. Absent other information, pairing reds with red-meat courses and whites with lighter courses, like fish, is traditional. Today, many people will order a bottle of red and white for the table. If you don't know wines well, do a bit of research before you arrive at the restaurant. In business, you try not to give up control of the wine list if you're hosting or tasked with ordering it.

How do you say no to alcohol at a work event? I always feel pressured when others partake. You are not alone, friend. It can feel like peer pressure when your colleagues are saying yes, and you're asking for a glass of water or ginger ale. First, no shame. Millions of people abstain from alcohol for any number of reasons. And there are even plenty of people who drink socially but not *on the clock*. Being honest and true to your choice while not judging others if they choose to drink alcohol is the key to moving through the situation and hopefully receiving the same respect in return. Here are some sample scripts to help when you feel the pressure:

YOU: "Seltzer for me, please."
HOST: "No wine for you, Jed? Come on, it's a Château Le Pin! When do you ever get the chance to have one of these?"
YOU: "That is a *very* nice bottle of wine and while I appreciate the encouragement, I'm going to stick with my seltzer tonight."

GOAL: You want to compliment the generosity, convivial spirit, and rarity or quality of the offer (if there is any), especially if your host is providing it, but it's still okay to decline alcohol even if it's one of the rarest in the world.

PACING YOURSELF

Pay attention to the pace of your eating and drinking during a business meal. There are no expectations that you finish your meal at exactly the same bite as your boss or client, but it is nice to keep pace with your dining companions so that you can all move through the meal together. If you are a particularly slow or fast eater, practice matching the pace of those around you when you eat in non-business-meal situations. There is no need to sit idle or to rush through the meal, shoveling food into your mouth. Here are some tips for slowing down or speeding up your eating without rushing.

TO SLOW DOWN	TO SPEED UP
Chew and swallow each bite before preparing the next.	Prepare the next bite while you chew.
Take the time to talk between bites.	Eat while you listen to others talk.
Periodically set your utensils down.	Stop talking and focus on eating.

COURSES YOU MAY ENCOUNTER

Casual dining may consist of anywhere from one to three courses, whereas semiformal occasions can range from three to five courses, and formal occasions could have anywhere from three to six or more courses served. Very few at-home dinners are six-course, gourmet meals these days—though some might like to attempt the challenge! (We salute you.) Whether you are at a restaurant, at someone's home, or choosing a menu for an event, the following are the courses you may encounter.

HORS D'OEUVRE Generally, a one- or two-bite item that's served before a meal and is passed by a server or set out either in groupings or at a buffet for guests to serve themselves. Platters of crudités, shrimp cocktail, satay or caprese skewers, chips of all kinds with dips, bowls of spiced and sugared nuts, cheese, and charcuterie boards are all regularly seen at work events and even at meals hosted by a colleague in their home.

AMUSE-BOUCHE French for "to amuse the mouth," an amuse-bouche is typically just one bite. It is meant to delight, prepare your palate, and leave you wanting more. It's normally reserved for meals with four or more courses (it being first) and is served at the table. Often sent out by the chef, it's not something you will select or see on your bill. Typically, this course is served at a high-end restaurant, not in someone's home.

APPETIZER/FIRST COURSE Antipasti, starter, first course, or appetizer, this is usually the first plated menu item. It can be heavy or light, hot or cold, but it should balance and work with the other courses. While soups and salads can be courses on their own, separate from an appetizer, many people choose to serve (or order) either dish as an appetizer. These small plates can be anything from spring rolls with a dipping sauce to crostini with thick spreads or an assortment of meats, fruits, and cheeses. For anything even remotely semiformal, they will likely be eaten with a fork and knife or a spoon (or specialty utensils). When dining out, it's fine from an etiquette perspective to choose an appetizer as your entrée, but double-check with the waitstaff that it's okay.

SOUP AND SALAD Soup is usually served early in the meal, as opposed to after an entrée, whereas salad can be eaten before or after an entrée. You may find an etiquette fanatic or foodie who will debate the merits of the "French" style (salad after the entrée) versus the "American" style (salad before the entrée). Don't let the pompousness of such statements intimidate you; it's a matter of personal preference, not correctness.

FISH A lighter protein, fish was regularly served as its own course before a meat entrée when long, multicourse meals were in fashion. Today, it is often a main course, with shellfish being more common as a first course. Fish is often served with specialty utensils, whether crackers or picks or a fish fork and fish knife. A discard bowl should be provided for bones, heads, tails, or shells. See *Emily Post's Etiquette, The Centennial Edition* for how to debone a fish.

MAIN COURSE/ENTREE This is the one course you will have no matter where the meal occurs. The main course is sometimes called the most filling course and often consists of some type of meat or protein-heavy item served with one to two side dishes, or a one-pot dish (such as shepherd's pie).

DESSERT, COFFEE, AND AFTER-DINNER DRINKS Dessert might range from fruit and cheese or cookies to pies, cakes, tarts, truffles or chocolates, pastries, and all puddings, trifles, and ice creams or sorbets, even nuts. Espresso, cappuccino, macchiato, regular drip coffee, decaf coffee, and tea or infusions are all options after dinner. Though not traditionally served after dinner, tea is becoming a common option, especially herbal varieties. When serving coffee, include sugar, sugar substitutes, cream, milk, and nondairy milk. After-dinner drinks, like port, sherry, and brandy, can add a distinctive touch to a fine meal, but do not order one if your host has not. Only order an after-dinner drink that contains alcohol if your host has offered it.

THE MENU

When you are dining out in business, there are some etiquette considerations regarding the menu and ordering. We'll look at what hosts and guests should consider when ordering a business meal. Before the meal, check in with your colleagues or boss about which courses and beverages are the best options. Doing so will prevent you from being out of sync with the group. If you're not hosting, follow your host's lead at the table. If they order an appetizer and an entree, it's fine for you to do so as well. If they do not order an after-dinner drink, don't order one for yourself. A host will offer if there is something they won't partake in but would like guests to feel comfortable ordering. "Please feel free to order dessert and any after-dinner drinks you'd like."

HOW TO CHOOSE

AS A GUEST The most important thing to look for when ordering from a menu is something you will enjoy; something familiar and manageable is a safe bet. It's best to pick midprice items from the menu unless your host indicates otherwise. If your host has suggested a special on the menu, or something the restaurant is known for, don't be shy about ordering that item. In many ways, this is the "go-ahead" you've been given.

AS A HOST when ordering, take the lead on menu conversation and considerations. Make some comments about what guests are welcome to order or about what you're planning to order. "I'm going to do the mussels as a main dish, even though it's an appetizer; please don't hesitate to order both a main and an appetizer if you wish." As the host, be prepared for a guest to order anything, including the most expensive item. While most guests need encouragement to do so, it's best to be prepared that they might, rather than count on them not to.

> **PRO TIP**: Don't cede control of the wine menu; we've learned over the years that a particular type of jerk thinks it's funny when ordering wine for the table to choose the most expensive bottle, sticking their host with the bill. Downright rotten! This is bad behavior, not a funny joke. Avoid being the punch line by playing your role and ordering yourself.

ALLERGIES AND RESTRICTIONS If you have a food allergy or certain dietary restrictions for personal, health, or religious reasons, it is best to let the server know so they can alert the kitchen. These are different from preferences and for safety reasons always come first.

SUBSTITUTIONS If you require substitutions, it's best to find one dish on the menu that you can eat and have it as your backup dish in case the kitchen does not allow substitutions. With that in mind, it's okay to ask, "Would the chef be willing to prepare this without cream?" or "Would the chef be willing to pair the carrots and green beans with the chicken instead of the Brussels sprouts?" If the answer is no, you've got your backup choice ready to go. Whenever possible, keep it simple, and order off the menu.

HOW TO ORDER WELL

AS THE HOST Ask first if your guest or group wants you to order for them. This doesn't mean you choose menu items but that you will place your guest's or the table's order with the server by saying, "My guest/my colleague/the gentleman/the lady . . . will have . . ." or "For the table, we'll have . . ." You do not address the person you are ordering for by a pronoun when placing the order, as in, "he/she/they will have . . ."

When ordering for a larger table or family-style meal, try to be ready with as much information as possible so you can communicate it clearly and efficiently. Be sure to get any restrictions and some basic suggestions from the group first and then choose a mix of dishes. Be careful not to order just one special diet dish. You don't want the person with the restriction at the table to be limited to one option (which others will share). Monitor how quickly food gets eaten, and order more if needed.

AS THE GUEST Ordering for ourselves is usually easy enough—we just have to remember to look at the server, speak clearly, and say please and thank you, especially if we ask for any special accommodations. "May I please have the whipped potatoes instead of the baked potato?" "Yes, of course." "Thank you!"

RESPECTING THE STAFF

Give your server the utmost respect and consideration as they do their job, no matter the establishment or your role as host or guest. Other people will notice if you treat waitstaff badly, and it will not look good on you. How you treat the people who serve you indicates to people how you think of yourself and how you see others. Ways to treat your server include the following:

- Saying good evening/afternoon/morning and listening for any specials or other information your server may have, rather than jumping straight into placing your order.

- Be patient or understanding if something cannot be accommodated. "Would you be able to . . . ?" or "Would it be possible to . . . ?" instead of "I want" makes a difference, as do the magic words "please" and "thank you."

- Make eye contact; it is the primary way to signal a server. If necessary, half-raise your hand to signal a server over. Do not snap, clap, whistle, point, or call out to them.

- Try to be efficient with your server and ask for things all at once, rather than repeatedly calling them over, which slows down overall service in a restaurant.

- Don't make dismissive gestures instead of speaking to a server. For example, don't wave someone off with your hand; instead, turn to them and say, "No, thank you" or "I'm all set, thanks."

- When a server is pouring wine or water, do not cover your glass with your hand or turn an empty wineglass upside down to indicate you don't want any. Simply speak to your server: "None for me, thank you."

- Always tip for sit-down service. If you have a problem with the service, you should tell management, not stiff someone on a tip. The *minimum* tip for sit-down service is 15 percent, which should be applied even if you're upset with the service. Speaking to the manager is how to handle a problem—let your words speak for you, not your money. Twenty percent is most commonly seen today and is easy math. See Tipping in the Reference Guide, page 243.

- Always acknowledge each interaction with eye contact, a nod, or a thank-you; any and all are great.

CONVERSATION AT THE MEAL

One of the big differences between casual conversations over meals and business conversations during meals is that at business dinners we traditionally wait until the main course has concluded to conduct business, and the host is responsible for broaching the topic.

Because there is no way to know if the business end of the meal will go well, it's important to save this portion of conversation for the end of the meal. Not only does it prevent people from souring on their meal and being turned off their food if it doesn't go well, but it also provides an opportunity to keep the meal itself a social event, a get-to-know-you, treat-you-to-something moment suspended outside of the risks of business. If business has been brought up before dessert, it's likely a fairly safe topic, and the host feels confident that discussing it will not ruin the meal.

If your host hasn't mentioned business before dessert, don't worry about doing so. If dessert arrives and your host has not mentioned business, it's a good sign that this was a get-to-know-you meal. No, you shouldn't start discussing the deal or business; instead, wait and set up a formal meeting.

Take note, hosts may choose to discuss business earlier in the meal at business lunches, where time is at a premium and the environment is likely to be less formal. For more conversation tips, see chapter 6, "Conversation Skills at Work."

HOW TO DEFLECT IF YOU CANNOT DISCUSS SOMETHING

Noncommittal responses can be the best tools you keep in your back pocket during a business-social event. You might need to deflect a conversation topic for privacy reasons, timing concerns, or because you're not the decision-maker. It's best to know how to deflect when the topic becomes something you cannot comment on. Here are some phrases you can use to help you politely deflect:

- "I really appreciate you sharing that with me."

- "I am not at liberty to speak for the company on that matter, but I would love to address it with the proper channels/person."

- "Thank you for sharing that. I will have to circle back with XYZ and let you know our position."

- "I understand. Unfortunately, I am not the right party to address the issue at this time."

Offer one of these, and then change the subject.

THE END OF THE MEAL

There are a few details to consider to ensure you end the meal and conclude the business well. Here are some tips for wrapping up as the host or the guest.

THE HOST ENDS THE MEAL

The host is the one who is responsible for signaling the meal is over, and this is often a good indication that the business discussions are also finished. After business wraps, the host will often turn back toward more personal conversation to end the meal on a light note. "I'm glad we've had a chance to see how we might work together. And I'm always happy to have met another golfer; I can't wait to get out on the course this year once this snow finally melts . . ." This also gives the host a lighter conversation to follow while they deal with the check, if it will be handled at the table.

THE CHECK

In business, the check is not something you'll ever "fight" over; it will be clear from the invitation who is paying at a business meal. Typically, whoever is trying to win the business is going to be hosting and doing the treating. There are some occasions where this might be reversed, and there will be times when both parties are on equal footing and are developing partnerships rather than winning business. But for the most part, if you're being interviewed, if you're a client, and when things are internal and you're a subordinate, you're being treated. But if your manager or boss just says, "Hey, wanna grab a bite at the deli?," that's likely getting lunch on your own dime, unless they expressly say, "Can I treat you to a sandwich today?"

As the host, ask for the check with a simple yet friendly "When you have a moment, may I please have the check?" Never demand the check or snap your fingers to get your server's attention. It's always a polite request. When it arrives, you may review it to ensure it looks correct. If you have any issues, it's best to deal with them away from the table so your guests don't have to wait while you run through the itemized bill with the server or a manager. Discretion is the better part of valor—no need to make a show of paying, either. The more discreetly you take care of it, and the more smoothly you get back to your guests, the better.

TIPPING

Did someone come to the table to take your order and bring your food? And clear your dishes, bring you a check? That's sit-down service and for it you always tip at least 15 percent at a restaurant. A 20 percent tip is more common today, and it's easier math. But, you never omit the tip. If you are upset with the service, speak with a manager away from the table. If you treat a business contact to a meal that isn't sit-down restaurant service, a discretionary tip of up to 10 percent will do. We often get asked: *Do I have to tip on alcohol?* The answer is, yes. And *Do I tip on tax?* You don't have to, but most people do.

CLOSING THE MEAL

The bill is paid, the last sips drunk, now's a good time to say casually, and if it fits the mood, things like, "Jenn, this was a beautiful dinner; it was fascinating to learn that you cooked in Greece for a year while studying abroad," or "Alex, I'm going to have to check out treading, it might be just the ticket for my lower back." While you could also reference something more business-related, referencing something you learned about your guests during the meal is a bit more personal and shows that you know how to end things on a friendly note. If we weren't trying to build this relationship, we'd just set up a phone call to discuss the business matters. This meal was also about relationship building.

As the guest, follow your host's lead; if the conversation has turned back toward lighter or more personal topics, don't dive back into business.

SAYING THANK YOU

The host and the guest say thank you at the end of the meal. As the guest, take a moment to compliment the establishment and the food. As the host, comment on the company and appreciate their availability: "Thank you both so much for taking the time to meet like this, I have so enjoyed getting to know you."

As the guest, thank your host for their hospitality: "Nancy, it was such a pleasure. Thank you so much for dinner. The meal was amazing, and it was great to get to know you better as well. Completely aside from the business at hand, this was wonderful."

Note that you always want to acknowledge someone's thanks before you offer your own in return. "You are most welcome/It was my pleasure and thank you so much for . . ."

Some business meals will really benefit from a handwritten thank-you note. If your host took you to a particularly nice establishment (or hosted you at home) or the meeting was a particularly special, unique, or important opportunity, these would be reasons to write that handwritten note.

REFERENCE GUIDES

PLACE SETTING GUIDES

Use the following visuals to help you remember how to navigate your table setting.

BREAD AND DRINKS

Make a circle with your thumb and forefinger, allowing the other three fingers to stand up straight. Left = *b* (bread). Right = *d* (drinks).

BMW

Bread, Meal, Water to remember that bread goes on the left, the meal in the middle, and water on the right.

FORKS

Read your setting like the word *FORKS*. First on the left is F = forks, O = plate, because a plate looks like an *O*, R = right of plate, K = knives, S = spoons.

OUTSIDE IN

You eat from the outside in per utensil grouping. As each course is cleared, the relevant utensils are also taken away, leaving you with only what is needed for the rest of the meal.

NAPKIN MANNERS

- The napkin is set to the left of the place setting or in the center.

- If you are given a choice of a light or dark napkin, choose the one that most closely matches your clothes. This way, lint or small threads from the napkin won't be as likely to show after the meal.

- Place your napkin in your lap upon taking your seat, and, when possible, use it to cover your entire lap, not just one leg.

- Clean your lips or the edges of your mouth with a light dab or small wipe as needed. Don't make such a mess eating that the napkin becomes covered with food halfway through the meal.

- If you drop your napkin on the floor—not uncommon—you may ask for a fresh one. It's best not to touch things that have touched the floor when dining with others.

- If you need to remove something you cannot swallow, use your napkin to cover your mouth. Then, transfer the item quickly to the edge of your plate. Do not spit or disgorge into a napkin.

- Lay your napkin loosely to the left of your setting if you need to excuse yourself from the table and once you are finished with the meal.

TABLE SETTING DIAGRAM

FORMAL SIX-COURSE MEAL Here we display all six courses' worth of utensils for a meal that consists of an oyster dish, soup, fish course, entree course, salad, and dessert. You could also, as Emily suggests, place only three (not counting dessert) courses' worth of utensils out at a time and possibly bring out the soup spoon and oyster fork with their respective dishes. You might have more than one wineglass (and of course sherry and Champagne glasses are only set if they are to be used).

1. Bread plate & butter knife
2. Dessert spoon
3. Dessert fork
4. Water glass/goblet
5. Sherry glass
6. Wineglass
7. Champagne glass
8. Napkin
9. Fish fork
10. Entree fork
11. Salad fork
12. Charger/place plate
13. Salad knife
14. Entree knife
15. Fish knife
16. Soup spoon
17. Oyster fork

FORMAL FOUR-COURSE MEAL For a four-course meal, we are likely to see all utensils on the table, though it isn't a must. Remember to set only the glasses you will be using. As always, the dessert spoon and fork could be set out or brought out with the dessert.

1. Bread plate & butter knife
2. Dessert spoon
3. Dessert fork
4. Water glass
5. Wineglass
6. Wineglass
7. Napkin
8. Salad & appetizer fork
9. Entree fork
10. Charger/place plate
11. Entree knife
12. Salad & appetizer knife
13. Soup spoon

THREE-COURSE MEAL As a three-course meal could be casual, semi/informal, or formal, you may or may not see a bread plate and butter knife, the dessert fork and spoon (displayed nontraditionally here), or the charger. You might have more than one type of wine but you will typically just be served one, either red or white.

1. Bread plate & butter knife
2. Dessert spoon
3. Dessert fork
4. Water glass/goblet
5. Wineglass
6. Napkin
7. Salad & appetizer fork
8. Entree fork
9. Entree knife
10. Salad & appetizer knife

ONE-COURSE MEAL A casual setting might utilize a placemat (though they can be used for semi/informal meals as well), and only our napkin, entree fork and knife, and a water glass will be set. It's unlikely that for a casual meal we will use a charger or underplate. In casual settings, sometimes the fork is placed on the napkin. Technically a formal meal can be a single course, however this is more common at holidays like Thanksgiving, than business meals.

1. Water glass/goblet
2. Napkin
3. Entree fork
4. Entree knife
5. Placemat

TIPPING

SIT-DOWN SERVICE	TAKEAWAY OR PARTIAL SERVICE
15% minimum, 20% standard, Nondiscretionary	Up to 10%, Discretionary

SEATING CHARTS

When seating your guests, any guests of honor are seated to the right and left of the hosts, with the first guest of honor on the host's right and the second guest of honor on the host's left. From there a host should place guests around the table based on who they think are likely to enjoy each other's company.

CHAPTER 11

Leadership

Good leadership is good business. Great leadership is great business. Great leaders always seek to get the best out of their team, and one of the best ways to encourage the best is to bring out your best. Let's look at leadership from an etiquette perspective and see how you can lead by example to get the results you seek, and why it has such a big impact when it comes from you, the boss.

A great boss is both practical and empathetic, thoughtful and understanding, balancing the demands and goals of the company or job with the reality of working with people, not with robots or AI. Leaders know people are complex, require direction, feedback, encouragement, support, and thoughtful consideration. Leaders constantly adjust and find ways to fine-tune everything from the work product to team morale. They understand that success is determined by the relationships that businesses are built on.

LEAD BY EXAMPLE

To lead is to show someone the way, literally. At the heart of good leadership is inspiration and goal setting, followed by direction to reach those goals. In good leadership, we see social responsibility. By its very nature, leadership means others will be involved, following the lead. If you want your team to have the benefit of great business etiquette skills, you must first exhibit them.

In our Emily Post seminars and training, we tell folks that this is not a time to fake it but to fully embrace and embody the attributes you want to set as the standard for those you work with to emulate. All the time. In *all* your interactions. It feels like a lot when we say it that way, doesn't it? Like you have to be perfect? No. There is room for error in how you treat people. We're all human. But you should always be guided by having high ideals for *your* behavior. Perfection is not a target to hit; no one can. But it should always be the goal, because then you're taking every instance as an opportunity to be the best example for your team. At a fundamental level, this is not something you can take a break from.

The good etiquette you employ must be genuine to have a positive impact. The sincerity in your effort and approach in how you treat people makes all the difference. It is difficult to be sincere and consistent in demonstrating good behavior while excusing your own bad behavior. The accountability we are discussing here must come from a willingness within. When you inevitably mess up—maybe you'll snap at someone, dismiss someone without realizing it, or make a joke you shouldn't have—you can display both understanding and genuine regard with a sincere apology. Powerful leadership is showing that even when you make a mistake, there is a professional and meaningful way forward that can strengthen bonds. It's remarkable what a bit of humility can do for an entire organization.

We've said it before: etiquette is a powerful tool for self-reflection and improvement, and it is much less effective at building relationships and fostering a sense of community when used to judge or exclude others. This is important to understand. If the leader is using etiquette as a tool for self-assessment, then the employees will start using etiquette as a tool for self-assessment. They will see their boss, manager, or employer practicing the art of self-correction, and they will self-correct, too.

Be vocal about it. Let your team see you using the five-step process (see chapter 2) or analyzing your own professional appearance. You don't have to berate yourself in your office mirror with the door open, but you can say things like, "Boy, I realized it's time to order new work shirts; I'm starting to see the first signs of wear on my favorites" while you grab a coffee in the kitchen. This small example of a willingness to self-assess will help others improve their behavior. Etiquette is much harder to explain than to show. Show your team, and they will follow suit. By demonstrating good behavior, you prove that these expectations are achievable.

A GREAT LEADER'S GREAT ETIQUETTE

No person is too small or too far removed for a great leader to include them in professional courtesies. These are extended to everyone, be it an important long-term client, the applicant riding the elevator with them on the way to an interview, or an employee's sister visiting town who has stopped by to see the office.

A GREAT LEADER SHOWS UP They spend face time with their colleagues and clients and know the people and things happening around them. When you've got your finger on the pulse of your company's community, your employees and direct reports can trust that leadership is actively paying attention. This not only builds employees' confidence in their job security but also builds their confidence in following you and letting you lead them.

A GREAT LEADER IS AN ACTIVE LISTENER This means that you both understand and process what is being told to you, that you respond and engage in a way that lets people know they have been heard. You bring your full attention to your interactions with others at work.

A GREAT LEADER IS AN EXCELLENT HOST Whether you're hosting an employee in your office for a review, a company dinner party, or clients in the boardroom, a great leader knows how to be a great host (see page 214 for a list of great hosting behaviors). Their awareness, sense of hospitality, and attention to detail put their "guests" at ease, regardless of the business at hand.

A GREAT LEADER IS A GRACIOUS GUEST Knowing that just because you are at the top doesn't mean you are always in charge is key to switching from that leading and hosting role into a gracious guest role. The humility of letting others lead when the time is right is a wonderful trait in a great leader.

A GREAT LEADER ENCOURAGES One of the finest roles a leader can play is in noting the good things that happen. Harness the power of the compliment and show both awareness of and appreciation for work well done.

A GREAT LEADER COMMUNICATES CLEARLY Whether verbally or via the written word, great leaders must be able to get the message across in a way that it can be understood. They craft language carefully and choose methods that match the content of the communication.

A GREAT LEADER KNOWS HOW TO OFFER CONSTRUCTIVE CRITICISM Earning enough trust to be a trusted critic is not an easy task. Thoughtful, honest criticism is easier to take when it's balanced with a healthy respect.

A GREAT LEADER KEEPS ETIQUETTE AT THE FOREFRONT OF EVERY INTERACTION They value the opportunity to treat everyone they encounter with consideration, respect, and honesty, regardless of the relationship or the job.

LANGUAGE AWARENESS FOR LEADERSHIP

When you are in a position of power, it is particularly important to pay attention to how that power differential affects your conversations with employees and direct reports. If you want to be a great leader, you need to recognize that conversational hazards such as gaslighting, othering, and making privileged statements have an even greater impact when *you* say them, and are maybe even harder for others to point out to you because of your position. Understanding what these sound like and how to avoid them will greatly help you communicate better with your team and better support them in ways that are deeply important to workplace relationships.

GASLIGHTING occurs when a person seeks to make someone doubt their own perceptions, memories, or sense of reality. The affected person says, "This happened," and the person responding to them essentially says, "No, it didn't" or "You're wrong." It differs from the affected person seeking your input by asking, "Am I reading it wrong?" or "Help me get some perspective?" A good response when someone shares their experience, no matter how unsure you are of what they tell you is, "I'm so sorry to hear it." Or if appropriate, "Is there something I can do to help?" In cases of harassment of any kind, suggesting someone speak to HR or report the issue is always going to be good move.

OTHERING happens when you make assumptions that the person you are engaging with isn't part of the same social group, community, or organization as you, or isn't from the same place. Saying to someone who looks or sounds different from you "Where are you from?" or "Wow, I've never heard a name like yours before. It's so beautiful" may seem innocuous, but it can be received as *You're different* or *You're an outsider*. Understanding this can help you avoid making the mistake.

PRIVILEGE can be and sound like many different things, but it mostly comes across as a lack of awareness that you have benefited in a way others may not have. Lots of things that are out of our control can make our lives easier or harder—our health, gender, age, sexual orientation, race, religion, ability, class—and nearly anyone can make a statement of privilege and not realize it. Understand what privileges you've experienced so that you can be aware of it in conversation with others. Remind yourself that not everyone has had your lived experience, and remember, the easiest privilege to check is your own. "I thought this was funny, but before we send it out, I'd really appreciate a few other perspectives."

STARTING FROM SCRATCH: A RICH OPPORTUNITY

Leaders are visionaries. Their purpose is to ideate and execute. Starting from scratch with any business or position is a glorious opportunity to set yourself (and your team) up for success by selecting and maintaining good leadership standards from the get-go. As a leader working with a blank slate, you get to dream up and execute your vision of the best version of this particular role. And then it's up to you to live up to the position you've created for yourself.

WORKING FROM CORE PRINCIPLES

Using consideration, respect, and honesty as a structure for working with others in a new role can help to guide you through new waters. Unsure if your new work schedule works for your team? Run it through the five-step process (see chapter 2), or at least ask yourself who is involved and how they are impacted by this schedule. By applying the core principles and looking at your suggestions, and even your decisions regarding how your business and management function, you will keep your professional endeavors operating through a lens of consideration, respect, and honesty, with etiquette as a core component.

BUILDING SOCIAL CAPITAL PROFESSIONALLY

Social capital is the value that is created in networks or relationships that allows them to function. It's what creates the potential for people to lean on each other for resources, information, or maybe even favors. It's like a bank where you are making deposits in the form of positive interactions and withdrawals in the form of negative interactions. The more positive interactions you deposit, the more social capital you have. And it works in professional environments just as it does for social ones. The more you spend on the negative, the less you have in the bank of social capital. Think of it this way: you want at least three positive interactions for each negative thing you have to address. As a leader, there will be many negative things you have to deal with, so the more you can have and deposit positive interactions, the more social capital you will have when tough things come up.

HOW TO BUILD SOCIAL CAPITAL

Offering to help others and serving as a resource to your team is a great way to do it. In most cases, the offer alone builds social capital with the other person, regardless of whether they take you up on it. *Wow, Darren's great. He's always offering to help.* Listen well and attentively. Show appreciation. Smile and make eye contact. Basic good etiquette habits will keep your account in the bank of social capital well funded.

HOW YOU DEPLETE YOUR SOCIAL CAPITAL BANK ACCOUNT

If you spend too much time griping, complaining, or talking about non-work-related things, you might wear thin your social bank account. It's okay to say the negative thing occasionally, and there will be times when critical feedback is necessary, but make sure you're providing proper context and balancing it with more positive interactions and conversations. Overly critical behavior will leave you short of funds quickly.

CHANGING THINGS UP

It can be difficult for a leader to enter an already-established system. If the former leader was beloved, people might have a hard time adjusting to new leadership, and if they were dreaded, you might end up bearing the costs of a bad leader when their behavior wasn't your fault. Taking over or turning that ship around isn't impossible, but it requires care and patience.

RESPECTING TRADITION

Respecting tradition can be an excellent bridge to building great relationships with an existing team as you come into a new role. Adopting traditions before changing them can be a way to transition from a previous person's leadership into your own. It also shows respect for how things have been done, even if you plan on changing them.

There are certainly cases where a change in leadership, tradition, and the way things are done is enthusiastically welcomed, but in the cases where it's not, showing a willingness to understand and even participate in the "old way" (as long as it's not harmful to anyone) can give you a better sense of what your team experienced. It can even help you hone your ideas for how to move forward more effectively and efficiently.

Lean into traditions that transcend the local environment. Focusing on the durable manners that have guided the larger professional world for generations (greeting and parting well, effective compliments, punctuality, etc.) is another way to establish a link with what was good that has come before you. It will also connect your team to standards that matter to a larger business community and reinforce that there are valuable things you can share with your team, even if you are new to them.

CHANGE CAN BE GOOD

However good or bad things have been, a moment of transition allows for the possibility for change to be good and for things to improve. In a moment of change, the often unwritten rules around social expectations can be looked at, named, clarified, refined, developed, improved, or instituted. We suggest a six-part leadership strategy to help change be a positive thing.

1. **COMMUNICATE NEW EXPECTATIONS CLEARLY** Clear communication and appropriate timing are keys to good transitions. Change won't occur if you can't communicate it to those who will be responsible for enacting it.

2. **FOCUS ON DO'S AS WELL AS DON'TS** Especially if you are looking to course correct or reinvigorate a group. Give positive direction and clear, concrete examples so everyone can understand and participate in the expected best-practice behaviors.

3. **OFFER AMNESTY FOR PAST ACTIONS** This is a great chance to start afresh. Remember that under a new system or expectation, we want to encourage people to rise to the desired result, not keep them under the thumb of an old system or expectation. There is a difference between punishing someone for a previous failure and reasonably using the instance to inform future choices. In the former, you're not allowing room for growth or change. In the latter, you can adjust the particular task or how it's handled to suit the company's needs while leaving room for the person who failed to regain trust and opportunity moving forward.

4. **OUTLINE CONSEQUENCES AND REWARDS MOVING FORWARD** Spelling out consequences and rewards moving forward is a great way to lean into the principle of honesty. Clearly defining rules, expectations, consequences, and rewards is only fair. This is a basic, standard operating procedure, and it exists for a reason.

5. **HOLD THE LINE WITH UNDERSTANDING RATHER THAN FORCE** It's not "my way or the highway" or "just do as I said!" It's "I hear you, and I appreciate knowing how you feel about it. I'm still confident about moving forward as we discussed."

6. **FOLLOW-THROUGH AND FOLLOW-UP** Change only works if all parties commit to the new standards. Follow-through needs to happen for there to be any ability to assess whether the change worked for the better. Follow up on how a change is working and how it's being adopted. Reflecting on it and fine-tuning it is important. It also demonstrates flexibility and a willingness to correct course when needed.

WORKING WELL ACROSS GENERATIONS

In today's workforce, it's no secret that there are often members of three or even four different generations working alongside one another. Someone born in the 1950s and someone born in the 2000s will have different expectations of each other based on vastly different lived experiences. Getting the most out of this situation, *and there is much to be gained,* requires social intelligence. A deep understanding of manners can help achieve that social intelligence.

The company you work for didn't grow by staying the same, nor did it likely grow by eschewing all methods and systems from the past. Traditions stick around for a reason, and manners can change over time. Both can be true at the same time and serve us well and help us strengthen relationships.

Leaders can utilize multigenerational workforces to show younger generations both the successes and the failures of the past, demonstrating the company's ability to be reflective and thoughtful. This teaches the value of perspective over time, while at the same time encouraging changes and improvements when necessary.

Emily Post embraced change and looked at younger generations as the ones who would dictate future etiquette. She did this confidently, knowing practicality is often at the heart of good etiquette. If something was practical and useful enough—without harming others or damaging relationships—it would likely get adopted into everyday normalcy. If a tradition didn't serve the public well, it had lost its effectiveness and was worth changing, adjusting, or dropping.

Leaders can take a page from Emily's book and find comfort in knowing that no single generation has it right. There is no perfect way. In the best situations, we learn from each other in a multi-directional way. When we are willing to learn from one another, we afford each other the respect needed to do the job.

WE MAKE IT TOGETHER

Be open. Whether you are a boomer or zoomer, the best way to work between generations is to get curious and use the divide like a puzzle to solve. There will be times when it's best for an employee of any age to participate in the system they've been assigned, and other times when you can be more nuanced, recognizing that Bill does great when you email him but rarely responds to business texts promptly. Or that giving Jennica five minutes of your time in the morning to chitchat about her life means that she's more likely to focus the rest of the day, even though you were brought up to never discuss personal lives at work. By acknowledging the places where we can be flexible and maybe even learn a bit about how another generation works, we open ourselves up to a rich intergenerational work environment that is understanding of people in general.

WHAT TO WATCH OUT FOR

As a leader, there are unique behaviors to watch out for that can easily develop when we are in a position of authority. Some can develop anytime and in any position, but they will quickly kill the positive impact of any great leader.

BEWARE THE JERK IN YOU. We all have one, and some of us have a few. Patience can be one of the best antidotes to our jerkiest selves. Your work relationships will be so much better off if you're able to hear your jerk voice and stop it before it reaches your mouth. Choose instead to wait quietly and let the jerk voice rant in the distance of your mind, while you pay attention to the person who is speaking. Even if you don't agree with what they're saying, you can always respond to the person who has triggered your inner jerk by saying, "Let me think about that and get back to you." Using a noncommittal response that acknowledges the other person but suggests you take the time you may need to respond more thoughtfully or at a better time. This is a way to keep your inner jerk from getting out in the moment.

The jerk in us all can show up for so many reasons: because we're tired, because we think it sets us apart, because we missed the life lesson that taught us to be humble and understanding, because it's Wednesday, because your mom said something mean the night before, because this person reminds you of someone who was cruel to you, because darn it, we worked hard on that pitch and were proud of it, and so many, many more. There's a jerk in all of us, but a great leader checks that voice before it ever escapes. And knows how to issue an apology if the jerk gets out.

PLAYING FAVORITES. A good leader is great at utilizing and highlighting all team members to the best of their ability. Just because one person works in a way you appreciate or is easier to get along with than another doesn't mean you lean on this person as much as possible. Just because you like or appreciate certain people at work doesn't mean you make mini teams of just your favorites to get the job done. Doing so greatly diminishes the likelihood of bonding with or seeing others at work more fully. It can be easy to lean into your easiest and most enjoyable colleague relationships. However, a good leader focuses on and puts to good use all of their team members.

OVERMANAGEMENT. A good leader allows their employees or direct reports to do their jobs. While direction and constructive criticism will play a role in managing others, if you are too involved, too controlling, or think that only your ideas will work and should be executed, you'll end up negating the purpose of both of your roles at the organization. Your role is to guide people, not take over their work.

UNDERMANAGEMENT. It's okay for a management role to come with perks, but those perks shouldn't start to look like you're not working. If you're a manager who has enough time to futz around on the internet or be at your desk but not doing anything related to the company, it means you're not showing up for the job. The same goes for the manager who doesn't work with their team. To state the obvious: ignoring requests to meet, not giving feedback that moves projects forward, and essentially avoiding the responsibilities of a leader is bad. And it doesn't serve *you* well. Something is wrong when you've stopped caring enough not to be doing your job. It's worth taking a moment to think about why you aren't applying yourself. We all can get off kilter occasionally, but if you find yourself avoiding your day-to-day responsibilities, it's time for a big self-check-in.

DEMEANING AND SUPERIOR ATTITUDES. In addition to failing to hold back the jerk inside, demeaning and superior attitudes are not the marks of a good leader. Thinking you're above others is the fastest way to break trust and erode relationships at work. It's great to be proud of your work, but as a leader, that work results from managing *others* well, which means they are doing a lot of the work of moving things forward. You role is to facilitate and ensure that they have the time, resources, and support needed to complete a task. But thinking you're above everything and everyone will bring it all crashing down around you. Instead, knowing the jobs of the people you manage and what they need from you to perform well is key to being the kind of support a leader should be to a team. *I'm better than you* has no place in a great leader's world.

DON'T JUST KNOW IT, PRACTICE IT

Leadership comes in many forms; you can be a leader with your behavior from any position in an organization. Professional etiquette is not just something you know once you reach a certain promotion level; it is something you practice in every interaction. Does John have good etiquette if he knows how to write a good thank-you note but never does it? Good etiquette begins with knowing something but doesn't make its impact until action is taken. It is in the *doing* that we find good etiquette.

This is a daily practice of treating others with care and awareness, not just knowing that it is important to do so, but doing so, again and again. We invite you to take on that daily practice of good etiquette.

REFERENCE GUIDES

GOOD LEADERSHIP ATTRIBUTES

Investing in the following areas from day one is worthwhile not only for yourself but for how you establish and lead your team.

- Good listening skills

- Appropriate communication

- Professional appearance and attire

- Time management

- Accountability

- Gratitude

- Greeting and parting

- Public speaking

- Offering constructive feedback

- Taking responsibility

- Business meal manners

INTERGENERATIONAL WORK BREAKDOWN

Use the chart below from Mindtools.com to gain a broad sense of what some of the generational differences actually are for the five generations working together professionally today.

	THE SILENT GENERATION	BABY BOOMER GENERATION	GENERATION X	GENERATION Y/ MILLENNIALS	GENERATION Z
Born	1922–1945	1946–1964	1965–1980	1981–2000	1995–2015
Core Values	Respect for authority, compliance, dutiful custom	Optimism, acceptance, workaholism, stimulation	Stimulation, self-reliance, informality, skepticism	Realism, self-direction, goal focused, purpose	Uniqueness, authenticity, creativity, shareability
Work Ethic	Discipline, hard work, loyalty	Questions authority, self-centered, crusading causes	Task oriented, autonomous, work-life balance	Multitasking, "What's next?" eagerness	Flexibility, self-reliant, personal freedom
Communication Preferences	Written, formal	One-on-one, telephone	Direct, email, text messaging	Text messaging, social media	Digital natives, handheld devices
Feedback Preferences	No news is good news, take pride in a job well done	Not keen on feedback	Direct	Require lots, instantaneous	Bite-size, immediate, real time
Stereotypes	Old-fashioned, practical, rule followers	Ambitious, optimistic, wealthy	Self-centered, risk takers, cynical	Job hoppers, tech dependent, work to live	Constantly connected, distracted, apathetic, multitaskers

THINKING FORWARD

Emily Post etiquette has a long history of acting as a finger on the pulse of American etiquette rather than a dictator of it. Emily herself was focused on looking to younger generations to determine the etiquette of the day and point the way to the future. In the spirit of acknowledging that etiquette can and should evolve over time, we would love to know your opinion on customs that should be changed or adjusted to better suit the lived experience and social standards of the day.

Here are some areas we are particularly interested in. However, we welcome your thoughts and suggestions for adaptations to traditions on other topics, if you have them.

1. What is a good definition of business attire today?

2. Does a handwritten thank-you note send a more meaningful or lasting message than a well-worded email?

3. As virtual assistants and AI become more prevalent, what responsibility do we have to let others know we are utilizing these services?

4. What's the appropriate balance between personal life and work life, and how do we separate the two?

5. Is a text now preferable to a voice call as a first means of contacting someone on their phone?

Please submit your thoughts to ThinkingForward@emilypost.com. Thank you for your time and participation.

ACKNOWLEDGMENTS

It takes many hands to produce a book like this, and we would like to thank the following people for their help and support in making *Emily Post's Business Etiquette*.

First, we'd like to recognize Emily Post, our great-great-grandmother, for setting an example to emulate and for establishing a legacy that could continue. We are consistently reminded of how relevant her advice from 1922 to 1960 remains, and we are grateful for the opportunity to carry on her work.

Second, we'd like to thank our Post family members, both Cindy Post Senning, Ed.D., and Peter Post, of the Emily Post Institute, as well as Tricia Post, John Senning, Peggy Post, Allen Post, Billy Post, and Maureen Post for their endless support and encouragement. We are so grateful to our fourth-generation family members.

We'd like to thank our agent Katherine Cowles of the Cowles Literary Agency. It has been such an honor and a pleasure to work with you over the years. We are endlessly grateful for your support.

The entire team at Ten Speed Press, especially Kimmy Tejasindhu, Kaitlin Ketchum, Ashley Pierce, Lizzie Allen, Andrea Lau, Dan Myers, Jina Stanfill, and Andrea Portanova. Thank you to copyeditor Julie Ehlers and proofreader Mikayla Butchart.

The Team at Emily Post Institute who supported us through an intense year of work: Susan Iverson, Chris Albertine, Kristi Spencer, and Claire Trageser.

We'd also like to thank Anna Post, for sharing her experience and views with us. As well as Catherine Wilson and Lee Ann Barkhouse, for their contributions to seating protocol. Emily Voorde, founder and CEO of Into Strategies, for helping us create a more inclusive book. And Nicole Alley, for her contributions to our work on leadership. We'd also like to recommend the following works: *Respect & Honor* by Robert Hickey, *The Happiness Advantage* by Shawn Achor, and *The Cost of Bad Behavior* by Christine Porath and Christine Pearson.

Finally, we'd like to thank our families: especially Puja Gupta Senning, who helped create the space for this book to come to fruition; Dan's kids Anisha, Arya, and William; and Lizzie's dog Sunny who sacrificed his long walks for book editing sessions on the couch. We could not have done it without you and your support.

INDEX

business attire, 45, 50
business cards
    exchanging, 198
    importance of, 111
    information on, 111
business casual, 45, 50

C

calendars, 48, 101–6
Canva. *See* messaging and work management
    apps
casual attire, 46, 50
chair, holding for someone, 222
change, 249–50
child, birth of, 167
chinos, 37
chivalry, 209–10
clients and customers
    activities with, 206
    confidential information and, 141
    introductions and, 194
    meals with, 208
    meetings with, 179
    visits from, 150
coffee, 231
collars, 36
communication methods
    choosing, 85, 86
    formality chart for, 117
    turnaround times for, 123
    See also specific communication methods
company culture, 146–47
company picnics, 207
company trips, 207–8
compliment sandwich, 133
conference calls, 188–89
confidential information, 141

congratulatory notes, 114, 120, 173
consideration, as core principle, 7, 8
contacts
    categories of, 86
    exchanging, 200
    managing, 85–86
    See also networking
conversations
    active listening, 128–29
    attention during, 129
    corrections, 139
    criticism and feedback, 133
    deflecting, 234
    discretion and, 141–42
    exiting, 138, 143
    facial expressions and, 127
    gestures and, 128
    gossip, 135–36
    humor and, 132–33
    importance of, 126
    introducing a topic in, 143
    joining a group, 143
    magic words in, 136
    at meals, 233–34
    in passing, 137
    personal space and, 127
    posture and, 126
    privacy and, 141–42
    profanity and vulgarity in, 140, 142
    redirecting, 143
    in restrooms, 164
    self-introductions in, 143
    serious, 137
    skilled talkers and, 129–30
    three tiers of topics for, 134–35
    voice for, 127
    word choice and, 130–32
cooperation, 149
corrections, 139, 152–53, 197

hold, putting someone on, 97
home office, 162
honesty, as core principle, 7–8
honorifics. *See* titles
hors d'oeuvres, 203, 230
humor, 132–33
hygiene, 30–31, 51

I

identity, respecting, 151–53, 171
"I don't know," saying, 130, 132
image
    assessment, 27–29
    attire and, 42–43
    digital, 46–48, 110
    improving, 29
    maintaining, 29
    presenting best, 27
    See also appearance
"I'm sorry," saying, 136. *See also* apologies
inclusion, 10
inflection, 34
interviews
    arrival at, 66, 67
    asking questions during, 69–71
    ending, 71
    follow-up after, 71–72, 74–75
    introductions at, 67
    preparation for, 63–66
    responding to questions during,
        68–69
    video, 68
introductions
    business cards in, 198
    casual, 195–96
    via email, 92–93
    formal, 194–95
    at job interviews, 67

    at meetings, 181
    mistakes during, 196–97
    self-, 143, 197–98
    semiformal, 195–96
    via text, 101
invitations
    for meetings, 176–77, 189
    sample, 213
    for social events, 203–5, 215
    See also RSVPs
"I" statements vs. "you" statements, 131

J

jackets, 39–40
jeans, 37, 49
jewelry, 38
job offers
    declining, 132
    ending job search after, 73–74
    giving notice to current employer, 74
    responding to, 70–71, 73
job search
    applications, 57
    ending, 73–74
    recruiters, 56–57
    rejections, 75
    starting, 56, 80
    See also cover letters; interviews; job offers;
        resumes
jokes, 132–33
"Junior," use of, 151

K

khakis, 37
kitchens, 163

for waitstaff, 232–33

for workspaces, 148–49, 159, 172

responsibility, taking, 131

restrooms, 164

resumes

chronological, 62, 77

customizing, 63

functional, 62, 77

importance of, 57

information on, 61–62

objective of, 60

organizing, 62–63

standards for, 58

structure of, 60

retirements, 168–69

RSVPs, 167, 168, 172, 183, 201, 204–5, 215

S

salads, 230

SalesForce. *See* messaging and work management apps

sandals, 38

scarves, 41

scheduling, 102–4

seating arrangements

for meals, 221, 241

for meetings, 177–79, 180

self-introductions, 143, 197–98

semiformal attire, 44–45, 50

"Senior," use of, 151

shared spaces, 162–65

shirts, 36–37

shoes, 38

shorts, 37

shoulder padding, 39

Silent Generation, 255

"sir," using, 153

skirts, 37–38, 40

Slack. *See* messaging and work management apps

slacks, 37

small talk, 134, 199–200

smiles, 158

snack bars, 164

sneakers, 38

social capital

building, 248

definition of, 248

depleting, 248

social events

best practices for, 212

eat and drinking at, 220

exiting, 211, 212

follow-up after, 211–12

guest role at, 201–2, 213

host role at, 201–2, 212–13

invitations for, 203–5

networking at, 202–3

speech giving and, 210–11

types of, 201, 205–8

valet service at, 211

social media

image and, 47, 110

messaging via, 84, 110

profiles, 47

soup, 230

spam courtesy, 84

speakerphones, 96, 165

speech giving, 210–11

stationery, 111–17, 118. *See also specific types*

stuttering, 33, 34, 127

substitutions, 232

suffixes, 151

suits, 39–40

sunglasses, 49

superior attitude, 253

sympathy notes, 170–71

ABOUT THE AUTHORS

LIZZIE POST

Lizzie Post, great-great-granddaughter of Emily Post, is a co-president at the Emily Post Institute. She manages the company's publishing efforts and delights in being a cohost of the Institute's weekly podcast, *Awesome Etiquette.* Lizzie has authored and co-authored several books on etiquette, covering a range of topics from weddings to legalized cannabis use. A regular source on the topic of etiquette in the media, she has a column with AARP.com and she has been featured by *The Today Show,* the *Tamron Hall* show, NPR's *1A,* the *New York Times, Here & Now,* NFL Films, the *Wall Street Journal,* the Associated Press, and others, and has written for *The Atlantic, Good Housekeeping, Women's Running,* and *Houzz.com.* She lives in her home state of Vermont with her dog, Sunny, and her cat, Taco.

DANIEL POST SENNING

Daniel Post Senning, great-great-grandson of Emily Post, is a co-president at the Emily Post Institute. He manages the company's training programs and enjoys answering questions as a co-host on the Institute's weekly podcast, *Awesome Etiquette.* Daniel has authored and co-authored several books on etiquette, covering topics from business to digital manners, and delivers seminars and speeches on these topics around the world. An active spokesperson for the Institute, he regularly speaks with media outlets about business, technology, and dining etiquette. Daniel has appeared on *The Today Show,* The History Channel, and ESPN and has been interviewed by publications including the *New York Times, GQ, Time* magazine, and the *Wall Street Journal.* Daniel lives in Vermont, with his wife, Puja, and their children, Anisha, Arya, and William.

TEN SPEED PRESS
An imprint of the Crown Publishing Group
A division of Penguin Random House LLC
tenspeed.com
penguinrandomhouse.com

TEN SPEED PRESS and the Ten Speed Press colophon are registered trademarks of Penguin Random House LLC.

Typefaces: Monotype's ITC Berkeley Oldstyle Pro, Monotype's Amadeo and Schick Toikka's Chap

Library of Congress Control Number: 2025931447

Hardcover ISBN 978-0-593-83634-7
Ebook ISBN 978-0-5938-3635-4

Acquiring editor: Kaitlin Ketchum | Project editor: Kimmy Tejasindhu | Production editor: Ashley Pierce
Designers: Lizzie Allen and Andrea Lau
Production: Dan Myers
Copyeditor: Julie Ehlers | Proofreaders: Mikayla Butchart and Eldes Tran | Indexer: Ken DellaPenta
Publicist: Jina Stanfil | Marketer: Andrea Portanova

Manufactured in the United States

1st Printing

First Edition

The authorized representative in the EU for product safety and compliance is Penguin Random House Ireland, Morrison Chambers, 32 Nassau Street, Dublin D02 YH68, Ireland, https://eu-contact.penguin.ie.